The Curse of Eve,
the Wound of the Hero

THE MIDDLE AGES SERIES

Ruth Mazo Karras, *Series Editor*
Edward Peters, *Founding Editor*

A complete list of books in the series
is available from the publisher.

The Curse of Eve, the Wound of the Hero

Blood, Gender, and Medieval Literature

Peggy McCracken

PENN

UNIVERSITY OF PENNSYLVANIA PRESS

Philadelphia

10 9 8 7 6 5 4 3 2 1

Published by
University of Pennsylvania Press
Philadelphia, Pennsylvania 19104-4011

Library of Congress Cataloging-in-Publication Data

McCracken, Peggy.
  The curse of Eve, the wound of the hero : blood, gender, and medieval literature /
Peggy McCracken.
    p. cm. (The Middle Ages series)
  ISBN 0-8122-3713-7 (cloth : alk. paper)
  Includes bibliographical references and index.
    1. Literature, Medieval—History and criticism. 2. Blood in literature.
3. Sex role in literature. I. Title. II. Series
PN682.B56 M38   2003
809'9335—dc21   2002072134

For Doug

Contents

PREFACE   ix

1. ONLY WOMEN BLEED   1

2. THE AMENORRHEA OF WAR   21

3. THE GENDER OF SACRIFICE   41

4. MENSTRUATION AND MONSTROUS BIRTH   61

5. THE SCENE OF PARTURITION   77

6. THE GRAIL AND ITS HOSTS   92

CONCLUSION: BLEEDING FOR LOVE   110

NOTES   119

BIBLIOGRAPHY   155

INDEX   173

ACKNOWLEDGMENTS   177

Preface

Blood seems to be everywhere in medieval culture. Christian writers debate the nature of the blood of Christ in the doctrine of transubstantiation, and some of them describe the abuse of Christ's blood in anti-semitic stories of blood libel. In secular society, status and privilege are inherited through bloodlines, or won with the blood shed in battle; medical treatises define the body's health with reference to the consistency, abundance, and composition of blood.

Medieval religious, legal, and medical discourses describe blood as both figurally and literally effective. That is, blood is a potent metaphor as well as a literal agent: the blood of Christ figures salvation, and it is literally consumed by Christians in the eucharist; bloodlines are a figural representation of the actual union of male and female blood in conception; menstrual blood pollutes symbolically, yet it can be used as a cure in some medical recipes.

The subject of this book is gender and blood. It argues that gendered cultural values are mapped onto blood and that cultural values are inscribed into a natural order when they are described in terms of blood. I also suggest that the values of men's blood are always dependent on the values, both positive and negative, associated with women's blood, and that the most prominent form of women's blood is menstruation, a category that for the Middle Ages includes menstrual blood, the blood of parturition, and any genital bleeding. It is no surprise that in medieval culture, as in many modern cultures, menstrual blood is regarded as a polluting blood, a blood that does both symbolic and practical harm. At the same time, though, menstrual blood is not only a polluting blood in medieval culture—it can be used in medicinal cures, as I mentioned above, and it usefully purges the female body of excess blood.[1] In other words, although the view of menstruation as "the curse of Eve" dominates many medieval discourses, there are also other, more positive meanings for women's bleeding in medieval culture, and in this ambivalence it is like many other cultures.[2] My subject is this ambivalence, and in the chapters that follow I seek to understand the multivalent ways in which literature imagines a relationship between blood, gender, and cultural values.[3]

While influenced by the values of blood as they are defined in learned and popular medical and religious discourses, literary texts imagine blood in related but sometimes rather different ways. More important, for my purposes, literature reveals the extent to which gendered cultural values are indexed to blood. For example, literary texts promote a definition of masculine military heroism that is based on the valorization of men's bloodshed on the battlefield, a valorization that demands the exclusion of women's blood from the public arena in which social and political hierarchies are defined. As I suggest in Chapters 1 and 2, in the opposition of public masculine bloodshed and hidden women's blood, stories about chivalric battles and warfare promote the association of all women's blood with menstruation and define all women's blood as a blood that should remain hidden and private.

Medieval fiction also imagines familial relationships, and particularly parental relationships, in terms of blood, and, I argue in Chapter 3, it explores the privileges that are grounded in gendered definitions of blood relationships. Narratives about sacrifice describe a father's relationship to his son as a shared blood, a blood that defines a father's prerogative to dispose of his child, and even to sacrifice his child for the sake of a higher good. But some of these stories question why the blood a mother shares with her child cannot justify such a privilege.

Literary texts debate the relative values of father's blood and of mother's blood not only in relation to parental privilege, but also in narratives about conception, as I suggest in Chapters 4 and 5. Stories about women accused of giving birth to a monstrous child question what a mother brings to lineage, and define a mother's suspect contribution to conception in terms of corrupted blood. Another group of stories defines the scene of birth as a forbidden scene and links the prohibition to the visible evidence of the shared blood bond between mother and child that subverts the exclusivity of the father's blood bond with his child.

Medieval fiction also represents blood in the religious context of martyrdom, which I discuss in Chapter 1, and in the eucharistic ritual, which is the subject of Chapter 6. Grail romances juxtapose the blood of the wounded guardian of the grail with the blood of Christ and characterize the blood from the grail king's wound "between the two thighs" as a sanctifying blood in opposition to the blood of women and, perhaps implicitly, in opposition to the blood of Jewish men. Ultimately, though, this gendering proves unstable and points to the way that all gendered values associated with blood are constructed values, even though those values may be defined through an authorizing attachment to biological truths.

In this study, I read medieval literary texts in relation to medieval historical, medical, and religious discourses about blood. However, I also use a number of studies of the uses and values of blood in nonmedieval and even nonwestern cultures to contextualize my analysis of blood. "Comparative inquiry," writes Howard Eilberg-Schwartz, "generates second-order reflection that transforms the way in which interpreters think about and therefore analyze cultural traditions."[4] I have found the work of anthropologists and students of religion helpful in identifying paradigms for understanding medieval representations of blood. This is not to say that ideas about blood are universal, or that the biological functions of the body have universal meaning, but rather to suggest that ways of understanding bodies and blood are not always culturally bound, and that explicit understandings of blood, and particularly of the symbolic meanings of blood, in cultures from outside medieval Europe may suggest models for understanding implicit meanings of blood in medieval culture.

In speaking of medieval culture, I do not mean to imply that that the Middle Ages has one monolithic form that extends from late antiquity to the Renaissance. In fact, I explore evolving ideas about blood beginning in Chapter 1. I do, however, focus on a wide range of texts in this study, moving among narratives from the twelfth through the fifteenth centuries, with a brief foray into early modern England. In its broad focus, this study runs up against Charles de Miramon's warning of the danger of flattening historical variation by compressing periods and kinds of discourse.[5] Most of the texts I will discuss have their sources in earlier, sometimes oral traditions, and they debate concerns that are hard to localize firmly within a few decades. However, one of the points I try to make in this study is that attitudes about blood are persistent over long periods (even up to the present, as I claim in Chapter 1), and, whereas I try to account for variety and dissent in medieval attitudes about blood, I also focus on dominant ideas that endure in medieval (and sometimes modern) culture. While I would not claim that modern American culture is the direct heir of medieval European culture, I am interested in showing the persistence, and sometimes the variations, of representations that have been little studied up to now. So, while I have depended on Miramon and others for historical contextualizations, I have also tried to suggest how a study of the values of blood in medieval culture might suggest ways of seeing modern values associated with blood in a new light, and how modern representations of blood might suggest new perspectives on medieval blood.

I

Only Women Bleed

In 1975 Alice Cooper released a song entitled "Only Women Bleed." It is a song about the emotional and physical abuse of women by the men they love, and it is a song that betrays surprisingly medieval-sounding descriptions of gender relations. Here is the first verse:

Man's got his woman / to take his seed
He's got the power / oh, she's got the need
She spends her life through / pleasing up her man
She feeds him dinner or / anything she can
She cries alone at night too often
He smokes and drinks and don't come home at all
Only women bleed / Only women bleed / Only women bleed[1]

I am fascinated by this song because of the way it associates women and blood in an exclusive relationship: "only women bleed." Of course, Alice Cooper is using blood as a metaphor here—when he says women bleed, he means that women suffer. Men don't bleed, they inflict wounds on women. But the representation of women's blood in this song seems to be motivated by more than the simple metaphorical equation of blood and suffering. The fact that women bleed, and bleed regularly, makes blood a readily available vehicle for the representation of sentiments, emotions, or feelings associated with women, and the fact that only women bleed regularly makes women's blood a readily available vehicle for the representation of their difference from men. This is not to say that the association of women's blood and women's suffering is a self-evident or essential equation, but rather, that gendered values are mapped onto blood so that women's blood, or women's bleeding, is seen to mean something different from men's blood or men's bleeding. The gendering of blood defines not only explicit power relationships between individuals ("He's got the power / oh she's got the need. . . . Only women bleed"), but also culturally endorsed values and sexual identities: the way that the protagonists in the song are never named suggests the way that "he" and "she" name categories of experience rather than individuals who experience suffering or who inflict violence.

"Only Women Bleed" identifies women's blood in opposition to men's violence, and it assigns a value to women's blood: women bleed and they suffer. To the extent that women's blood of sufferance recalls the biblical account of the suffering inflicted on women as a result of original sin, the song makes an implicit link between women's suffering and the biology of women's blood—women bleed because they suffer from the curse of Eve. I do not think that Alice Cooper has written a song about original sin, or even about menstruation, but the values assigned to women's blood in "Only Women's Bleed" explicitly associate women's blood with suffering and abjection. That association, I will argue, has a very long history, and is part of a persistent definition of the values of women's blood in relation to the value of menstrual blood.

Virgin's Blood

If, as Alice Cooper suggests, women's blood is intimately associated with suffering, that association would seem to be born out—though not exactly in the way Alice Cooper means—in the thirteenth-century *Queste del saint graal*. In this romance, the virgin sister of the grail knight, Perceval, voluntarily allows her blood to be drained from her body and offered as a cure to a leprous lady. Only a virgin's blood can heal the afflicted lady, and she has killed many young women in her search for a cure. As it turns out, only the blood of Perceval's sister can save the lady from the leprosy that devours her body, and Perceval's virgin sister dies giving her blood for the cure. When the lady is bathed in the sacrificed virgin's blood, she regains her health.[2]

The account of Perceval's sister's death is similar to the female martyrdoms recounted in the many *vitae* that tell the stories of saints whose blood is spilled for God.[3] Many of these dying women are virgins, and the blood of a martyred virgin, as in *La queste*, seems to have a particular sanctity. But what is the difference between the blood of a virgin and the blood of a nonvirgin? From the perspective of hagiographical narratives, the difference is not in the blood itself, but in the state of the body that sheds the blood—the intact virgin's body incarnates a unique purity and the virtue of the body guarantees the virtue of the blood. At the same time, though, a virgin's blood could be seen as literally different from that of a nonvirgin. The twelfth-century nun Hildegard of Bingen postulated that the menstrual flow of virgins is less abundant than the blood flow of other women, for example.[4] So a virgin's blood could be seen as quantitatively and, as in *La queste*, qualitatively different from other women's blood: only a virgin's blood can cure leprosy.[5]

If the uniqueness of a virgin's blood derives from the female body dedicated to chastity, the virgin body that conceives a child poses a particular challenge to medieval categories of purity in relation to menstruation. Medieval descriptions of the Virgin Mary emphasize the miraculous purity of her maternal body and insist on her perpetual virginity, her sealed womb, and her own conception and birth without sin. Mary's eternally intact body demonstrates not only that she was innocent of sexual sin, but also that she was not tainted by original sin and the curse of Eve, and this definition of Mary's purity seemed to suggest, at least for some theologians, that she could not have menstruated. At the same time, though, Christ's essential humanity depended on Mary being more than simply a vessel for a divine birth, and Mary had nursed her child—how could she lactate if she did not menstruate, since milk is produced by the maternal body's transformation of menses?[6]

Women's blood—menstruation and the blood of parturition—have long been associated with pollution in the Judeo-Christian tradition.[7] The ritual prohibitions surrounding women's blood set forth in Leviticus continued to be observed or at least acknowledged in the Middle Ages, as is demonstrated by an often-cited letter from the end of the sixth century attributed to Gregory the Great. Gregory discusses taboos associated with women's bodies in the early church and he claims that menstruating women should not be prohibited from entering a church or from receiving the eucharist (implying that they were).[8] Gregory's instructions to disregard notions of ritual impurity also apply to men's bodies: in response to the question of whether a man may receive the sacrament after a nocturnal emission, Gregory claims that "natural superfluities or weaknesses" should not prevent participation in the eucharistic ritual, either for priest or for celebrant.[9] Gregory thus suggests a conceptual parallel between menstruation and the involuntary loss of semen.

But while menstrual blood may be paired with semen in codifications of pollution in Leviticus and in Gregory's refutations of cultural taboos, the qualities of semen and menstrual blood are far from similar in most medieval theories of the body. In reproductive theory, menstruation and semen had very different values for medieval writers, who largely followed Aristotle's view of the male body as hotter than the female body and thus able to refine nutrients first into blood, and then into the semen that imparts human form to the formless menses.[10] Semen, like breast milk, was considered a form of blood in the Middle Ages, but semen was seen as a pure form of blood that demonstrates the superiority of the hot, dry male body over the humid, cold female body that is incapable of giving form to its blood.

In texts written for or about religious men and women, the discussion of bodily emissions follows a similar gendered hierarchy based on the mastery of fluids. Treatises on virginity rarely mention female bodily emissions; in Jocelyn Wogan-Browne's phrase, "virginity [is] imagined in bodies without menstrual and menopausal phases."[11] However, men's loss of bodily fluids continues to trouble clerical writers, and theological discussions of nocturnal emissions equate masculine sanctity with the ability to control the body's fluids. That is, the man most devoted to spiritual purity does not experience nocturnal emissions.[12]

Although women are not expected to control menstruation as a physical demonstration of their spiritual development, the cessation of menstruation can be seen to mark the female body as a holy or sanctified body. Peter Brown cites the example of St. Eupraxia, who slept on ashes to tame her body when she began to menstruate, and Caroline Walker Bynum has richly documented the amenorrhea that characterized the extraordinary closure of some medieval female saints' bodies.[13]

There would seem then to be at least three ways of characterizing saintly female bodies and their blood, though these were not necessarily well known or universally accepted models for religious women: the pure body that does not bleed because it is not tainted with the curse of Eve through original sin, like the Virgin Mary's body; the body worshipfully devoted to mystical ascetic practice and whose amenorrhea is a sign of sanctity; and the martyr's body that bleeds, but not with menstrual blood. In the first two examples, amenorrhea is a sign of purity; in the third, the blood of martyrdom is different from menstrual blood—but how different is it?

Some stories of female martyrs linger over women's bloodshed and recount in detail the torture and mutilation of the female body. The blood of martyrdom is holy blood, whether it is shed by women or by men, but some *vitae* may suggest a link between women's bloodshed and menstruation. Francesca Sautman has pointed to the way that, in some stories of female martyrdom, the flow of women's blood recalls the blood of menstruation or parturition. She notes that this blood is surrounded by taboos similar to those that mark menstruation: torturers do not dare look upon the female martyr's blood, and she cites the example of the *Life of Saint Margaret* where the narrator recounts that "when [the torturers] had seen blood flow from everywhere in the tender flesh, they covered their eyes and their heads, for they could not look on it" ("quant il veient de la char tendre / De totes pars le sanc espandre / Lur oils et lur chières [covreent]/ Que esguarder ne la poeent").[14]

I do not mean to suggest that all representations of women's blood must be interpreted as figural representations of menstruation. Nor do all representations of menstruation define it as a polluting blood that must remain hidden—medieval culture also allows for more positive views of menstrual matter. It is an organic material that has healing qualities in some medical recipes; for example, Hildegard of Bingen identifies menstrual blood as a cure for leprosy. Another twelfth-century woman also promoted the positive values of women's blood: in her third letter to Abelard, Heloise claims that women can tolerate wine better than men because their bodies purge monthly.[15] But in many medieval discourses menstruation is a polluting blood, a feature of the imperfect female body whose imperfections mirror the perfections of the male body.

Recent scholarship on menstruation is still influenced to some extent by Mary Douglas's 1966 study on pollution systems. In *Purity and Danger* Douglas argued that the cultural coding of a substance as a pollutant is based on a shared perception of that substance as anomalous to a general symbolic or cultural order. Anomalous substances are coded as "dirt," as symbolic "matter out of place"—pollutants are thus simultaneously a product of a specific symbolic order and a danger to it. Menstrual blood, like other bodily wastes (urine or feces, for example) is anomalous, "out of place," because it escapes the natural boundaries of the body by which it is normally contained.[16]

Douglas later modified her argument to claim that although all pollutants are anomalous in terms of a given symbolic order, not all symbolic anomalies must be coded as polluting. They are simply "powerful," and that power may be granted a positive or negative value within specific cultures.[17] Recent studies have critiqued Douglas's idea of a single, monolithic cultural symbolic system and have suggested that within a single culture, matter may be "out of place" in one symbolic subsystem and securely at home within an alternate subsystem.[18] In other words, although menstruation is considered a polluting substance in many cultures, including medieval Judaism and early Christianity, to focus too closely on pollution systems is to ignore the positive cultural values that may be associated with menstruation in those and other cultures.

Indeed, to broaden the question of how blood is valued in different kinds of discourses is pertinent to the exploration of the value of menstrual blood in medieval culture. It allows us to perceive that menstrual blood can be seen as both polluting and healing, as a sign of fertility and as a sign of death, or as a curse and as an ingredient in a love potion. It also suggests the way that the gendering of bloodshed in romance narratives enacts a curious reversal of the values associated with the body in other medieval symbolic systems.

The Value of Blood

In order to extend the frame of reference for thinking about the gendered values of blood, it may be helpful to step outside of medieval culture and to examine some rituals in which gendered blood is seen to reflect gendered cultural values. In particular, ritual practices that explain male genital bleeding as a counterpart to women's menstruation may offer useful paradigms for thinking about the ways in which medieval texts define gendered cultural values in terms of blood. I turn first to a study of the evolving significance of circumcision in rabbinic Judaism (second through sixth centuries C.E.).

Lawrence Hoffman has characterized the symbolic meaning of circumcision as follows:

Circumcision symbolized the gender status in rabbinic society where men and women were emerging in binary opposition: men whose very flesh was thought to be marked with the covenantal sign, and women who were covenanted only secondarily, by virtue of their fathers and husbands; men who were charged with knowing God's commandments, teaching them to new generations of men-to-come, and women who were not; men who officially attended covenant meals—the seder and the circumcision feast—and women who did not. The whole system becomes manifest in the duality of male and female blood, the former . . . being positively viewed as salvific, the latter earning the opprobrium of rabbinic commentators, who continued to treat it as the priests had, as laden with impurity and ringed with taboo. This male/female dichotomy [was] encoded in the blood symbolism of circumcision on the one hand and menstruation on the other.[19]

Hoffman explains this dichotomy—men's blood is salvific, women's blood is polluting—as a perceived opposition between "men who are in control of their blood, [and] so of themselves, and therefore of society; and women who, lacking control of blood and therefore of self, are thus denied control of society as well."[20] Hoffman's reading of the symbolic opposition between the blood of circumcision and menstrual blood, that is, between men's blood and women's blood, shows how this opposition grounds conceptual frameworks that oppose men's control to women's unruliness, and that construct men's blood as purifying and women's as polluting. The gendered values of blood thus identify, justify, and even naturalize gendered social values.

A similar opposition is at work in cultures very different from the one discussed by Hoffman, but whose ritual blood-letting practices construct gender difference through a focus on control and lack of control. In a much discussed literature focusing on traditional cultures in the Pacific Islands and Australia, scholars have debated the significance of so-called male menstruation, the ritual practice of penile incision whose effects are described in terms similar to those in which the purgative function of female menstruation is represented. In these rituals, the penis is cut, allowed to bleed, then bandaged. Seclusion precedes and follows the ritual, and the blood spilled in the operation is considered highly polluting.

In New Guinea, the ritual of penile subincision is actually called "male menstruation," and according to its practitioners it purges the body: the blood released from the penis carries away impurities in the same way that menstruation is seen to cleanse women's bodies.[21] Ritual male "menstruation" resembles female menstruation, with one important difference. When the man "menstruates," the impurities he purges from his body are characterized as female, that is, he expels explicitly female elements from his body.[22] The ritual penile incision thus imitates women's menstruation while at the same time it affirms difference from women; it regenders the body masculine by purging femaleness. In New Guinea and in many other cultures, there are virtually no rituals in which women try to rid their bodies of masculine components, either spiritual or physical. Menarche rituals are most often performed mostly by women in isolation from men, and in order to celebrate fertility. [23]

In these examples of ritual male blood-letting, the controlled bloodshed of men reaffirms the value of masculinity, and masculine privilege is defined in opposition to feminine abjection—women cannot purge themselves of femaleness. In other words, ritual bloodshed defines a gendered hierarchy in which men, who control the expulsion of female elements from their bodies, are superior to women, who do not control their bloodshed and who cannot expel female elements from their bodies.[24] In this cultural construction of gendered bloodshed, as in the symbolic meanings surrounding the blood of circumcision studied by Hoffman, women's blood seems to demand a symbolic counterpart that is characterized by values that are uniquely masculine.

At least one scholar of initiation rites sees this a little differently. In his study of male puberty rituals—primarily circumcision and penile incision—Bruno Bettelheim focuses on rituals involving male genital bleeding.[25] Bettelheim hypothesizes that since initiation rites of both boys and girls may serve to promote and symbolize their acceptance of socially prescribed sexual roles, and since vaginal bleeding at adolescence unequivocally demonstrates the attainment of sexual maturity in girls, men may have wished to provide themselves with an equally obvious sign of maturation. He further suggests that one of the purposes of male initiation rites may be to assert that men, too, can bear children.[26]

Bettelheim's emphasis on puberty rites involving male genital cutting as an envious imitation of women's menstruation suggests that the competitive appropriation represented by male rites of initiation that include cutting the penis may be seen as a symbolic appropriation of genital bleeding as a masculine value. That is, if menstruation is a potent and visible sign of female sexual maturity and reproductive capacity, then the ritual appropriation of that representation depends on its redefinition as a masculine attribute—as controlled bloodshed. So in other words, the control of blood is not a "natural" positive value to be opposed to the negative value of uncontrolled blood, but rather, control is established—through rituals and through fiction—as a value in the opposition of men's blood and women's blood. Female bleeding seems to demand a counterpart, and it is the disturbing value of women's blood that must be countered with a different value: the ability to control bloodshed.[27]

Medieval narratives do not represent rituals that involve genital cutting, but they do represent the values associated with men's blood and women's blood in oppositional terms, and the martyrdom of Perceval's sister in *La queste del saint graal* offers one example of the gendered value of blood in medieval texts. Perceval's sister dies while giving her blood to save a leprous lady, and the virgin's sacrifice would seem to be a salvific sacrifice: not only is the lady cured, but the virgin's voluntary gift of her blood prevents a battle in which Galahad, Perceval, and Bors would have had to fight against overwhelming odds to save her from that fate.

The grail knights are prepared to take on a battle with the leprous lady's men to protect Perceval's sister from the custom that demands that each virgin who comes into the country fill a basin with her blood. Galahad protests that Perceval's sister is too young and fragile to survive the bleeding, but the virgin claims that her own blood must take the place of the blood that the knights would shed in battle:

"By faith," she says, "if I should die for this cure, it would be an honor for me and all my family. And I must do it, partly for you and partly for them. For if you go into battle tomorrow as you have done today, inevitably there will be a greater loss than my death."

("Par foi, fet ele, se je moroie por ceste garison, ce seroit honors a moi et a tot mon parenté. Et je le doi bien fere, partie por vos et partie por ax. Car se vos assemblez demain ausi come vos avez hui fet, il ne puet estre qu'il n'i ait greignor perte que de ma mort.")[28]

The story of Perceval's sister's blood is the story of a martyrdom, and like other representations of blood in the grail quest (I will return to some of these in Chapter Six), it is firmly situated within Christian blood symbolism. Perceval's sister dies giving her blood to save another woman, and to some extent she is a sort of Christ figure, since her blood heals the leprous lady, although it does not guarantee the lady's salvation.[29]

Through her self-sacrifice Perceval's sister joins the ranks of the holy men and women who populate this romance, but even though her martyrdom endorses the Christian ethos represented by the grail quest, her death is never explicitly explained as part of the struggle between good and evil, as are most events in the story. And although her blood cures the leprous lady, after the virgin's death a storm arises and destroys the healed lady's castle, killing her and all her household. Perceval's sister's death thus accomplishes no enduring good, since the lady she saved dies in a divine punishment for the murder of all the damsels she had killed in her quest for a cure. The maiden's blood has value, but not lasting value—it does not ultimately save the leprous lady from death.[30]

In romance narratives women's bloodshed is often caused by violence and coercion, and in this respect, romance characters like Perceval's sister may resemble martyred saints. But unlike hagiographical narratives, romances do not represent women's bloodshed as having a lasting effect, either symbolic or actual. In romance narratives women's blood may be salvific, as in Perceval's sister's cure of the leprous lady, but its effect is local and specific. Romance representations of bleeding women locate these characters in an economy of exchange that is based on self-sacrifice, and they offer the portrait of a female martyr whose death has no enduring significance.

Bloody Sheets I

If women's blood represents suffering, that suffering may have immediate consequences, as in the healing of the leprous lady, but the effect of women's blood of sufferance is not represented as part of a myth of social order. That representation is reserved for men's blood. As Andrew Lynch notes: "Blood is the basic currency of fights and quests, their operative factor as much as their issue, and often unrealistically prominent in fights that end without a death."[31] Men bleed prominently in medieval fiction to prove valor, to avenge unjust wrongs, and to impose justice.

In many chivalric narratives, honor and heroism are proven in battles between knights for the right to possess women.[32] And in chivalric contests in which women are the prize, the quest for honor through the bloodshed of battle seems to demand the suppression of women's blood. Chrétien de Troyes's *Chevalier de la charrete*, for example, is a twelfth-century romance in which the disputed exchange of women between men is debated in terms of blood and, implicitly, in terms of the value of women's blood in relation to the value of men's blood.

Le chevalier de la charrete is the earliest extant story about the adulterous love of Lancelot and Queen Guenevere, and the story of Lancelot's great love for the queen is simultaneously a story about his great exploits as a knight. The romance begins with the kidnapping of Queen Guenevere by Sir Méléagant. Sir Lancelot goes to the queen's rescue, and confronts Méléagant in a battle to determine Guenevere's fate. Lancelot wins the contest and liberates the queen, and Guenevere rewards her knight with an invitation to a secret meeting at the window of her bedchamber. Lancelot appears at the queen's window in the dark of night and, empowered by his great love for the queen, he manages to separate the bars that block the window and enter Guenevere's chamber, where he spends the night with her in bed. But when Lancelot pried open the bars on the window, he wounded his fingers, and during the night the blood from his wound stains the queen's sheets. Lancelot leaves the queen before daybreak in secret without noticing the wound, and the queen herself doesn't see the stains in her bed until Méléagant enters her chamber, sees the bloody sheets, and accuses the queen of sexual infidelity with Sir Kay, who lies wounded on a bed in the queen's chamber and whose sheets are also stained with blood. The queen denies that Kay has been in her bed, but Méléagant's father, King Bademagu, accepts the validity of his son's accusation and permits a judicial battle to determine whether the queen is guilty of adultery with Sir Kay. The accusation against the queen is dropped only when Lancelot champions the queen in a second battle with Méléagant.

A similar episode is recounted in another twelfth-century romance, Béroul's *Roman de Tristan*, but the identification of the blood that stains the queen's sheets is not disputed in the *Tristan* story—the blood on the sheets and the blood drops on the flour that covers the floor between Iseut's and Tristan's beds are clearly identified as Tristan's.[33] In Chrétien's romance, however, the question of whose blood stains the queen's sheets structures a contest between men (who may become the queen's lover?) that will determine a truth about the queen's body (has the queen made love?).

In Méléagant's view the bloody sheets signify adultery, but Guenevere offers an alternative reading of the stained bed linens. When the queen sees the stains on the sheets of her bed and Kay's bed, she claims that the blood must be her own:

Then, for the first time, the queen saw the bloodstained sheets on both beds. She was astonished and turned scarlet with shame. "As the Lord God is my witness, this blood you see on my sheets never came from Kay," she said. "No, last night my nose bled, and that blood is, I suppose, from my nose." She believed she was telling the truth.

(Lors primes la reïne vit
et an l'un et an l'autre lit
les dras sanglanz, si s'an mervoille;
honte en ot, si devint vermoille
et dist: "Se Damedex me gart,
ce sanc, que an mes dras regart,
onques ne l'i aporta Ques,
einz m'a enuit senié li nes;
de mon nes fu au mien espoir."
Et ele cuide dire voir.)[34]

The queen's explanation for the blood on her sheets is rejected outright. Méléagant calls it nonsense: in his words, Guenevere's claim that the sheets were stained by her own blood is empty, literally a void (*neanz*, v. 4786).[35]

The easy dismissal of the queen's defense is curious. There is no obvious reason why a nosebleed wouldn't explain the bloody sheets, yet this explanation is rejected out of hand. It is not even repeated for King Bademagu when he arrives in the queen's chamber to judge the evidence for his son's accusation of adultery. The whole episode is structured around the explicit question of whose body bled in the queen's bed, but it seems that only a man's body can provide a credible answer because the blood can only be read in the context of a competition to possess the queen: the blood on the sheets proves adultery. This reading of the blood reverses the association of bed sheets and women's blood found in the widespread custom of displaying blood-stained bed linens after a wedding night as proof of a woman's virginity and sexual initiation. This episode identifies men's blood as the sign of sexual possession, and Méléagant's accusation defines the possession of the queen as an overt contest between knights: Guenevere cannot have bled in her own bed, the blood on her sheets is evidence of the queen's adultery with Kay, and Méléagant will do battle with Kay to prove the adultery, and to prove his own right to the queen's sexual favors.

The wounded Kay cannot fight, but Lancelot takes his place and proves Kay's innocence in his battle with Méléagant. Lancelot thus proves that the blood on the queen's sheets cannot belong to the wounded knight, but the question of who bled on the queen's sheets remains unanswered for the characters who initially refused to believe that Guenevere had a nosebleed. Presumably the queen's explanation for the blood on her sheets is accepted after Méléagant's accusation is proved false, but the story does not explicitly indicate that the characters finally acknowledge the truth of the queen's claim to have had a nosebleed; in Paul Strohm's words, Guenevere's bed must remain "a hot spot of alternative interpretation."[36]

The unresolved question of whose blood stained the queen's sheets may point to the narrator's reluctance to explore in too much detail the mechanics of an episode in which the queen's lover defends her against the charge of adultery. It certainly points to the way that the accusation against the queen is appropriated into a contest between knights. Yet at the same time, because the blood on the queen's sheets is in fact evidence of adultery, as the reader/listener knows, and because there is never any explicit acknowledgment that Méléagant accepts the queen's explanation, the romance implicitly continues to ask the question with which the episode began: whose blood stains the queen's sheets, and what evidence does it offer about the queen's sexual transgressions?

When I teach Chrétien's *Chevalier de la charrete*, my students sometimes wonder why Guenevere doesn't explain the bloody sheets by claiming that she has her period. This lie would be just as logical, and perhaps more plausible, than the nosebleed explanation. Presumably Méléagant would not demand a physical examination, and the queen would be able to explain the blood on the sheets in a way that ought to cut the conversation short.[37]

Freud might say that this is in fact the explanation the queen offers, that the blood from her nose symbolically replaces menstrual blood in her explanation for the bloody sheets.[38] Like modern psychoanalytic theory, premodern medical theory links menstruation and nosebleeds: women's bleeding from the nose or the breast was thought to be the result of a menstrual disorder.[39] The analogy between a nosebleed and menstruation is surely motivated by the fact that both are characterized by an uncontrolled flow of blood that does not result from a wound or a disease.[40] But of course a nosebleed could be experienced by both men and women, and indeed, medieval courtly literature recounts a number of nosebleeds, but no examples of menstruation, a blood experienced only by women.

In the world of courtly romance, the queen does not menstruate—bodily functions are not subjects of courtly discourse. The kings, queens, noble ladies, and knights of medieval romance are characterized by love and chivalry, sometimes by deceit and betrayal, but never by urination, defecation, or menstruation. Yet the bloody sheets episode in Chrétien's *Chevalier de la charrete* seems to point toward a more generalized absence, not just of menstrual blood but of all women's blood: in the world organized by battles and the exchange of women between knights, only men bleed.

If the bloodshed of knights maintains or reestablishes social order, the bloodshed of women might be seen as subversive of the symbolic system in which heroism is defined. To the extent that the value of bloodshed is tied to injury and the danger of death, women's bleeding bodies may be viewed as profoundly threatening to the symbolic status of bloody heroism: the body that can regularly bleed but not die challenges the heroic nexus of blood, death, and glory promoted in romance narratives about battles undertaken to restore justice, win women, and gain honor. And to the extent that the valorization of men's bloodshed demands the suppression of women's blood, the representation of the gendered value of bloodshed in romance narratives enacts a curious reversal of the values associated with the body in other medieval symbolic systems. I have already suggested that the scrutiny of the blood that stains Guenevere's bed sheets as evidence of sexual possession rewrites the common display of women's blood on bed sheets as evidence of the sexual initiation of a virgin. But the prominent representation of men's blood in battles also revises the characterization of gendered bodies in medical and in theological discourses, where the idealized male body is usually described as sealed, intact, and conservative; by contrast, the female body is unruly, uncontained, and permeable.[41] While women can aspire to an intact body and even to an idealized masculine integrity through the preservation of virginity, this ideal is not usually promoted in stories about love, chivalry, and adultery—in Chrétien's *Chevalier de la charrete*, the adulterous queen Guenevere is hardly a virgin. Yet in romance narratives, the female body is—in relation to the loss of bodily fluid—sealed, intact; the male body is permeable, promiscuous in its bleeding.

This is not to say that the bleeding male body of chivalric romance is a feminized body. The knights who meet each other in battle should be closely matched opponents, otherwise the battle has no meaning. The victor wins heroic status, but the defeated knight also retains status: many romances recount battles in which a vanquished knight proclaims that there is no shame in being defeated by a great knight whose prowess is known throughout the world—a great knight like Lancelot, for example. In other words, bloodshed in battle is not associated with femininity; rather, it is subsumed into a model of masculine heroics. And the value of masculine bloodshed as the controlled, public bloodshed of battle seems to depend on its difference from women's blood, an uncontrolled bloodshed that remains private and hidden.

Women's bloodshed is not always private and hidden, as the example of Perceval's sister demonstrates. But the values of women's blood seem to be limited or localized in a way that the values of men's blood are not. And the values of men's blood seem to depend on the limited representation of women's blood—why can't the blood on the bed sheets have come from Guenevere herself? Because women's blood does not have lasting significance in contests between knights to possess women, honor, and glory. But what happens when women bleed in the heroic space of men? What happens when the blood spilled on bed sheets is identified as a woman's blood? The idealized portrait of the bloodless Queen Guenevere can be read against the representation of a bleeding female body in *Le roman de Florence de Rome*, a later narrative in which bloody sheets may be seen to structure a dispute about the possession and exchange of a woman.

Bloody Sheets II

The Old French *Roman de Florence de Rome* recounts the familiar story of a woman who is falsely accused of sexual infidelity to her husband.[42] She is presumed guilty, banished from her husband's court, and ends up in a foreign land where she is received as a distinguished guest, even though her identity remains hidden. Florence joins the household of a castellan and is befriended by his daughter, Beatrice. The castellan's seneschal, Macaire, tries to seduce Florence, who rejects him. Macaire insists, and tries to embrace Florence, who hits him with a bone and knocks out some of his teeth. Florence leaves the seneschal and goes to bed, where she is joined by her dear friend, Beatrice. While the two young women sleep, Macaire pursues his vengeance.

One day Florence was in her bed with her dear friend Beatrice, the daughter of the castellan who had treated her so well, and Macaire, who planned great treachery, hid all alone behind a curtain. He held in his hand a knife with a sharpened point, and he planned to do great treachery with it, as he subsequently did—may God condemn him! The young lady—may God help her!—slept in the royal chamber I am describing, in a rich and beautifully covered bed. It was large and wide, as is appropriate for a noble house. First Beatrice had fallen into a light sleep, then Florence, who was very tired, went soundly to sleep that night. . . . Macaire advanced, full of great evil, pulled down the cover, and struck the young girl [Beatrice] in the center of her chest. He struck her so hard that she did not scream or cry out, nor did she move foot or hand. She was struck so hard that she died there, and her soul left her body. The blood that flowed out of her shamed the bed; there was nothing under her that was not completely stained with it.

(Car un jour fu Flourence dedens son lit couchie
Avoecques Biautris, qui moult estoit s'amie,
La fille au castelain qui li fist courtoizie;
Et Maccaires estoit par se grant trecherie
Derriere le ghourdine tous seuls sans campaignie,
En se main un couttiel a la pointe aguizye,
Dont a faire penssoit une grant trescherie,

Enssement conme il fist, —li corps Dieu le maudie!
En la cambre royaus, dont je vous segnefie,
Dormoit la damoizielle, que Dieus soit en aÿe,
Dedens un riche lit, ouvré bien par maistrie:
Grans fu, larges et lez plus que je ne vous die,
Enssi conme il affiert a si noble mainsnie.
Biautris fu devant douchement endormie,
Flourence estoit derriere, qui toutte estoit haittie,
Et dormoit fermement en ycelle nuittie. . .
Maccaires s'avancha, plains de grant diaublerie,
Si a le couvreture un paul a mont sacquie,
La puchielle fery droit entre coer et fie.
Tellement l'assena qu'elle ne brait ne crie
Ne sacqua piet ne main, si bien fu atacquie
Que la endroit moru; l'ame s'en est partie.
Li sans qui de li yst a le kieutte honnie;
N'y a chose sous li n'en soit toutte souillie.) [43]

Florence is charged with the murder and condemned to be burned, but after hearing her eloquent plea of innocence the castellan allows her simply to leave his domain.

The blood on Florence's bed sheets does not offer the same mystery as the blood in Guenevere's bed; the source of the blood in Florence's bed is hardly in question, since the corpse of the murdered Beatrice is still there. However, the narrator's description of the blood that soaks the bed and the reasons behind the murder falsely attributed to Florence point to a structure similar to the one that organizes the battle over the blood on Guenevere's sheets.[44]

"The bed was shamed with blood all over, and the sheets were red" ("De sancq estoit honnis / Li lis tout environ et li linchieux rougis" [ll. 3623–24]). The shameful blood is the blood of murder and, to the extent that it is a woman's blood, it might also suggest the blood of menstruation. More important, though, the woman's blood that stains the bed is different from the masculine blood that is identified on Guenevere's sheets. It does not mark a transgression that threatens the exchange of women, as in *Le chevalier de la charrete*, where Méléagant takes the position of the cuckolded husband and accuses Guenevere of adultery with Sir Kay, whose blood, Méléagant claims, stains the queen's sheets. In *Florence de Rome* the woman has taken herself out of the structure of exchange between men: she has refused Macaire's seduction and prefers to sleep with her good friend, Beatrice.

The romance does not describe a sexual relationship between the two women, but they are clearly marked as a couple and Macaire, as a rejected outsider. Moreover, Macaire's failed seduction—unlike Méléagant's failure to possess the queen—is not part of a contest with other men. Florence is married, but she has been abandoned by her husband, and if her rejection of Macaire indicates a preference for another suitor, the position of the rival would seem to be occupied by Beatrice. But in the world of chivalric contests between men, a female rival for the possession of a woman creates an unintelligible triangle. The situation imagined in this text—a man who is rejected by a woman who sleeps with another woman—is illegible in a narrative structure in which relationships between knights are defined by the disputed possession of women. In other words, the bloodshed in *Florence de Rome* is situated outside of the structure in which knights undertake battles to win justice, fame, and the right to possess women. The blood on the sheets of the bed shared by Florence and Beatrice is neither the pretext for nor evidence of a heroic contest—it is women's blood.

Florence is banished from the castellan's court, and she eventually proves her fidelity to her husband and is reunited with him. The falsely accused woman is reintegrated into a structure in which the possession of women is disputed between men, but Florence's shifting position inside and outside the heroic economy based on the exchange of women reveals that romance narratives include multiple sexual economies: they include stories of women possessed and defended by men through bloody battles, stories of women repudiated by men because of false accusations of infidelity, and stories of men rejected by women who share their beds with other women. However, in the narrative structure of romance only one of these stories is a heroic story, only one kind of bloodshed is heroic bloodshed, and only one sexual economy is coterminous with the definition of justice through chivalric battle.

Bodies and Blood

The disputed origin of the blood on Queen Guenevere's sheets, taken as evidence of a crime, provokes the bloodshed (or the potential bloodshed) of the knights who fight to prove her guilt or innocence of adultery. Men's blood, as I have suggested in this chapter, structures contests between knights that determine truth, impose justice, and define social order. Men's blood thus participates in intersecting symbolic systems. That is, men shed blood—their own blood and the blood of adversaries—in local battles that have broad significance. Whether or not the blood on Guenevere's sheets is Kay's blood is decided in a battle between Lancelot and Méléagant, but the consequences of the queen's adultery extend far beyond the battle and threaten her husband's authority and even royal power.

Women's blood seems to have a much more limited symbolic potential, at least in medieval fiction. Women's blood remains tied to women's bodies. Women's blood can be martyr's blood, the blood of a suffering body, as the example of Perceval's sister demonstrates, or even as Alice Cooper suggests in "Only Women Bleed." But women's blood cannot guarantee justice or mark a covenant. In medieval fiction, only men bleed in ways that have consequence beyond their own bodies, in ways that bring about lasting change and recognition. Women's blood is linked to the body, and to embodiment; its effects are seen to affect the body, not society, as the example of Perceval's sister may suggest: the virgin's blood cures the body of the leprous lady, but cannot save her from moral and physical destruction. Another grail romance, the thirteenth-century *Perlesvaus* offers another example of the association of women's blood with embodiment itself.

Gauvain is the protagonist of much of this romance, and he arrives at a castle held by Marin le Jaloux, whose name indicates his nature. Marin himself is absent, and his wife greets Gauvain reluctantly. She is happy to welcome such a great knight, but she is apprehensive about receiving him in her husband's absence because the jealous Marin sees Gauvain as a threat to his wife's chastity, claiming that "Messire Gauvain never declared his love to a lady or to a maiden without having his way with her" ("Messire Gavains ne porta foi a dame ne a damoisele qu'il n'en feïst sa volenté.')[45] The lady receives Gauvain with courtesy, and the knight responds with restraint. However, an evil dwarf goes to Marin le Jaloux and falsely reports that his wife has slept with Gauvain. Marin returns to his castle and accuses his wife of infidelity. She denies that she has betrayed him, but her husband does not believe her. He has her stripped to her chemise and pulled by the hair into the forest. He forces her to stand in a cold lake beside a spring and begins to beat her. He strikes her on the back and on the breasts until the water of the spring is red with blood. Then Messire Gauvain arrives.

Gauvain offers to defend the lady in battle with Marin, and the two knights draw back for the charge:

The knight draws back for the charge, as Messire Gauvain goes toward him as fast as his horse can go. Marin le Jaloux flees Monseigneur Gauvain when he sees him coming, and avoids his blow. He lowers his lance and goes toward his wife, who sat crying like one who was innocent. He strikes her in the middle of her body and kills her.

(Li chevaliers se tret arriere por prendre son eslés, e Messire Gavains vient vers lui qanque chevaus li pot rendre. Marins le Jalox fuit Monseigneur Gavain qant il le voit venir e eschiue son cop. Il besse son glaive e va vers sa fame, qi se dementoit en plorant comme cele qui cope n'i avoit. Il la fiert parmi le cors e ocit. [*Perlesvaus*, 77])

Gauvain's failure to save the lady remains unexplained in this scene.[46] Gauvain himself does not understand the knight's violent conduct or his refusal of the chivalric code; and unable to bury the dead lady, Gauvain leaves her body in a chapel and continues on his way. A priest he encounters later in the romance explains the murder in terms of the religious economy of sacrifice.[47]

"Sire," said the priest, "there was great joy in the significance of her death, for Joseph tells us that the Old Law was destroyed by the blow of a lance without resuscitation, and in order to destroy the Old Law, God suffered the blow of a lance in his side, and with this blow and with his crucifixion the Old Law was destroyed. The lady signifies the Old Law."

(Sire, fait soi li prestres, ce fu molt grant joie de la senefiance de sa mort, car Josephes nos tesmoige que la Viez Loi fu abatue par un coup de glaive sanz resociter, et por la Viez Loi [abatre] se sofri Diex a ferir en coste du glaive, et par ce coup fu la [Viez] Loi abatue et par son crucefiement. La dame senefie la Viez Loi. [*Perlesvaus*, 110–11])

The priest goes on to explain that the murdered woman's son, whom Gauvain met later in the forest, represents the Savior, who was born in the Old Law.[48]

In the *Perlesvaus*, the lady and her jealous husband become allegorical figures in a drama of sacrifice and redemption. This romance is filled with episodes of bloody aggression and revenge: Arthur is cured of a wound with the blood of the knight who wounded him (38–39); King Gurguran has his dead son's body boiled, cut into small pieces, and sent as a ritual meal to all the men of his land (105); and Perceval punishes his defeated enemy, the Sire des Mores, by decapitating his knights and collecting their blood in a barrel, then hangs the Sire des Mores by the feet with his head in the blood until he drowns (234). And in the Christian symbolic economy of the *Perlesvaus*, men's blood enacts revenge and justice, and men's blood is a salvific blood; it represents and performs the battle for Christian justice and Christian salvation. Women's blood remains tied to the body and to embodiment: women's blood represents the blood of the Old Law, the law of the body that is transcended by the spirit through the salvific blood of Christ in the many representations of the eucharist in this romance.

If the value of women's blood remains tied to the body and to the significance of the suffering body, and the value of men's blood is defined in contests with other men, those respective values are of course determined by the ways in which gender roles are defined in medieval culture. After all, Guenevere doesn't try to defend her own innocence in battle, Florence does not challenge Macaire to prove his treachery, and the wife of Marin le Jaloux cannot undertake her own defense. Women do not usually go into battle in medieval fiction or in medieval culture. Indeed, nowhere is men's blood more valorized and women's blood more marginalized than in representations of war, the subject of the following chapter.

2

The Amenorrhea of War

BLOOD AND WAR would seem to be a natural pair—it is hard to imagine a battlefield without blood, as a whole spate of recent movies about World War II have graphically reminded us. Military heroism seems to demand bloodshed, or at least the possibility of bloodshed. But only one kind of blood is conventionally shed in war: men's blood. To be sure, women are hurt, killed, raped, and wounded in war, but women's wounds and women's deaths are usually classed under the heading of atrocities; they are the result of illegitimate violence that takes place outside the battlefield.[1] Legitimate violence, authorized by a higher good that requires heroic struggle and sacrifice, is traditionally the domain of men in most cultures: only men should die in combat; the blood of war is men's bloodshed.

In the United States, women are legally excluded from active combat in the Navy, Marine Corps, and Air Force. The United States Army is not prohibited by law from sending women into combat, though the army has repeatedly stated that it will not put female soldiers on the battlefield.[2] Several reasons are cited for the exclusion of women from warfare in the U.S. armed forces—to a large extent, the argument that "women can't fight" is marshaled on the evidence of bodies: women's bodies may become pregnant, and pregnant bodies do not belong on a battlefield; women's bodies are seen as weaker than men's bodies and unsuited to the conditions of combat; women's bodies are seductive and distract men from the business of war.[3]

The place of women in the military continues to be debated, and the terms of that debate are continuously restated, proved, and disproved.[4] However, my point here is not to argue for or against women's participation in combat, but rather, to explore the way that women's exclusion from war is defined as natural. In particular, I want to examine the association of women's blood with women's reproductive biology, and the extent to which that association defines the difference between women's blood and the bloodshed of men. The different values associated with women's blood and men's blood invent and reinforce the notion of a "naturally" gendered social order in which men fight and women don't.

G.I. Jane

A recent representation of gendered military heroism offers a striking example of the way that women's blood is seen as utterly, if not scandalously, inappropriate in a combat setting. Ridley Scott's 1997 film, *G.I. Jane*, tells the story of a woman who joins the Navy SEAL elite combat training program.[5] Lieutenant Jordan O'Neil (Demi Moore) is chosen to participate in the training, and her success or failure will demonstrate whether or not women are able to take on the demanding physical requirements of combat. Lt. O'Neil takes the challenge seriously. In the training exercises she refuses any concession to the fact that she is a woman and complains when she is not held to the same standards as her male counterparts. She also insists on sharing the men's barracks. The anxiety that this causes among the male recruits is shown to focus on blood: the men with whom she will share quarters express a mixture of outrage and horror when they see that Lt. O'Neil is putting what one recruit calls "her stuff" into her locker: "What about the tampons?" he cries to the other men. "Don't you care about the tampons?"

Lt. O'Neil surprises everyone by successfully completing the rigorous physical training that eliminates 60 percent of the men in her group, and her success is underlined in a subtle and ambivalent way in the movie. During a physical examination, the woman doctor who examines her explains to Lt. O'Neil in somewhat clinical terms why she no longer menstruates: "It's called amenorrhea when you lose your period. It's because you drop body fat, but that's not at all unusual for female athletes."

It is of course true that women athletes' experience of amenorrhea is not unusual; women cadets at West Point have also ceased menstruating during training.[6] It is, however, unusual that menstruation, even the absence of menstruation, gets mentioned in a mainstream movie. And why is it necessary in the logic of the film to point out Lt. O'Neil's amenorrhea? Hollywood movies are, as a genre, usually very reticent about bodily functions—rarely do we see characters urinating, defecating, or menstruating on screen. *G.I. Jane* makes a point of representing menstruation, but only in order to show its absence. Any blood Lt. O'Neil sheds must have come from the cuts and abrasions she continues to accumulate in training exercises.

The idea of a woman in combat—even a woman who does not menstruate—continues to be a controversial idea in this movie, despite Lt. O'Neil's successes, and, perhaps predictably, what most characters in the story see as the female recruit's "unnatural" ability to fight like a man is ultimately linked to what they also see as her "unnatural" sexuality. Lt. O'Neil is photographed in what is considered a compromising situation: a beach party with the woman doctor, who is a lesbian. Lt. O'Neil is immediately identified as a lesbian; she is accused of conduct unbecoming an officer and suspended from active duty. Lt. O'Neil's heterosexual credentials have already been emphatically and anxiously established earlier in the film; the photograph of her with the lesbian doctor is deliberately misinterpreted and used to force Lt. O'Neil out of SEAL training, as is discovered later in the movie. But in its intense scrutiny of the female reproductive body in the references to O'Neil's amenorrhea and to her sexuality, the film reveals a profound anxiety of its own about a woman who performs as a man, a woman who bleeds profusely from her wounds but not from her genitals, a woman who escapes what the film constructs as the "natural" categories of sex and heterosexuality. This is a sign of the movie's profound ambivalence about the very message it purports to offer: women's ability to perform in combat as women. But it is also an example of the anxious suppression of women's blood in the construction of masculine military heroism. *G.I. Jane* exposes a perceived incompatibility between women's blood and heroic bloodshed, which is usually defined as masculine. And this incompatibility points to what we might call the amenorrhea of war: the necessary absence of women's blood in the valorization of the productive values of men's bloodshed.

War and Menstruation

As contemporary debates about women in battle demonstrate, the gendering of military heroism comes into question precisely when women do enter the battlefield. And despite the recorded presence of women in battles throughout western history, the traditional exclusion of women from warfare is one of the arguments inevitably advanced for prohibiting women from combat service in the modern military: "The historical record is quite clear. War and soldiering, with few if any substantial pre-twentieth-century exceptions, have been an exclusive male preserve. One can point to the Amazons of Greek mythology but few real exceptions are recorded."[7] In fact, the exclusion of women from war has a long and disputed history, and premodern narratives offer many examples of women warriors. These narratives include historical chronicles, legends, and fictional accounts, but they all imagine women as warriors whose exploits deserve elaboration. At the same time, though, these accounts all insist on the extraordinary nature of the successful woman warrior, and they use a variety of narrative strategies to question whether women's participation in combat is "natural." One way in which women are shown to be inadequate or out of place in battle is through the association of women and the debilitating functions of the female reproductive body.

Medieval Irish stories recount battles fought to avenge insults and wars undertaken in retaliation for transgressions against the king or against his clan, or as the result of a theft. The *Táin Bó Cúalnge* is one such story. Three versions of the *Táin* survive from the Middle Ages; they record oral sources that date from as early as the seventh or eight century.[8] A twelfth-century redaction of the *Táin*, found in the Book of Leinster, is the most extensive version of the story and includes an episode absent from the other two versions of the story: the female protagonist, Medb, is unable to continue fighting during a battle because she begins to menstruate.

The *Táin Bó Cúalnge* is a story about the theft of a bull and the war that results. The idea for the cattle raid is provoked by an argument between Medb and her husband, Ailill, over which of them is the richest. They assemble all their possessions and find that they are equal except for the bull possessed by Ailill, and "It was to Medb as if she owned not a penny of possessions since she had not a bull as great as that."[9] Medb asks if there is not another bull in Ireland to match it, and learns that the Ulstermen possess a bull than is even better than Ailill's. When an attempt to borrow the bull fails, Medb assembles men from four provinces of Ireland to take the bull (Donn Cúailnge) from Ulster. After many battles, Medb takes the stolen bull back to Connacht, and as she defends the retreat with her forces she is suddenly incapacitated by her menstrual period.

Then Medb covered the retreat of the men of Ireland and she sent the Donn Cúailnge around to Crúachu together with fifty of his heifers and eight of Medb's messengers, so that whoever might reach Crúachu or whoever might not, at least the Donn Cúailnge would arrive there as she had promised. Then her issue of blood came upon Medb (and she said: "O Fergus, cover) the retreat of the men of Ireland that I may pass my water." "By my conscience," said Fergus, "It is ill-timed and it is not right to do so." "Yet I cannot but do so," said Medb, "for I shall not live unless I do." Fergus came then and covered the retreat of the men of Ireland. Medb passed her water and it made three great trenches in each of which a household can fit. Hence the place is called Fúal Medba.

Cú Chulainn came upon her thus engaged but he did not wound her for he used not to strike her from behind. . . . Then Fergus began to survey the host as they went westwards from Áth Mór. "This day was indeed a fitting one (for those who were) led by a woman," said Fergus. . . . "This host has been plundered and despoiled today. As when a mare goes before her band of foals into unknown territory, with none to lead or counsel them, so this host has perished today."

(And sain geibis Medb scíath díten dar éis fer ṅHérend. And sain faítte Medb in Dond Cúalnge co coíca dá šamascib imbe & ochtor dá hechlachaib leiss timchell co Crúachain. Gipé rašossed, gipé ná rossed, go rossed in Dond Cúalnge feib ra gell-si. Is and drecgais a fúal fola for Meidb [⁊ itbert: "Geib, a Ḟerguis," bar Medb], "scíath díten dar éis fer ṅHérend goro šíblur-sa m'ḟúal úaim." "Dar ar cubus,' ar Fergus, 'is olc in tráth⁊ ní cóir a dénam." "Gid ed ní étaim-sea chena,' bar Medb, 'dáig nída beó-sa meni šíblur-sa m'ḟúal úaim." Tánic Fergus ⁊ gebid scíath díten dar éis fer ṅHérend. Siblais Medb a fúal úathi co nderna trí tulchlassa móra de co taille munter in cach thurchlaiss. Conid Fúal Medba atberar friss.

Ruc Cú Chulaind furri ac dénam na huropra sain ⁊ níra gonastarsum; ní athgonad-sum 'na díaid hí. . . . And sain ra gab Fergus ac tachim in tšlúaig ac dula a Áth Mór síar. "Rapa chomadas in lá sa indiu ám I ndíaid mná,' [ar Fergus]. . . . Ra gattá ⁊ ra brattá in slúag sa indiu. Feib théit echrad láir rena serrgraig i crích n-aneóil gan chend cundraid ná comairle rempo, is amlaid testa in slúag sa indiu.")[10]

To my knowledge this is the only representation of menstrual blood in the context of war in all medieval fiction, and even here the language of the text is not entirely clear. The passage initially describes Medb's debility as her "urine of blood" (*fúal focal*, translated above by Rahilly as "issue of blood"), an ambiguous phrase that seems to name both menstruation and urine.[11] In the two subsequent uses of "fúal" in this passage, the word is used alone and simply means "urine" (translated above as "water"). The cause of Medb's debility seems to be both menstruation and urination and suggests that the cleric who recorded the story may have had a fairly inaccurate understanding of women's bodies. But to the extent that the passage first links Medb's debility to menstrual blood, it associates women's biology and the incapacity to engage in combat:

Medb has to leave off the business of war while she attends to her sudden flow of blood. The switch to urine alone in subsequent descriptions of Medb's bodily functions may be associated with the power of her flow, which creates great trenches.[12] But while Medb's output is indeed prodigious, Fergus's claim that women are unable to lead troops ("As when a mare goes before her band of foals into unknown territory, with none to lead or counsel them, so this host has perished today") suggests that the monumental dimensions of Medb's flow might also be seen as an exaggerated representation of the uncontrollable functions of women's bodies.[13]

The debilitating effect of Medb's menstruation corresponds to another prominent characterization of debility as feminine in Old Irish literature. In a story whose outcome is echoed in the *Táin*, Crunnchu goes to the provincial assembly of Ulster, where he boasts that his wife Macha can outrun the king's horses. The pregnant Macha begs to be spared the race—she is near delivery—but because of his boast, her husband will die if she cannot win. Running alongside the chariot pulled by the king's horses, she gives birth to twins and curses the men who would not defer the race.

Then she raced the chariot. As the chariot reached the end of the field, she gave birth alongside it. She bore twins, a son and a daughter. The name Emain Macha, the Twins of Macha, comes from this. As she gave birth she screamed out that all who heard that scream would suffer from the same pangs for five days and four nights in their times of greatest difficulty. This affliction, ever afterward, seized all the men of Ulster who were there that day, and nine generations after them. Five days and four nights, or five nights and four days, the pangs lasted. For nine generations any Ulsterman in those pangs had no more strength than a woman on the bed of labour.[14]

Macha's childbirth pains are similar to Medb's menstruation in that they are simultaneously associated with power (she wins the race) and debility (she curses the Ulstermen with incapacitating birth pains). The *Táin Bó Cúalnge* uses the motif of the warriors' periodic debility: when Medb begins the cattle raid, the Ulstermen cannot fight because they are debilitated by the pangs of childbirth, the result of Macha's curse. The *Táin* promotes the idea that women's bodies are unsuited to leadership in battle through the representation of the female body's natural functions as debilitating in the context of war: women's blood—the blood of menstruation and the blood of parturition—is shown to be incompatible with battle.

Women Warriors

Medieval representations of women warriors do not always focus on women's biological functions as evidence of a natural feminine inability to participate in combat. They do, however, often point to a basic incompatibility between women and war even as they represent successful women warriors. Icelandic sagas offer an example of this kind of representation. Recorded in the thirteenth century, sagas recount stories from around the time of the christianization of Iceland, 900–1000. A number of sagas recount the stories of maiden warriors, young women who put on men's clothing and participate in battle.[15] These women are often successful in combat, sometimes they are ultimately defeated or even killed by their male adversaries, but they are generally reintegrated into traditional roles by the end of their stories—they marry and produce children.[16] Hervör, Angantýr's daughter, is one such maiden warrior. She is "as strong as a man; as soon as she could do anything for herself she trained herself more with bow and shield and sword than with needlework and embroidery."[17] She goes to her father's tomb, claims his sword (which belongs to her as his only child), disguises herself as a man, and enters the service of King Gudmund. She later joins the Vikings and goes out raiding, but she wearies of this life and goes home to do needlework. She is subsequently married to Höfund, son of King Gudmund.

The extent to which these fictional accounts of women warriors were modeled on the actual experiences of women in war is unknown.[18] Grave goods provide some clues about women's participation in war, but the evidence is ambiguous. Weapons have been discovered in female graves from the Viking Age, and the grave goods may indicate that the woman buried with the arms used them in battle during her lifetime. However, the weapons may also have symbolic functions that do not imply that the buried woman actually used weapons, so archeological evidence cannot provide firm support for how closely sagas about women warriors may reflect the experiences of women in war.[19] There is evidence, though, that a woman who went to war was perceived to transgress conventional gender roles.

Around 1200, Saxo Grammaticus forcefully condemns women who would go to war in his *History of the Danes*. Saxo discusses a number of warrior women from Denmark's legendary past in the first part of his *History*, and he concludes with a condemnation of the association of women and warfare.[20]

In case anyone is marveling that this sex should have sweated in warfare, let me digress briefly to explain the character and behavior of such females. There were once women in Denmark who dressed themselves to look like men and spent almost every minute cultivating soldiers' skills. . . . Loathing a dainty style of living, they would harden body and mind with toil and endurance, rejecting the fickle pliancy of girls and compelling their womanish spirits to act with a virile ruthlessness. They courted military celebrity so earnestly that one might have guessed they had un-sexed themselves. . . . As if they were forgetful of their true selves they put toughness before allure, aimed at conflicts instead of kisses, tasted blood, not lips, sought the clash of arms rather than the arm's embrace, fitted to weapons hands which should have been weaving, desired not the couch but the kill, and those they could have appeased with looks they attacked with lances.

(Et ne quis hunc bellis sexum insudasse miretur, quaedam de talium feminarum condicione et moribus compendio modicae digressionis expediam. Fuere quondam apud Danos feminae, quae formam suam in virilem habitum convertentes omnia paene temporum momenta ad excolendam militiam conferebant. . . . Siquidem delicatum vivendi genus perosae corpus animumque patientia ac labore durare solebant totamque femineae levitatis mollitiem abdicantes muliebre ingenium virili uti saevitia cogebant. Sed et tanta cura rei militaris notitiam captabant, ut feminas exuisse quivis putaret. . . . Hae ergo, perinde ac nativae condicionis immemores regoremque blanditiis anteferentes, bella pro basiis intentabant sanguinemque, non oscula delibantes armorum potuis quam amorum officia frequentabant manusque, quas in telas aptare debuerant, telorum obsequiis exhibebant, ut iam non lecto, sed lecto studentes spiculis appeterent, quos mulcere specie potuissent.)[21]

For Saxo Grammaticus, as perhaps for the authors of the sagas, the transgression of proper gender roles is what makes the woman warrior an inappropriate anomaly.

This judgment is echoed in fictional accounts of successful women warriors. In the twelfth-century *Roman d'Eneas*, based on Virgil's *Aeneid*, a Trojan tells the warrior, Camille, that she should be doing her fighting in bed, not on the battlefield ("Feme ne se doit pas combatre, / se par nuit non tot an gisant"[22]). And while some Old French *chansons de geste* recount stories in which entire armies of women go to battle, these stories also recount women's warfare as a pursuit that causes them to neglect their "natural" roles as mothers. Catherine Jones has noted that in the thirteenth-century *Ansëys de Mes*, when twenty thousand women unite to avenge the deaths of their husbands, lovers, sons, and brothers, their action is represented as a conscious imitation of masculine behavior and appearance.[23] Jones also points to the way that descriptions of women warriors focus on physical attributes, like their beautiful or noble bodies, while descriptions of men in battle focus on social status, like nobility, a gendered difference that has also been noted in descriptions of women warriors in romances like *Le roman d'Enéas*.[24] In *Ansëys de Mes*, the "unnatural" presence of women in war is underlined in the consequences of the battle. Although the women are able fighters, so many of them are killed in battle that the men of Flanders have to import women from England to repopulate the country.[25]

These Old French representations of women in war identify women warriors as unnatural, as neglecting their "natural" roles as mothers and as lovers. And accounts of Norse women warriors, like the story of Medb, point to women's inability to wage war even as they represent women warriors. It seems that there are at least two ways to see the narrative construction of women's unsuitability for war. In the sagas, as in Saxo's account and in *Le roman d'Eneas* and *Ansëys de Mes*, women take on men's dress to "un-sex" themselves, to take on men's roles. The woman who discards feminine attire and takes on men's clothing to fight as a man is also found romance narratives like the thirteenth-century French *Roman de Silence* or *Yde et Olive*. However, in these stories women do not merely put on masculine clothing when they take on masculine endeavors; they disguise themselves as men and take on male identities. Yet despite her successful masculine impersonation, the heroine of *Le roman de Silence* ends her military career much like many saga heroines do: the woman warrior is restored to her proper gender identity, appropriate clothing, and "natural" sexuality as the story recounts the redressing of the heroine as a woman and her marriage.[26]

In *Yde et Olive*, the woman disguised as a knight is not reintegrated into society as a wife; rather, she is transformed into a man so that she can marry the woman to whom she has been betrothed while passing as a man. From the point of view of the relationship between women and war, the two kinds of ending are not really very different: women are excluded from the battlefield either through a reintegration into the proper gender role through marriage or through a transformation into the proper gender for battle. In both cases, women disguise themselves as men in order to participate in war, and the need for any explanation for their success in battle is avoided by their transformations—back into a woman and wife or into a "real" man.

Stories about women warriors who adopt men's dress all emphasize to a greater or lesser extent that when women participate in combat they take on men's roles, and the crossing of strictly defined gender boundaries is of course what causes the anxiety about women in war, whether in the Middle Ages or today.[27] Medieval texts usually try to contain the subversiveness of cross-dressing women warriors by reintegrating them into marriage and maternity, and women's participation in warfare is thus to some extent limited to a transitional period, to a period of anomalous dress and activity that has a definite end.

But as the *Táin* demonstrates, there is another way to imagine women's exclusion from warfare as a "natural" exclusion, and that is through the emphasis on the bleeding female body as a body that is not suited for combat. The warrior Medb does not put on men's clothes, nor does her sexuality seem to be compromised by her position as a warrior (Medb's sexual exploits, like her urine flow, have legendary proportions in this story). This story defines the unsuitability of women in combat through a focus on the woman's body and its functions. The female body is not reformed or suppressed or disguised by men's clothes or by its ability to enact men's exploits; nor is it reintegrated into a proper gender role through marriage and reproduction, as in some sagas. Rather, the warrior's female body is represented as a body debilitated by its female biological functions; it is a body that cannot fight because it must bleed.

But why should women's blood become the focus of the gendering of military heroism? To be sure, some women are physically ill during menstruation, but even in contemporary debates about women in combat, this physical incapacity is rarely discussed openly and never, it seems, scientifically. (A West Point cadet observed, "There's no latrine on a tank. If a woman is going through her menstrual cycle there's no opportunity for her to take care of herself."[28])

The example of Medb's menstrual debility is clearly an exaggerated one—her monumental flow of blood and urine leaves valleys in its wake. But the association of amenorrhea with the body whose strength exceeds its femininity, as in the example of Lt. O'Neil in *G.I. Jane* or even, I suggest, Joan of Arc, also represents menstruation as the primary marker of a "natural" incompatibility of women's bodies and war. That is, these representations of women warriors—representations of extraordinary women whose place in combat is contested even as they are represented as successful on the battlefield—suggest the importance of women's blood in the anxious definition of the battlefield as the terrain of masculine heroism.

Maiden's Blood

Joan of Arc is perhaps the most famous example of a woman warrior in Western history, though Joan's military career was in fact rather short: it began with the relief of the English siege of Orléans in 1429 and ended with her capture in 1430.[29] Joan was tried and condemned for heresy, and on May 31, 1431, she was burned. Twenty-five years later a new trial nullified the condemnation of 1431. In Joan's 1455–56 nullification trial, testimony was gathered from those who had known Joan during her short lifetime. These witnesses testified to Joan's purity, piety, and to her skill as a military leader. Among those interviewed during the rehabilitation trial was Jean d'Aulon, Joan's personal valet, whose testimony revealed that the maiden did not menstruate.

He also testified that he had heard it said by several women, who saw the Maid undressed several times and knew her secrets, that she never suffered from the secret illness of women and that no one could ever notice or learn anything of it from her clothes or in any other way.

(Dit encores plus qu'il a oy dire à plusieurs femmes, qui ladicte Pucelle ont veue par plusieurs foiz nue, et sceu de ses secretz, que oncques n'avoit eu la secrecte maladie des femmes et que jamais nul n'en peut riens cognoistre ou appercevoir par ses habillemens, ne aultrement.)[30]

This claim could address several concerns: it could explain away some potentially awkward personal arrangements in Joan's daily life among her soldiers. It could be intended to emphasize Joan's virgin innocence, or it may describe Joan according to the model of holy women whose severe ascetic practices reduced their bodily discharges.[31] Joan's amenorrhea may position her outside of gender and reproductive sexuality; in the context of Joan's cross-dressing, her amenorrhea could describe the perceived denaturalization of the female body that wears male clothes. As part of the testimony at the nullification trial, the assertion is clearly intended to contribute to a validation of Joan's mission and of her divine inspiration, but one thing that the claim certainly does accomplish is to remove women's blood from the battlefield. And indeed this is the explicit interpretation of one nineteenth-century account of Joan's history that describes the maiden as "Womanly in modesty, but exempt, by a particular design, from the weaknesses of her sex, she was also not subjected to those periodic and inconvenient dues, which, even more than law and custom, prevent women in general fulfilling the functions that men have taken over."[32]

Conflicting stories have been told about Joan of Arc since before her death, and Joan is such a famously disputed historical figure in part because she incarnates many of the tensions that troubled late medieval culture: the relationship of popular religion to the formal rituals of the church; the changing form of war, in which the use of mercenaries replaced feudal alliances; and of course a contested definition of royal succession.[33] Joan's story touches on all these tensions, but what is most striking about her trial and about late medieval and early modern accounts of her life is the way that anxieties about cultural institutions take the form of anxieties about Joan's perceived gender impropriety and possible sexual transgressions.[34] And this is true of both French and English sources, of texts written by the partisans of Joan and by her detractors. In the recorded debates about the origins of Joan's mission (was she inspired by God, or was she duped by the devil?) we see the ways in which the demonic and the holy, like the military and the domestic, are gendered concepts that script Joan's entry into history.

Joan's reputation for not suffering "the secret illness of women" suggests that blood is also gendered in her story, that gendered cultural values are mapped onto blood, so that blood itself comes to be seen as gendered and thus as a "natural" foundation for gendered cultural values. This gendering is particularly apparent in the rather late and unsympathetic portrait of Joan found in Shakespeare's *Henry VI, Part 1* (1591/92). Shakespeare's late sixteenth-century English perspective on Joan la Pucelle is not a contemporary account, of course, and it is not particularly accurate in its history of Joan, but it does highlight the way that anxieties about gender and battle can focus on blood.[35]

1 Henry VI is one of the few accounts of Joan's life in which it is the maid's military prowess, and not her cross-dressing, that seems to demand explanation. In an early scene in the play, Joan defeats the French dauphin in single combat to prove her personal prowess and her worthiness to lead troops. Whereas this is perhaps not a significant victory, at least from the perspective of the English, who see Charles as a weak and unworthy pretender, Joan also demonstrates her prowess in combat with the English general, Talbot, and the battle ends in a draw. This exaggerated skill with the sword is not described in medieval accounts of Joan's exploits, and Shakespeare's portrayal of Joan's skill explains the military successes of a woman who cannot, in Shakespeare's account, have benefited from divine aid.

The woman warrior is a figure celebrated in mythical and Biblical traditions—in *1 Henry VI* Charles admiringly describes Joan as an Amazon and claims that she fights with the sword of Deborah (1.3.83–84).[36] But by the late Middle Ages, it seems that *only* mythical women could be celebrated as warriors—medieval women who sought to go into battle were regarded with deep suspicion. This strict exclusion of women from the business of war was a somewhat recent development. Although war was always considered a masculine endeavor, chroniclers recorded the military activities of a number of women who were neither censured nor ridiculed for their pursuit of war.[37] Historian Megan McLaughlin notes that descriptions of the military activities of women are found in many medieval sources from the early Middle Ages: women went to war to defend castles when their husbands were absent, and as I mentioned above, there is disputed evidence that Viking women participated in warfare.[38] Aethelflaed, daughter of Alfred the Great of Wessex, appears to have fought alongside her brother in the tenth century, and a number of noblewomen from southern Europe are known to have joined in military campaigns with their husbands or to have mobilized retainers for warfare during the eleventh through thirteenth centuries.[39]

Because medieval military organization was essentially domestic in character, women had a relatively large opportunity to participate in warfare. The basic military unit through most of medieval Europe was the small group of warriors tied to a lord by bonds of personal loyalty or vassalage. Military education was also domestic in this period, and the training of children for knighthood took place in the home. McLaughlin suggests that the daughters of a noble house would have been exposed to military practices and heard military exploits praised from an early age. They thus had the opportunity to obtain some theoretical knowledge of the subject. The domestic organization of warfare, then, provided women with the chance to prepare themselves for battle. It may also have increased the likelihood that they would be accepted in that role by the men on the battlefield.[40]

But as domestic military units lost their predominant role in warfare in the later Middle Ages, the number of women warriors mentioned in the sources declined as well. McLaughlin argues that in the later Middle Ages, "normal" feminine behavior comes increasingly to be seen as opposed to military pursuits, and "warfare came to be seen not just as unusual, but as somehow unnatural for females."[41] The later Middle Ages were marked by a reorganization and professionalization of warfare throughout

Europe: in this as in other areas of medieval life, the trend was towards greater differentiation of the public and the domestic. Small feudal contingents continued to play a role in many military engagements, but they were increasingly overshadowed by units of a different origin and nature, less clearly tied to the household. As this happened, women lost their opportunity to participate in military activities.

Joan of Arc was not part of a noble household where she might have been involved in warfare as a domestic enterprise. Nor was Joan a mercenary, of course. She said she was called by God to fight for the dauphin, and Charles seems to have believed her, at least initially, and gave her arms and troops. By why did soldiers follow Joan? It would seem that if there was cultural resistance to the idea of a woman warrior in late medieval France, that resistance would surely be shared by soldiers. Kelly DeVries notes that no troops of the Hundred Years War had ever followed a woman into battle, and stories of women who had led troops in earlier periods were likely to have distant enough to have the status of myth, if they were remembered at all.[42] Yet apparently French soldiers were willing to follow Joan—why?

We do have testimony from men who fought under Joan. The soldiers claimed that they were inspired by her piety, and they further claimed that they never felt any sexual desire for her. Gobert Thibault, a royal esquire, described the attitude of the soldiers toward Joan, at a time when the only other women in the army were camp followers:

In the army she was always with the soldiers; I heard many of those closest to her say that they never had any desire for her; that is to say, they sometimes felt a certain carnal urge but never dared to let themselves go with her, and they believed that it was not possible to desire her; often when they were speaking among themselves of the sin of the flesh and were saying things that might arouse desire, if they saw her or came near her, they were not able to continue such speech and suddenly their carnal impulses ceased. I have questioned several of those who sometimes slept the night in Joan's company about this, and they answered as I have, adding that they never felt any carnal desire when they saw her.

(Dicit etiam quod in exercitu erat semper cum armatis; et audivit dici a pluribus eidem Johanne familiaribus, quod de ipsa nunquam habuerant concupiscentiam, esto quod aliquando adesset voluntas libidinis, nunquam tamen de ea presumpserunt, et credebant quod non posset concupisci; et multotiens, dum loquebantur de peccato carnis et de aliquibus verbis que trahere poterant ad libidinem, dum eam videbant et appropinquabant, non poterant de hoc loqui, ymo repente amittebant motum carnis. Et de hoc interrogavit plures qui aliquando cubuerunt de nocte in societate dicte Johanne, qui sibi respondebant ut supra deposuit, dicentes ultra quod nunquam habuerant concupiscentiam carnalem, dum eamden aspiciebant. Nec aliud scit de contentis in eisdem articulis.)[43]

If Joan's troops felt divinely inspired to follow her, it is Joan's mission from God that explains her success as a leader. Yet the soldiers' willingness to follow Joan may be explained by the familiar as well as the extraordinary. Joan of Arc was a woman, and she was a peasant—she obviously did not resemble the noble generals who directed the war. But as DeVries has argued, Joan was in fact like mercenary captains, leaders of the Free Companies who were by this time fairly common in war. These men led loyal troops successfully in battle and rewarded their successes with booty. Joan of Arc did not offer her troops material rewards, she did not allow them to loot or pillage captured lands—she offered them salvation. DeVries suggests that "in the fifteenth century, in an age of flourishing popular religion, personal devotion, mysticism, and adherence to several living saints, especially to *mulieres sanctae*, Joan's gift to her troops was sufficient to entice them to follow her with a loyalty unknown to any French noble leader of the time, even to the dauphin himself."[44] Joan herself would thus be doubly positioned by the rise of mercenary warfare: as war was increasingly the business of mercenaries rather than small groups of warriors associated with a household, women were increasingly marginalized from the activities of war; at the same time, it may have been the model of the mercenary captain that made Joan's leadership familiar and acceptable to soldiers fighting for the dauphin.

Joan's military exploits after Orléans did not match her success in delivering the besieged city, and she suffered a series of defeats before her capture. After she was taken, the French did not make any effort to rescue her, although the trial transcripts indicate that she expected such an attempt. It has been suggested that Joan's declining military successes had already shaken French faith in her calling, and her capture may have put into question the divinely sanctioned status of her mission.[45] The dauphin and the French nobles effectively distanced themselves from Joan after her capture, and even before, as Shakespeare suggests, though of course Shakespeare also shows Joan appealing to her demons to help her. *1 Henry VI*, like late medieval English chronicles, suggests that Joan's military successes can only be explained by witchcraft.

If McLaughlin's thesis about the changing nature of warfare—the move from war between households organized by feudal bonds to wars conducted largely through mercenaries—explains the marginalization of women from war during the late Middle Ages, Joan's successes would be suspect, anomalous and perhaps transgressive, but what explains the anxious demonization of Joan like that displayed in Shakespeare's *1 Henry VI*? The possibility that Joan was possessed by the devil rather than inspired by God is not unique to this theatrical version of Joan's life. A contemporary observer noted that, when the dauphin first heard Joan claim to have a divine mission to save France, he "thought her crazy, possessed by the devil, and completely audacious." [46] The fact that Joan attributed her successes to divine guidance invites an alternative supernatural explanation for her military career—if God was not responsible, it must have been the devil. Certainly the perceived gender transgression in Joan's adoption of men's clothing and in her masculine pursuit of warfare provokes anxiety about social order, religious order, and even the nature of sovereignty, but what *1 Henry VI* suggests with a particular insistence is the extent to which Joan's presence on the battlefield is seen to threaten the cultural values promoted by war.

For the early modern period, as for the Middle Ages, as even for twenty-first-century America, the emblem of war is bloodshed. Men shed blood to restore social order, to impose justice, and to right wrongs. Men shed blood to protect women; men shed their blood to protect their blood—their lineage or their patrimony. The heroism of war and bloodshed is a masculine heroism, the bloodshed of war is the privilege of men, and the blood of war is men's blood.

The presence of a woman warrior on the field of battle may be seen to threaten the practice of chivalric heroism as a masculine prerogative. To the extent that chivalry was associated with aristocracy, masculine privilege was under siege in a number of ways in Shakespeare's *1 Henry VI*, as Jean Howard and Phyllis Rackin have shown.[47] But the particular form in which the conflict between gendered forms of military heroism is imagined in *1 Henry VI* invites a consideration of the extent to which masculine privilege and identity are grounded in representations of blood and suggests that women's blood on the battlefield might threaten the masculine virtues constructed in war.

Although the fact that it is men who bleed in battle may mark the bloodshed of war as a masculine bloodshed, the blood of war is also gendered symbolically. In other words, the symbolic value of blood is linked to the gender of blood, but the gender of blood is revealed to be a symbolic value as well. So whereas in the *Táin*, a woman's bloodshed demonstrates both the power to destroy and the incapacitation of Medb, who bleeds and cannot fight, in Shakespeare's story about Joan, the gendered value of bloodshed is more precariously related to the body that sheds it. For example, in *1 Henry VI*, when the English general Talbot's son, John, joins his father on the battlefield, Talbot praises his son's military performance in terms of an initiation—John Talbot fights his first battle. But Talbot describes the event in the terms of a sexual initiation in which John occupies the position of a woman. Talbot boasts to his son of having wounded "The ireful Bastard Orléans, that drew blood from thee, my boy, and had the maidenhood of thy first fight" (4.6.16–18). In Talbot's analogy, the first blood that John sheds in battle is like the blood that a maiden sheds in her first experience of intercourse (and may suggest the way in which the homosocial bonding of the battlefield is expressed in sexualized and gendered terms). But this is women's blood; it is a blood that is usually seen as the mark of sexual possession by a man. John's maidenly bloodshed is further emphasized by Joan when she later boasts that when she encountered John, she said to him, "Thou maiden youth, be vanquished by a maid" (4.7). Indeed, John Talbot's maidenhood displaces Joan's in Shakespeare's play, where Joan is characterized by the English as a whore, the mistress of the Bastard of Orleans (a common English characterization of Joan), and where Joan herself claims to be pregnant in an attempt to avoid the flames.[48]

John's maiden bloodshed suggests the instability of the gendering of the blood that supports military heroism. It suggests the possibility that the bloodshed of war is not uniquely or unambiguously men's blood. It might be men's blood that is like maiden's blood—it might be like women's blood. This ambiguity is countered by an anxious negotiation of the place of Joan's blood in the context of masculine military heroism. But this is not an anxiety unique to *1 Henry VI*. We also see it in some of the medieval accounts of Joan of Arc's mission to save France.

Joan was wounded twice, once in the shoulder and once in the thigh.[49] Her blood does not receive special attention in descriptions of her wounds: in accounts by her contemporaries, Joan's bloodshed is like any other soldier's blood. It is in her lack of blood that she is extraordinary—as in Jean d'Aulon's testimony that Joan did not menstruate.

Shakespeare does not of course represent a menstruating Joan of Arc, but he does give particular attention to Joan's blood. In *1 Henry VI*, the maid's blood links her to witchcraft and to demons. Talbot wishes to draw Joan's witch's blood: "Devil or devil's dam, I'll conjure thee," he says, "Blood will I draw on thee—thou art a witch—And straightway give thy soul to him thou serv'st" (1.7.5–7). Talbot may refer to the idea that whoever draws a witch's blood is protected from her magic, but his names for Joan, "devil or devil's dam," that is, devil or devil's mother, suggest that the blood he wishes to draw is mother's blood, witch's blood—it is female blood, and a blood associated with reproduction.

If Joan's blood is mother's blood, it is the blood of a corrupt mother. When the fiends that Shakespeare identifies as responsible for Joan's successes abandon her, she appeals to their past relationship in a description that suggests just the kind of maternal relationship that Talbot identified earlier when he called Joan a "devil's dam," a devil's mother. Joan pleads with the fiends: "O, hold me not with silence overlong! Where I was wont to feed you with my blood, I'll lop a member off and give it to you" (5.3.13–15). Joan's offer of blood may reflect the belief that witches have an extra nipple with which they nurse demons. And breast milk is a form of mother's blood in premodern reproductive theory: in lactating mothers menstrual blood is turned into the breast milk that nourishes a child.

It is no accident that the demonization of Joan in *1 Henry VI* is so closely associated with her blood and with maternal imagery. If, as many critics of the play have observed, Joan is a foil for the English general, Talbot, and if Talbot's virtues are emphasized in Joan's faults, then Talbot, the loving father whose son refuses to leave him on the battlefield, even in the face of death, offers yet another contrast with Joan, the devil's dam, whose fiends abandon her to the fire.[50] The threat that the Maid's prowess poses to masculine military heroism is contained in the representation of Joan's blood as a corrupt mother's blood, a fiendish and bodily woman's blood. Shakespeare's representation of Joan as a bleeding demonic mother stands in sharp contrast to the bloodless Joan described by the Frenchman Jean d'Aulon. But both accounts suggest the symbolic power of blood, and both suggest the extent to which the value of blood is a gendered value.

Intimate Blood, Intimate Killing

In insisting on the symbolic gendering of blood and on the way that women's blood is imagined in relation to the masculine heroic space of the battlefield, I do not wish to gloss over the very real blood and the very real violence of war. In combat, bloodshed and violence are not experienced symbolically but are part of what Joanna Bourke calls "intimate killing," face-to-face combat with an enemy who must be killed. "The characteristic act of men at war is not dying, it is killing," Bourke claims, and sanctioned bloodletting is the privilege only of warriors.[51]

One of the accusations leveled against Joan of Arc, linked to the other offenses cataloged during her trial—leading an army, wearing men's clothes—was the charge of cruelty: Joan did not hesitate to spill blood, both the blood of her enemies and the blood of her allies.[52] In the nullification trial, Joan's defenders do not respond directly to the accusation of cruelty, but several of the treatises that comment on the trial address the question of Joan's bloodthirsty mission. They stress that Joan herself was horrified by bloodshed; Jean d'Aulon claimed that she could not stand the sight of blood.[53] Moreover, they suggest, she could not herself have drawn blood since she carried her shield in one hand and her standard in the other.[54]

Joan's willingness to shed blood seems to come into question because she is a woman. To spill blood in war is not an offense when men take up arms—it is only when a woman enters the battlefield not to bring peace, but to fight, that bloodshed becomes an unjustifiable cruelty.[55] In other words, Joan's interrogators, like her defenders, seem to be at a loss to explain a woman's willingness to kill. What lies behind the question of Joan's cruelty—along with the broader issues of which it is a part—is the question of women's "natural" aggressiveness, which is tied to notions of proper gender roles. Can women kill?

Not surprisingly, perhaps, this is a question that continues to resurface in modern debates about women and combat. Women, it is claimed, do not experience or respond to aggression in the same way that men do—women are programmed to nurture, not to kill.[56] There are, of course, a number of historical examples of women who have fought bravely in combat situations. How can these examples be explained in light of women's "natural" inability to kill and to respond to aggression with aggression? Curiously enough, one way to explain women's ability to fight, like their inability to fight, is by recourse to reproductive biology: a woman will act aggressively to protect her children and her home.[57] Maternal instinct explains the transformation of the usually passive woman into the effective combatant. Yet the appeal to a female psychology defined by biological reproductive roles situates women ambivalently with respect to killing. They can't fight because they're mothers—they nurture, they don't kill; they can fight because of a maternal instinct that will lead them ferociously to defend their homes and family against threats from the outside. In other words, menstrual blood would seem to mark women as unsuited for war, whereas the blood of parturition seems to condition women as potential fighters.

Neither fictional accounts nor explicit debates about women and war make or defend such a distinction in terms of blood. Nor is menstruation the primary reason cited for women's exclusion from battle in the modern military, although it is often mentioned in support of the argument that women's bodies are not meant for fighting. However, what the long history of women and war suggests is that the battlefield is never so masculine a site as when it is invaded by women, and that the anxious defense of military heroism against feminization operates symbolically—through a focus on women's blood. War always involves bloodshed, and stories about women and war recount the gendering of bloodshed, and ultimately of blood itself, in a hierarchy of values in which only the heroic bloodshed of men represents a worthy sacrifice on the battlefield.

If the mother who would kill is both unimaginable as a soldier and the ultimate example of a combatant, the mother who would kill her own child solicits no ambivalence. In most accounts of maternal infanticide, this mother who would kill is a monster, an aberration of nature. Although a father may be divinely inspired to kill his child in a sacrifice to a higher good, a mother's murder of her own child is almost never called a sacrifice. And if the exclusion of women from combat maintains "men's privileged access to the rights of being a combatant,"[58] the exclusion of mothers from sacrifice maintains fathers' privilege to dispose of their children and guarantees their privileged access to the higher goods served by sacrifice, as I argue in Chapter 3.

3

The Gender of Sacrifice

IN THE TWELFTH-CENTURY *Philomena* attributed to Chrétien de Troyes, one of the changes the author makes to his Ovidian source is his identification of Procne as the murderer of her son.[1] Whereas Ovid recounts that Procne's sister, Philomena, cuts off Itys's head, in Chrétien's rewriting of the story it is the mother, Procne, who kills her son, and the two women then dismember, cook, and feed him to Tereus, Procne's husband, in revenge for his rape of Philomena. This change is part of what has been identified as a demonization of the character of Procne in Chrétien's version of the story, where she is a mother who cannot be swayed from murder even by the pleas of her son, but the identification of Procne as the murderer of her child also situates both the crime and the vengeance within the nuclear family—a wife's vengeance against her husband explains her infanticide.[2]

Revenge explains most examples of maternal murder in medieval literature. Gudrun, in the Scandinavian *Edda*, is another mother who cooks her son and feeds him to his father in revenge for the murder of her brothers.[3] This story is told a little differently in the *Thiðrejssaga* and in *The Nibelungenlied*, where Grimhild/Kriemhild sends her son to die at her brother's hands in order to set in motion a battle in which she hopes to take revenge for her brothers' murder of her husband Siegfried, but the mother still arranges the death of her child as part of a vengeance against her husband.[4] The most famous story of a mother's infanticidal revenge is, of course, the story of Medea, an example, like that of Philomena, inherited from classical literature.[5] Medea murders her children when their father, Jason, abandons her; and although in a number of medieval retellings of her story, including Christine de Pizan's *Book of the City of Ladies*, Jason's disloyalty to Medea is emphasized and the infanticide is absent, Medea's murder of her children is part of her story in Christine's *Mutacion de Fortune* and in the fourteenth-century *Ovide moralisé*, the text that also includes Chrétien's *Philomena*.[6]

Fathers also murder their children in classical and medieval fictions, and I will discuss a well-known example below in the legend of Amicus and Amelius. But unlike examples of maternal infanticide, a father's murder may be explained as a sacrifice, not a vengeance: a father may kill his child in the service of some higher good or higher purpose. Biblical examples are the most important models of paternal sacrifice for medieval writers: Abraham is a father who is willing to sacrifice his son to honor a covenant with God, and Jephthah sacrifices his daughter to keep a promise to God. There are no Biblical examples of mothers who sacrifice their children; when a mother kills her child, the infanticide is always a murder. Not all paternal murders are sacrifices, but it seems that no maternal murders can be explained by sacrificial logic, the logic that explains a child's death as necessary to accomplish a higher good or purpose. Mothers' murders are located in the realm of the domestic, not the divine: they offer revenge, not a covenant; they impose local justice, not the higher justice of divine right.

To be sure, a mother's consent to her child's death may be construed as a sacrifice, and in fact, the mother's submission to the death of her child may be seen as a culturally sanctioned model for a mother's participation in child murder, as Barbara Newman has shown in her study of medieval narratives in which a mother agrees to sacrifice her child to some higher good.[7] But in narratives that recount the mother's willingness to accept her child's death, the child does not actually die at the mother's hands. It seems that a mother can agree to a sacrifice, but she cannot enact it: the mother who would kill her child with her own hands does not sacrifice, she murders.[8]

The gendering of sacrifice in medieval narratives would seem to be consistent with sacrificial practice in most of the world's cultures: in virtually every culture that practices ritual sacrifice, mothers (or women who could be mothers) do not perform sacrifices.[9] Nancy Jay suggests that the exclusion of mothers from sacrificial ritual points to the symbolic definition of lineage as uniquely masculine. The exclusively male ritual of sacrifice symbolically transcends and displaces childbirth by valorizing social structures whose continuity flows through men, not women—as in a male priesthood, for example.[10] The exclusion of women from sacrificial ritual may thus be seen as an exclusion of women from the ritual definition of cultural values, and nowhere is that exclusion more apparent than in stories of child sacrifice—stories in which a "greater good" requires the death of a child.

Sacrifice is often seen to promote community or to contain violence in cultures that practice the ritual, but this "benevolent" view of sacrifice has been critiqued by Bruce Lincoln, who points to the fundamental inequalities that characterize sacrificial practices and to the hierarchies they define and enforce: "those categories of person who already enjoy disproportionate shares of all that this life has to offer—men, victorious warriors, or kings, e.g.—are able to define themselves and their favored entities as 'higher' than others and to reproduce their power and their privilege through the sacrifices they impose on those other, 'lower' beings."[11] If sacrifice involves giving up something for a higher good, it also ritually enacts a definition of what is "higher," and thereby imposes a value system that awards power and privilege to those who control sacrificial rituals. In other words, sacrifice enacts cultural values, but it also constructs cultural hierarchies and privileges. And in medieval literature, sacrifice is the privilege of fathers.

In this chapter I explore some ways in which literary texts imagine a parent's murder of a child, and I seek to understand why a father's murder can be called a sacrifice and why a mother's murder cannot. My goal is not to suggest how literary representations might correspond to actual practices of sacrifice in the ancient or medieval worlds, but rather to ask how sacrificial practice is imagined in medieval literary texts. In particular, I want to ask why maternal infanticide is never described as a sacrifice.[12] And I want to explore how the suppression of maternal sacrifice in medieval narratives inscribes a difference between what it means to be a father and what it means to be a mother. This is not to say that there is no difference between motherhood and fatherhood. Rather, I seek to understand how that difference is represented and how it is assigned value in medieval narratives about parental murder. I will suggest that the difference between maternity and paternity in sacrifice is defined in terms of blood: a father's blood, shared by the child, and a mother's blood, shed in childbirth.

This distinction—the masculine blood of lineage versus the feminine blood of parturition—risks explaining all representations of gender difference as part of the familiar medieval association of men with symbolic meaning and thought, and of women with materiality and the biological functions of the body. I do not wish to claim that women's exclusion from sacrifice is the consequence of their role in childbirth, that is, to offer a biological explanation for a symbolic meaning. Instead, I want to suggest that narratives about sacrifice may demonstrate one way that medieval culture, like modern culture, assigns symbolic values to the biological functions of bodies and uses the biological functions of bodies to represent symbolic values. Ultimately these stories demonstrate how the values associated with women's blood—menstruation and the blood of parturition—both construct and deconstruct the values embodied by men's blood.

The Drama of Paternal Sacrifice

The foundational myth of child sacrifice in medieval Europe is surely the Biblical story of Abraham and Isaac, a story common to the three monotheistic religions so consistently in conflict during the Middle Ages. Abraham's sacrifice is an interrupted sacrifice: God commands Abraham to sacrifice his only son; Abraham consents; and because of the father's demonstrated obedience, God withdraws his demand for Isaac's death and provides an animal for the sacrifice.[13] Yet the interruption of the sacrifice is not always the most important aspect of the story; the exemplary force of the story in medieval Christian contexts does not depend on the fact that Isaac is *not* killed by his father, but rather on the father's willingness to sacrifice his son and the son's willingness to be sacrificed, and these are the aspects of the story featured in fifteenth-century dramas about Abraham.[14]

The other Old Testament story that represents a father's sacrifice, the sacrifice of Jephthah's daughter in Judges 11, is not an interrupted sacrifice: the daughter dies at her father's hands.[15] Perhaps because the sacrificed dead daughter does not fit into Christian typology, this story is not the subject of dramatic development in the Middle Ages, though it is mentioned by the sacrificed virgin, Virginia, in Chaucer's *Physician's Tale*: "Thanne yif me leyser, fader myn," quod she, / My deeth for to compleyne a litel space; / For, pardee, Jepte yaf his doghter grace / For to compleyne, er he hir slow, allas!"[16]

Like the sacrifice of Jephthah's daughter and like the sacrifice of Virginia, the sacrifice of Isaac is the story of a father's sacrifice. Isaac's mother, Sarah, is absent from the Biblical account of the sacrifice in Genesis 22: Abraham neither seeks her consent for the sacrifice, nor considers her reaction to it.[17] However, in some of the medieval plays about the sacrifice of Isaac, Sarah is brought into the play indirectly, in the dialogue between the father and son. In the Chester play, when Abraham tells his son that he must die as a sacrifice to God, Isaac wishes for his mother's presence, since she would plead on bended knee for his life: "Would God, my mother were here with mee! / Shee would kneele downe upon her knee, / prayeinge you, father, if yt might bee, / for to save my liefe."[18] When in the Northampton play Isaac protests that his mother would not have let him leave home to be killed, Abraham replies that he loves Isaac as much as his mother does, but that God's will must be done ("I loue þe as wele as she doþe, in fay, / And ȝit þis dede most be do").[19] Isaac later pleads with his father not to let Sarah see his bloody corpse; rather he should tell Isaac's mother that their son has gone to live in another country ("But, good fader, tell ȝe my moder nothyng, / Sey þat I am in another cuntré dwellyng").[20] Abraham knows that Sarah will never believe that their son has simply run away: "What shal I to his moder say? / ffor 'where is he,' tyte will she spyr; / If I tell hir, 'ron away,' / hir answere bese belife—'nay, sir!'"[21]

In most of these dramas, Sarah appears in the story only as an absent referent, if she appears at all.[22] She represents parental love and domestic safety, and she must be protected from knowledge of the father's sacrifice and the covenant it will establish between the patriarch and his god. Only in the Northampton *Abraham* does Sarah appear as a character, and there she learns of the sacrifice only after God has spared Isaac. Even though Abraham claims that he must tell Sarah of God's command, he reveals the intended sacrifice of their son to his wife only at the end of the play after a ram has been divinely provided as a substitute for Isaac. Sarah responds with incredulity: "Would you have slain my son Isaac? Then I would have lost all my happiness. Alas, where was your mind?" Abraham's rebuke: "My mind? Upon the good Lord on high!" ("SARA. . . . Wold ye haue slayne my son Isaac? / Nay, þan al my ioy had me forsake! / Alas, where was your mynde? / HABRAHAM. My mynde? Vpon þe goode Lord on hy!" *Non-Cycle Plays*, 41, ll. 342–46).[23]

If, as Carol Delaney has suggested, the Abraham story is the foundational text for a pervasive notion of procreation that conflates masculine engendering, masculine authority, and the patriarchal family, Sarah's absence would seem to be a logical part of the dramatization of the story: the child engendered by the father belongs to the father who has the authority to decide his child's fate.[24] The mother's absence corresponds to her lack of authority over her child. And when Sarah appears as a character, as she does in the Northampton play, and also in the fifteenth-century *Mistére du viel testament*, although she eloquently states the pain she would have suffered if her son had died, she could not have prevented the sacrifice.

Indeed, in *Le Mistére du Viel Testament*, the play in which Sarah's role is the most developed, Abraham worries about what Sarah will say when she learns her son's fate, but he claims that he cannot tell her of his plan to sacrifice Isaac, for she would not understand:[25]

"Should I tell his mother? No, that would be futile, for a mother is always fragile and, if I give her to understand, she could come defend her son and save him from death. And in that case we would incur the anger of all powerful God. In short, I will obey, and today my son will die. But I won't say anything to Sarah until after the sacrifice, for I know only too well that her heart will break because of it."

("Le doy je point dire a la mére?
Nenny; point ne seroit utille,
Car tousjours la mére est fragille
Et, se je luy donnoye entendre,
Elle pourroit venir deffendre
Et garder son filz de mourir;
Par quoy, nous pourrions encourir
L'yre de Dieu, le tout puissant.
Bref, je seray obeissant;
En cestuy jour mon filz mourra;
Mais rien n'en diray a Sarra,
Jusque après le sacriffiement,
Car je sçay bien certainement
Que trop auroit le cueur grevé."
[*Le mistére du Viel Testament*, 2: 21–22, ll. 9787–9800])

In Abraham's decision not to tell Sarah of God's command, he explicitly recognizes her resistance to the heartbreaking infanticide, and he implicitly recognizes a mother's right to protest the death of her son. But he also claims that if Sarah refused the sacrifice they would incur God's anger. Abraham defines the father's sacrifice as accomplishing an act of higher good that a mother cannot understand, and he implies that Sarah is incapable of sacrificial thinking, that she cannot imagine that a higher good could be served by her son's death. And when Abraham returns home and explains to Sarah his decision not to tell her of the intended sacrifice, Sarah admits that she could not have shared Abraham's sacrificial logic: "Certainly if you had told me of it, I would not have given my consent." ("Certes, quant vous me l'eussiez dit, / Point consentue ne m'y feusse" [*Le mistére du Viel Testament*, 2: 76, ll. 10565–66]).

Abraham's decision not to tell Sarah about the sacrifice of their son suggests, as Delaney has argued, that men are the primary parents of their children, that men engender and therefore have the right to dispose of their children.[26] And the Biblical story of a father who agrees to kill the son that God has miraculously given him suggests that all children are gifts to fathers from God the Father.

Paternal Sacrifice and Fraternal Love

In another popular medieval story about paternal sacrifice, the legend of Amicus and Amelius, the father's infanticide is not averted, but his sacrificed children are miraculously resurrected after they are killed and their blood is used to cure their father's leprous friend. This legend was widely known in medieval Europe; it was recounted in most of the major vernaculars of the high Middle Ages, and in most of the major genres.[27] In all the versions of the Amicus and Amelius legend, the child sacrifice and the cure it enacts are the culminating events of the story, and the episode is preceded by the story of an extraordinary friendship between two knights.[28] In the late twelfth-century version of the story in Old French, on which I will focus here, the friendship is preordained: Ami and Amile are conceived at the same hour, born on the same day, and they resemble each other perfectly. The two boys are baptized together at Rome by the pope, but then they are separated. When they reach an age to be knighted, they seek each other out and go together to serve the emperor, Charlemagne.

Hardré, one of Charlemagne's vassals, is jealous of their beauty, valor, and friendship, and he attempts to have the knights killed. Hardré's plot is discovered, and in an effort to make peace among his vassals, Charlemagne approves the marriage of Ami and Hardré's niece, Lubias. Ami and Lubias leave court to claim the bride's property in Blaye, and Amile stays at court. One evening the emperor's daughter, Belissant, joins him in his bed without revealing her identity. Amile thinks she is a servant and makes love to her. Hardré hears the couple in bed, guesses Belissant's identity, and denounces Amile's betrayal to the emperor. Amile must then prove his innocence in judicial battle—impossible, of course, because he is guilty. Amile asks the emperor to delay the battle, and he leaves the court to seek the aid of his friend, Ami, who agrees to take his friend's place. Posing as Amile, Ami defeats Hardré in battle and proves that the charge against Amile is false. In recognition of Amile's apparent innocence and in recompense for the apparently false accusation, Charlemagne offers his daughter to the knight. Ami, still posing as Amile, promises marriage in his friend's place, even though he is warned by an angel that he will be punished for the false vow. He then returns to Blaye with Belissant, changes places with Amile, and the two men resume their proper identities and go their separate ways, each to live in his own land with his own wife.

Ami subsequently becomes a leper, is rejected by his wife and vassals, and wanders the countryside as a beggar until he arrives in Amile's lands where he is recognized and welcomed. An angel reveals to the leprous Ami that he can be cured by the blood of Amile's infant sons. Ami recounts the vision to his friend, and Amile kills his sons and bathes Ami in their blood. Ami is miraculously cured, the children are miraculously resurrected, the two friends set out on pilgrimage to Jerusalem, and they both die during the return voyage.

In all its medieval versions, the legend of Amicus and Amelius is a story about exemplary friendship.[29] As in many medieval narratives, feudal bonds are expressed as affective bonds: alliances between lords and vassals or between vassals are represented in terms of friendship or even in terms of love, and relationships between men are solidified through gifts of women—as in Hardré's gift of his niece to Ami or Charlemagne's gift of his daughter, Belissant, to Amile.[30] But what distinguishes the bond between Ami and Amile from other friendships is sacrifice. Ami sacrifices himself by accepting the punishment announced by an angel before he makes the false promise to wed Belissant, and he becomes a leper.[31] Amile sacrifices his children to cure his friend's leprosy. Ami's self sacrifice (he loses his lands, his family, and ultimately stands to lose his life) is complemented, even compensated by Amile's sacrifice of his children.

When Amile learns that the blood of his sons can cure Ami, he anticipates the pain that their deaths will bring him, and he regrets the crime that he will commit, but he is resolved to kill his children to repay the debt to his friend. He justifies his decision in a prayer:

"God, savior of us all," says Amile, "This man offered his body to protect me in the battle with the traitor, Hardré. I can give him health from the children that I have engendered; they are mine, I can say it truthfully, and the hour was good when God made them be formed. When my friend can recover from them what no living man can give him, except glorious God who saves all, I would not refuse, even if I were to be dismembered, nor for all the gold that anyone could give me, that my sweet sons have their heads cut off to aid Ami."

("Dex, dist Amiles, qui tout as a sauver,
Cist hom si mist son cors por moi tanser
En la bataille dou traïtor Hardré.
Quant je li puis de moi santé donner
De mes anfans que je volz engendrer,
De moi sont il, por voir le puis conter,
L'ore soit bonne que Dex les fist former.
Quant mes compains en puet ce recouvrer
Que hom qui vive ne li porroit donner,
Fors Dex de gloire qui tout a a sauver,
Je nel lairoie por les membres coper
Ne por tout l'or c'on me seüst donner
Qu'a mes douz fiz n'aille les chiés coper
Por Ami faire aïe." [*Ami et Amile*, ll. 2933–46])

Yet while Amile's decision to decapitate his sons to save his friend is indeed a reciprocal act, the two acts of friendship are not equal or even alike in the context of the story. Ami rejects a divine warning and makes a false vow to save his friend, while Amile obeys divine instructions to kill his sons to cure his friend.[32] Ami may be seen to have made a conscious decision to sacrifice himself to save his friend, but Amile's sacrifice demands innocent victims.[33]

In fact, the sacrifices are symmetrical only if the sons' lives are equal to what Ami has lost.[34] Ami "offered his body," Amile offers his children, and Amile's prayer suggests that the sacrifices are equivalent: the children are his to keep or to lose since he engendered them. Amile's eldest son awakes as his father laments the sacrifice that he must make, and the son reassures his father that Ami can be cured with the children's blood. The child approves the sacrifice in the same terms of possession used by Amile to justify his right to sacrifice: "Dear sweet father," the child answers immediately, "Since your friend will be cured if he is bathed in our blood, you can do as you wish, for we are yours, from your engendering" ("Biax tres douz peres, dist l'anfes erramment, / Quant vos compains avra garissement / Se de nos sans a sor soi lavement, / Noz sommez vostre, de vostre engenrement, / Faire en poéz del tout a vo talent" [ll. 3000–3004]). Amile's paternal rights include the right to kill his children in order to cure his friend and restore him to the health and privileges he sacrificed to friendship. To restore, in other words, the resemblance between the two friends.

Resemblance is a crucial part of the story of exemplary friendship—the friends are alike.[35] To restore Ami's life means to restore him to his likeness to Amile, that is, to restore his status as a lord, as a husband, as a father. The anointing with blood may also be seen to enact a symbolic redefinition of lineage: Ami and Amile are united in a common lineage by the blood of the children. I want to stress the symbolic nature of this joining, and the way that the positions the men occupy in relation to each other are defined through a patriarchal family structure. It would be possible to see Ami and Amile as symbolically enacting a fraternal relationship through blood, as becoming blood brothers.[36] Yet the relationship is constructed not through a sharing of their own blood, but through a sharing of the blood of Amile's children. The children's blood symbolically engenders a father, and when they are restored to life, the blood of sacrifice unites Ami and Amile in a procreative relationship: the reborn sons have two fathers, but no mother.[37] In restoring Ami to health, Amile restores him to the patriarchal authority that he enacts when he defines paternal prerogative as the right to kill his sons.

Friendship, not paternity, is the primary relationship valorized in the legend of Amicus and Amelius, yet the story of friendship is recounted as a story about paternity and the authority of the father.[38] Lubias, Ami's wife, slanders her husband's friend, tries to destroy the friendship between the two men, and in one version of the story she mistreats Ami's son, beating him so brutally that he dies.[39] In contrast, Belissant, Amile's wife, vows never to disrupt the friendship, and approves the murder of her children when she learns of the sacrifice her husband has made.[40] Unlike Sarah, who protests her son's death in the Abraham plays, Belissant is a wife who recognizes a father's authority over his children as an authority sanctioned by God, and the divine revelation of the cure and the miraculous restoration of the children support Belissant's view.[41] Children are a gift from God, and they are expendable according to God's instructions and their father's desire for his friend, as she claims in the Anglo-Norman *Amis e Amilun*:

"Jesus, the son of saint Mary, can give us children if he wishes, but if you had lost Amilun you could never have replaced him. Let us think no more of our children, if God wills it we will have more."

("Jhesu, le fiz seinte Marie,
Si li plest par son poer,
Nus porra enfanz bien doner;
Si Amilun perdu eussez,
Ja mes tel autre n'avriez.

Des enfaunz nient plus n'enpensum,
Si deu le veut, bien recovrom!")[42]

A mother's approval of the sacrifice of her child is not unusual in
medieval literature: in a number of medieval hagiographic and romance
narratives, including perhaps most famously Chaucer's *Clerk's Tale*, mothers agree to the deaths of their children—Barbara Newman has called
this narrative development the "maternal martyr plot." In these stories,
the renunciation of maternal affection is a sign of obedience to God, as in
the case of certain female martyr saints, or to a husband, as in the case of
Griselda. Newman shows how the maternal martyr plot represents the
love of children as something to be sacrificed to any "higher" good that
may conflict with it and how, paradoxically, the motif of child murder
comes to support the patriarchal family.[43] The submission of the mother
to the deaths of her children is thus a culturally sanctioned model for a
mother's participation in the murder of her child. It is a form of maternal
infanticide that *can* be explained as a sacrifice, but only indirectly: the
mother accepts the sacrifice of her child, but she herself does not kill her
child. Indeed, while Abraham's willingness to kill his son continues to
inspire figural appropriations and retellings, a mother's murder of her
children is usually narrated as an unnatural crime, a monstrous act that
cannot be explained in terms of a "higher" good.[44] And the gendering of
sacrifice is nowhere more apparent than in the Old French *Philomena*.

Maternal Murder

In *Philomena*, as in the Ovidian story on which it is closely based, Procne
and her sister, Philomena, kill Procne's son, Itys, and feed him to his
father, Tereus, in revenge for Tereus's brutal rape of Philomena. The
child's death is represented as a vengeance, not as a redemptive sacrifice,
and in this story infanticide and cannibalism represent the end of a dynas-
tic lineage, not the beginning of a new heroic and symbolic lineage of
men, as in *Ami et Amile*, or even the Abraham story.

Philomena, Ami et Amile, and the Abraham plays come from different
narrative traditions, but all these stories participate in constructing the
gendered values of sacrifice in medieval literature: *Ami et Amile* and the
Abraham dramas affirm the value of men's sacrifice, which enacts chivalric, amorous, and religious identities: men's sacrifices serve a higher good.

Philomena explores what happens when women intervene in this structure. In the terms of this text, the mother's murder does not serve the higher good of sacrifice—it is a murder, not a sacrifice—but through an explicit focus on a mother's sacrificial practice in an earlier episode in the story, the text also asks why the mother's infanticide cannot be seen as a sacrifice.

In *Philomena*, as in Ovid's story, Tereus takes Philomena from her father's home on the pretext of bringing her to visit her sister, Procne, who has married Tereus and gone to live in his lands. Instead of reuniting the two women, he takes Philomena to a secluded hut, cuts out her tongue, rapes her, and leaves her isolated in the forest, guarded by an old woman. He then returns home and tells Procne that her sister has died. Procne casts off her rich clothes and puts on mourning. And in the Old French narrative, in a scene not found in the Ovidian story, she offers a burnt sacrifice to Pluto, God of the dead.[45] The narrator describes the ritual acts of the sacrifice in detail:

The fire was laid and lit as she had commanded before the altar of that god, and in order to make more smoke, as custom dictated, the bull was brought to the fire. Then she promised and swore to the god to make a similar sacrifice on his altar every year so that he would honor her sister's soul in hell, and give her pleasure and rest. When the bull was completely burned, both flesh and bone, so that nothing was left that was not ash or cinder, she sprinkled the blood over it. Then she put everything in a white pot as cleanly as she could, and she buried the pot under a dark marble tomb. . . . Procne gives all her attention to making the sacrifice with great devotion, in order to draw her sister's soul out of that place where she was not; rather she was alive, and her life weighed heavily on her and every day her pain was renewed by the traitor, the evil-doer who was consumed with love for her and she hated that he took his pleasure with her by force, he who had betrayed her.

(Li feuz fu alumez et fais,
Si tost comme el l'ot commandé,
Devant l'autier a icel dé,
Et pour fere greignor fumee,
Si com chose ert acoustumee,
Fu li tors aportez au feu.
Lors fist aus diex promesse et veu
De faire sacrefice autel
Chascun an devant son autel,
Pource que l'ame sa serour
Gardast en enfer a honour,
Et a delit et a repos.

Quant tout fu ars, et chars et os,
Que nulle riens n'i ot remese
Que tout ne fu ou cendre ou brese,
Puis espandi dessus le sanc;
Apres mist tout an un pot blanc
Au plus netement qu'ele pot;
Puis a mis en terre le pot,
Souz un sarcus de marbre bis. . .
Ensi o grant devocïon
Metoit toute s'entencïon
Progne au sacrefice faire,
Pour l'ame sa serour soustraire
De la ou ele n'estoit mie,
Einçois vivoit et de sa vie
Li pesoit moult, et chascun jor
Li renoveloit sa dolour
Li traïtres, li vilz maufez,
Qui de s'amour iert eschaufez,
Et merveilles li desplesoit
Qu'a force tous ses bons fesoit
De lui cil qui l'avoit traïe. [*Philomena*, ll. 1022–69])

The description of Procne's sacrifice leads to a description of Philomena's continuing torment at the hands of Tereus. The sacrifice is a wasted effort, the narrator points out, since Philomena is not dead at all, but the narrative link between the sacrificial death ritual and the tormented life that Philomena continues to live seems to suggest a parallel structure: a ritual sacrifice follows the (false) revelation of Philomena's death, and a ritual death will follow the discovery that she is alive.

Procne's sacrificial offering to Pluto is not usually commented on by readers of the poem, but as an extensive addition to the Ovidian material it certainly demands attention.[46] And as an explicitly recounted ritual killing Procne's sacrifice invites a rethinking of the culminating act of the story, the murder of Itys. That is, the offering to Pluto and the murder of Procne's son might be seen as parallel narratives of sacrifice.[47]

When Procne receives Philomena's tapestry and learns that she lives, she goes to rescue her sister and takes her to a hidden room where they can speak in secret. Apparently the room is not hidden from Itys; the son comes to join his mother, and because he looks like his father, Procne conceives the idea that he must die to pay for his father's betrayal. Again, the child's death is called a vengeance, not a sacrifice, but the structure of the story aligns Procne's sacrifice of the bull when she learns of Philomena's death, with the murder of her son when she learns that her sister lives. Moreover, the preparation of the child's murder, while not repeating exactly the ritual acts of the sacrifice, is rehearsed in some detail, and its actions—cutting and cooking—suggest those of the sacrifice:

> She cut off the child's head and gave it to Philomena. Then together they prepared the flesh quickly and carefully. One part they put into roast, and the other part to boil. When the flesh was cooked and roasted it was time to eat it.

> (A a l'enfant copé la teste,
> Si l'a Philomena baillie;
> Si ont la char apareillie
> Entr'eles deus mout bien et tost.
> Partie an mistrent cuire an rost,
> Et an essiau l'autre partie.
> Quant la char fu cuite et rostie,
> Si fu de mengier temps et hore. [ll. 1332–39])

When Procne and Philomena kill Procne's son, Itys, the infanticide enacts vengeance, not redemption as in *Ami et Amile*; it is inspired by the devil, not sanctioned by God.[48] But why isn't the murder of Itys a sacrifice? Is the mother's murder of her son to remedy an injustice done to her beloved sister so different from the father's murder of his sons to heal a leprous friend? Indeed, what are the differences between Procne's murder of her son and Amile's murder of his children? The stories are similar in many respects; that is, they recount similar events, but with different outcomes. Ami and Amile are not brothers, but all the versions of their story insist on their fraternal resemblance, and the desire of each man to see the other leads to the quest that unites them, while Procne's strong desire to see her sister leads to tragedy. Ami suffers the bodily degradation of leprosy from which he is saved by the sacrifice of Amile's children; Philomena suffers the physical violence and humiliation of rape, but Procne's murder of her son is not a healing sacrifice, it is an act of vengeance. Why is the story of a sister's devotion to her sister harder to inscribe in a narrative paradigm of redemptive sacrifice than the story of a knight's devotion to his friend? To be sure the deaths of Amile's children are divinely sanctioned, and they are restored after the cure, whereas Philomena's murder is described as "unnatural" and inspired by the devil, but that difference may be seen as an effect, rather than the origin of the opposition between maternal vengeance and paternal sacrifice.[49] The parallel narratives of the mother's sacrifice and the mother's murder in

Philomena suggest that in the narrative logic of monstrous acts, only fathers can justify infanticide as a sacrifice.

Father's Blood and Mother's Blood

One way to understand the gendering of sacrifice is, as Delaney has suggested, to look at the ways that parental relationships are imagined.[50] In many cultures, a father's right to his children is conceived of as a legal right, an ownership conferred by an active engendering—this view is suggested in Amile's claim that his children belong to him because he engendered them. By contrast, the mother's relationship with her child is that of a caregiver, a guardian, a body: it is seen as a bond, not a right. These ways of describing parental ties do not reveal a truth about essential relationships; rather, they participate in a corporeal rhetoric that maps cultural values onto gendered roles in procreation. And the representation of family ties through the symbolic meanings of blood offers yet another example of the way that gendered hierarchies of authority and privilege are inscribed within the patriarchal family.

A child shares its father's blood. In the Northampton *Abraham,* when the father laments the necessity of killing his son, he claims that his blood abhors to see his son bleed, for it is all one blood ("My blode aborreþ to se my son blede, / For all on blode it is").[51] In *Le mistére du viel testament*, God claims that Abraham will build an altar on which he will sacrifice "his only son and his own blood."[52] When Abraham and God refer to Isaac as Abraham's "blood," the word "blood" figuratively names a familial relationship, as in the way a genealogy is described as a bloodline. In other texts, the father's bloodline is figured through resemblance, and paternal blood is made visible in the child's resemblance to his father.[53]

The shared blood that justifies a father's right to sacrifice becomes the motivation for a mother's murder in *Philomena*. When Procne decides to kill her son, she does not describe him as sharing his father's blood, but the son's resemblance to his father is what motivates her act, as she explains to the innocent boy:

"Ah," she said, "you look so much like the traitor, the infamous devil! You must die a miserable death because of your father's crime. You will pay for his crime. You will die wrongly for his act, even though you do not deserve it, except that I have never seen, nor did God ever make, I think, such a clear resemblance between two things, and for this reason I want to cut your head off."

("Ha, fet ele, chose samblable
Au traïtour, au vil dÿable!
Morir t'estuet de mort amere
Pour la felonie ton pere.
Sa felonie conperras.
Pour son forfait a tort morras,
Qi ne l'as mie deservi,
Fors seulement c'onques ne vi,
Ne Diex ne fist mon esciant,
Chose a autre miex resamblant,
Et pour ce te vueil decoler." [*Philomena*, ll. 1299–1309])

The child incarnates the father; he shares his father's blood. This visible evidence of the father's engendering is consonant with medieval reproductive theory: a child is engendered by its father's "seed," that is, his semen, and semen is considered a purified form of blood in medieval medical theory. In both the one-seed, Aristotelian idea of reproduction and the two-seed Galenic theory, it is always the father's blood (semen) that actively impregnates. The son is the father's, he is an metonymic extension of the father, he shares his father's blood, and the father's sacrifice makes visible that relationship and the institutions and hierarchies that it grounds.

A child also shares its mother's blood. In medical theory, that blood is the nourishing blood of menstruation and the blood of parturition, but this blood is not displayed symbolically in proof of lineage. Representations of women's blood are not usually found at all in medieval literary texts, except in stories about female martyrs or victims of violence. Yet the Old French *Jourdain de Blaye* offers a rare example of the representation of women's blood, the blood of parturition, which is shown to be a dangerous blood in this text.

Jourdain de Blaye is an epic poem from the end of the twelfth or beginning of the thirteenth century that continues the story of *Ami et Amile* with the adventures of Ami's son, Girart, and grandson, Jourdain.[54] It is a story that begins with a sacrifice: Renier, a vassal of the lord of Blaye, and his wife, Erembourc, sacrifice their young son to save Jourdain, the son of their feudal lord. After Jourdain is saved from death by the sacrifice of Renier and Erembourc's son, he goes through a series of adventures and ends up as a captive on a Saracen ship. While the ship is at sea, Jourdain sees a tree trunk floating by, he leaps from the ship into the water, and clutches the tree as a raft. When the Saracens pursue him,

Jourdain remembers that the sea cannot abide blood: "Mers ne puet sanc sueffrir ne tant ne quant."[55] So he deliberately cuts his hand, a storm is raised, and the sea tosses him onto land.

Jourdain enters the service of the king of this land, marries his daughter, and then decides that he must go to the rescue of Renier and Erembourc, who were also captured by Saracens. Jourdain sets out to sea with his pregnant wife, Oriabel, who insists on accompanying him. Oriabel gives birth to a daughter while they are at sea, and a storm threatens to capsize the boat, because "the sea cannot abide a person who bleeds"—in this case, Oriabel, who bleeds from childbirth.[56] After a thousand men are killed in the storm, Jourdain's companions insist that he throw his wife overboard. He refuses, they overpower him and demand that he comply. Jourdain reluctantly makes a watertight box for his wife, seals her in with money and letters of explanation, and casts her overboard. The sea is calmed and Jourdain is carried safely to shore, as is Oriabel, who ends up in Palermo where she is put into the care of a bishop.

The motif of the sea that cannot abide blood comes from the Apollonius of Tyre legend, on which many of Jourdain's adventures are based, and it is found in medieval versions of the Alexander story.[57] In the Apollonius legend, the wife of Apollonius gives birth on board the boat, but after the birth she appears to be dead, and since the sea will not tolerate a corpse on shipboard, she is cast overboard in a sealed coffin. Like Jourdain's wife, she is carried to shore and revived by those who find her.

In *Jourdain de Blaye*, the change in the Apollonius story (the wife must be cast overboard because she bleeds from childbirth, not because she is dead) echoes the earlier episode in which Jourdain deliberately cut his hand so that the sea would cast him out—but with a difference. The two episodes point to an important opposition between the representation of men's blood and the representation of women's blood. Jourdain controls his bloodshed: he deliberately wounds himself so that the sea will throw him onto land. Oriabel cannot control her bleeding, and she cannot save herself.

The parallel scenes of bloodshed in *Jourdain de Blaye* suggest the gendered values that inform heroic action in this and other stories of war and prowess: men shed blood deliberately in displays of prowess; men spill blood to rescue themselves and others. Women's blood demonstrates women's isolation from the structures that define cultural values and social order: Oriabel is the victim of her own bleeding body. She herself describes the childbirth on board ship as a "pechié," a sin: "This sea is

troubled because of my sin" (Par mon pechié est ceste mers tourblee"
[*Jourdain de Blaye*, l. 2240]).[58] And when she is saved from the sea, Oriabel repeats the explanation: "I was pregnant, I had great pain, and had
to deliver a daughter. The sea became troubled because of my sin" ("Mais
je fui grosse, grant dolor oi asséz, / Et d'unne fille me convint delivrer. /
Par mon pechié se tourbla ceste mers" [*Jourdain de Blaye*, ll. 2330–32]).

Oriabel's characterization of childbirth as a sin may refer to the ritual
pollution of the blood of parturition that is stressed later in the text.
When she is rescued from the sea, Oriabel declares her intention to rest
in isolation for a period of purification after which time she will go to
mass: "I want to lie in bed for nineteen or twenty full days, and then I will
go to mass, according to Christian custom, so that my body will not be
impure" ("Dis et nuef jours ou vint trestouz passéz / Voldrai jesir et puis
a messe aler, / Selonc l'uzaige de la crestïenté, / Que li mien cors n'en soit
point encombréz" [*Jourdain de Blaye*, ll. 2356–59]).[59]

The impurity of the postpartum female body is discussed in a number of medieval theological, philosophical, and fictional texts.[60] *Jourdain
de Blaye* imagines that body in explicit contrast to the male bleeding body.
It may also implicitly imagine the bleeding maternal body in relation to
sacrifice: Oriabel's bleeding postpartum body recalls the violence done to
the maternal body through child sacrifice, as Erembourc's lament to her
sacrificed son suggested earlier in the story: "It was for my misfortune
that I carried you inside me for nine months" ("Mar voz portai nuef mois
en mon costel" [*Jourdain de Blaye*, l. 654]). The mother's bond with her
child is figured in the maternal body, in the blood of parturition shared
by a child and a mother, and this blood is imagined as a dangerous blood,
a polluting blood, even a sinful blood.

The Blood of Sacrifice

Medieval narratives about sacrifice suggest that the blood of sacrifice is
gendered symbolically not according to the identity of the sacrifice—in
both *Ami et Amile* and *Philomena*, the murdered children are sons—but by
the identity of the sacrificer. In other words, the relationship of the sacrificer to the offering symbolically genders the blood of sacrifice. Blood
shed by the father is paternal blood—it demonstrates lineage and loyalty
between men or between men and God. It is blood that is shed deliberately and with intention; it is therefore blood that can mark a covenant, it

is a blood that can be spilled for a higher good. The blood shed by the mother is maternal blood, it recalls menstruation and the blood of parturition. It is then, in many medieval discourses, a polluting blood, a blood that cannot serve a higher good.[61] Mother's blood, blood shed by a mother, is not sacrificial blood, and a mother's murder of her child can only be explained as a demonic act of vengeance. Just as Abraham's willingness to kill his only son exemplifies a father's right to sacrifice his child for a higher good, Medea's murder of her children remains the defining instance of a mother's criminal infanticide.

The medieval retellings of the Medea story inspire the invention of anti-Medeas, literary figures like Griselda, according to Ruth Morse, who explains this movement as a transformation of the powerful and dangerous women into a woman celebrated for her passive endurance. Yet both Medea and Griselda are mothers who participate in infanticide: Medea kills her children for revenge against Jason, who has abandoned her; Griselda agrees to the deaths of her children in a demonstration of her obedience to her husband.

Griselda's story parallels Abraham's of course—with a difference. Both parents consent to their children's deaths in an act of obedience, but the higher good that demands obedience is different in each case. Abraham obeys God, Griselda submits to her husband's will. Abraham is willing to kill his own son, Griselda agrees to her husband's decision to kill their children. But both stories ultimately work to a common end: to establish the father's authority as patriarch.

Medea usurps that place and through the sacrifice of her children she challenges patriarchal authority with her insistence on another value: love for a husband. But the children she kills are always shown to die as a vengeance for Jason's lack of loyalty, rather than as a sacrificial offering that upholds bonds of love. The introduction to Chaucer's *Man of Law's Tale* is typical of this judgment: "The crueltee of the, queene Medea, / Thy litel children hangynge by the hals, / For thy Jason, that was of love so fals!"[62] Medea's infanticide, unlike Abraham's willingness to sacrifice Isaac or Amile's sacrifice of his sons, does not reaffirm the primacy of the father's blood, it does not confirm patriarchal authority, it cannot be explained as a sacrifice.

The difference between maternal murder and paternal sacrifice cannot simply be explained by narrative traditions, by the fact that Medea, like Philomena, is a figure from classical literature, whereas Abraham and Griselda are part of a Christian tradition. The twelfth- and fourteenth-century

Medea and Philomena stories are rewritten in a Christian culture, and the prominent story of a father's sacrifice in the story of Amicus and Amelius is, in its earliest form, a classical story that makes no mention of God's approval of the sacrifice.[63] The narrative logic that describes a father's blood relationship with his child as a metonymy, a shared blood, supports a father's right to sacrifice his own blood and can only explain a mother's infanticide as a criminal, polluting act. Medea must remain a maternal monster, but Griselda, the "maternal martyr," in Barbara Newman's phrase, transforms the figure of the murdering mother into the mother whose renunciation of maternal affection grounds patriarchal authority.[64] If the bleeding female body figures not only pollution and sin, but also affection and maternal bonds ("I carried you inside me for nine months," laments Erembourc to her sacrificed son in *Jourdain de Blaye*[65]), the narrative valorization of father's blood over mother's blood gives primacy to paternal right over maternal love, and to a father's "engendering"[66] over a mother's desire for justice. Stories about child murder identify sacrifice as the bloodright of fathers, as a visible demonstration of paternal lineage and patriarchal order that depends on the suppression of the mother's bleeding body.

4

Menstruation and Monstrous Birth

IN THE PRECEDING CHAPTER I claimed that the exclusion of mothers from sacrificial practice corresponds to a particular way of conceptualizing lineage. That is, the gendering of sacrifice corresponds to the gendered hierarchy promoted in representations of blood ties between children and their parents. A child shares its father's blood, and paternal blood symbolizes the patriarchal privilege to make covenants and to dispose of children. The blood that a child shares with its mother is the blood of parturition, a polluting blood that cannot mark a covenant. Yet although the blood of parturition, or even parturition itself, as we will see below, may be defined as dangerous to others, childbirth does not put women in an unredeemable state of impurity since they are reintegrated into their communities after a period of ritual isolation. Indeed, definitions of ritual impurity are usually accompanied by descriptions of rituals that restore purity. And rituals do not merely negate or neutralize impure status. They may also be seen as enactments of purity, as David Biale has emphasized with reference to the thirteenth-century *Sefer Nizzahon Yashan* in which women's purity rituals are equated with circumcision, a purity ritual of men.[1]

The *Sefer Nizzahon Yashan* is a polemical compendium which contains a disputation between Jews and Christians over the atoning qualities of the blood of circumcision in comparison to the water of baptism, and here the heretics (Christians) are shown to attack Jewish belief by questioning the gender inequality that the circumcision ritual enacts.

The heretics [say]: We baptize both males and females and in that way we accept our faith, but in your case only men and not women can be circumcised. One can respond: Women are accepted because they watch themselves and carefully observe the prohibitions connected with menstrual blood.[2]

Jewish women may claim the value of their blood and, by observing the ritual prohibitions surrounding menstrual blood, retain their bodily purity. The *Sefer Nizzahon Yashan* identifies parallel blood rituals that mark Jewish faith: the rite of male circumcision is paralleled by women's observation of the ritual prohibitions connected with menstrual blood, one of which is the interdiction of intercourse during menstruation. And this ritual observance is also seen to mark a difference between Jewish women and Christian women.

Differences between Jewish and Christian notions of ritual female purity may also be articulated in descriptions of sacrifice. Although sacrificial rituals are performed by a male priesthood in Judaism, in the twelfth-century *Chronicle of Solomon bar Simson*, a record of the massacre of the Jews of Mainz during First Crusade (1096), both mothers and fathers kill their children in a collective act of sacrifice. In this text, as in other Hebrew chronicles that record the same events, the violence inflicted by the crusaders is described as part of the continuing suffering of God's people. The *Chronicle* recounts how the Jews under attack offered themselves as a sacrifice before God, killing each other, their children, and themselves[3]:

> The women girded their loins with strength and slew their own sons and daughters, and then themselves. Many men also mustered their strength and slaughtered their wives and children and infants. The most gentle and tender of women slaughtered the child of her delight. They all arose, man and woman alike, and slew one another. The young maidens, the brides, and the bridegrooms looked out through the windows and cried out in a great voice: "Look and behold, O Lord, what we are doing to sanctify Thy Great Name, in order not to exchange You for a crucified scion who was despised, abominated, and held in contempt in his own generation, a bastard son conceived by a menstruating and wanton mother."
>
> Thus the precious children of Zion, the people of Mainz, were tested with ten trials as was our Father Abraham. . . . They, too, bound their children in sacrifice, as Abraham did his son Isaac. . . . Refusing to gainsay their faith and replace the fear of our King with an abominable stock, bastard son of a menstruating and wanton mother, they extended their necks for slaughter and offered up their pure souls to their Father in Heaven.[4]

The mothers' access to the higher good of sacrifice is explicitly endorsed here: both mothers and fathers kill, both mothers and fathers sacrifice their children. But the sacrificing Jewish mothers stand in contrast to the Christian mother named in this passage: the "menstruating and wanton mother," the mother of Christ. The claim that the Christian savior was conceived by a menstruating woman impugns the purity of both the son and his "wanton" mother, and emphasizes, by contrast, the purity of the sacrificing mothers. Unlike the Christian mother, the Jewish mothers observe the ritual prohibitions surrounding menstruation.

Intercourse during menstruation is proscribed by Christian as well as Jewish law in the Middle Ages. The early church fathers forbid coitus during a woman's menstrual period, and, although abstinence is also required during pregnancy, childbirth, and lactation, it is intercourse during menstruation that seems to have the most severe consequences.[5] Early medieval penitentials claim, for example, that conception during menstruation would result in a hideously deformed child.[6]

Concern for ritual purity seems to wane over the course of the Middle Ages, and by the fourteenth century intercourse during menstruation is considered only a minor sexual offense.[7] But at the same time that penitential concerns about ritual purity seem to become less intense, the notion of menstrual pollution becomes part of scientific discourse; that is, concerns about the dangers of menstruation become less prominent in penitential literature as they become more prominent in scientific literature.[8] Like earlier penitentials, thirteenth-century scientific literature proscribes intercourse during menstruation, and warns of the monstrous children that are conceived during a woman's period.[9] The late thirteenth-century *The Secrets of Women* and its commentaries offer typical cautions about the dangers of women's menstrual blood both to a child and to the man who might engender the child[10]:

In menstruating women the urine is bloody, and when a woman suffers menstrual pain she has watery eyes, the color of her face is changed, and she has no taste for food. A man should beware of having sex with women in this condition, and prudent women know how to keep themselves apart, and remain separated from men during their monthly flow. . . .

Note that when a woman has her menstrual period, humors ascend to the eyes, because the eye is a porous part of the body, and experiences things immediately. At this time the woman becomes pale in the face and loses her appetite because her cerebrum and sense of smell are affected. It is harmful to have sexual intercourse with these women, because children who are conceived tend to have epilepsy and leprosy because menstrual matter is extremely venomous. . . .

Menstruating women are somewhat sluggish and do not enjoy sexual intercourse and similar things. When men go near these women they are made hoarse, so that they cannot speak well. This is because the venomous humors from the woman's body infect the air by her breath, and the infected air travels to the man's vocal cords and arteries causing him to become hoarse. It is harmful for men to have sexual intercourse with menstruating women because should conception take place the fetus would be leprous. This also frequently causes cancer in the male member.[11]

Conception during menstruation is not the only cause of monstrous or leprous offspring identified in medieval medical texts.[12] *The Secrets of Women* discusses other conditions that may contribute to an abnormal conception: an insufficiency of matter, a surplus of matter, a slippery womb that does not retain enough semen, or intercourse in an "irregular" position.[13] But the association of menstruation and monstrous births remains a potent one, and a renewed attention to women's ritual purity marks the climate in which Pseudo-Albertus Magnus writes *The Secrets of Women*, a text whose ideas are then extended and elaborated by the authors of the fifteenth-century inquisitorial treatise on witchcraft, *Malleus Maleficarum*.[14]

With the exception of the Old Irish *Táin*, which I discussed in Chapter 2, medieval fiction does not explicitly represent menstruation, and medieval stories certainly do not recount episodes of sexual intercourse during a woman's period.[15] However, the logic of monstrous birth, the idea that a woman's corrupting menstrual blood might produce monstrous offspring, may subtly inform a group of narratives in which a woman is falsely accused of giving birth to a monster. The child is described as an animal-like being in Jean Maillart's early fourteenth-century *Roman du comte d'Anjou*, "a very ugly figure, black and hairy, with the head of a bear or a dog or some other animal" (d'une trop laide figure, / Noire et velue, qui a teste / D'ours ou de chien ou d'autre beste).[16] In this romance, as in other similar medieval stories, the description of the monstrous birth is a false slander intended to alienate an absent husband from his wife who has just given birth.[17] The monstrous child is meant to demonstrate the mother's nature: her corrupt bloodlines and her corrupting *menstruum*.[18]

In *Le comte d'Anjou* and in stories that recount similar episodes, like Chaucer's *Man of Law's Tale*, the birth of the monstrous child is not explained by intercourse during menstruation. The mother-in-law who invents the story explains the monstrous birth in various ways in the different versions of the story: as the consequence of the mother's unknown and presumably nonnoble origins, as the result of a demonic deception the wife has operated on her husband, as the product of the mother's sexual promiscuity, or as a sign of the mother's nonhuman, fairy nature. But the slander appeals to a menstrual logic that would have been available to the audiences of these stories and in which the monstrous birth might be explained by the child's conception during his mother's menstrual period. This logic is particularly pertinent in *Le comte d'Anjou*, a story that demonstrates a particularly obvious attention to maternal blood: the mother's corrupting bloodline is repeatedly invoked, and the ritual purity of the mother's postpartum body is repeatedly questioned.

In this romance, the story of monstrous birth is also a story about maternal purity. The mother and her perfectly normal child are sent into exile, and the various people they encounter during their journey notice the extreme youth of the child and conclude that his mother cannot have finished her postpartum lying-in, her *gesine*.[19] The repeated references to the lying-in period, a period of ritual isolation after childbirth, and the care that the mother receives because of the concern for her postpartum body reintroduce mother's blood into the story.

In *Le roman du comte d'Anjou* and similar stories, the false accusation of a monstrous birth and the emphasis on the mother's ritual purity may be seen as part of a debate about the value of mother's blood in a noble lineage, a debate in which the attributes of a bloodline are figured in the mother's *menstruum*. That is, the mother's contribution to lineage, like the father's, is carried through blood, and it is the value of that contribution that is at stake in the false claim that the mother has given birth to a monster and in the possible explanation of the monstrous birth as a result of an impure conception. If narratives about sacrifice represent a father's authority through the metonymic figure of the blood he shares with his child, *Le comte d'Anjou* and its analogues offer an alternative model for describing blood relationships, one that recognizes that a child shares its mother's blood, even as it questions the value of women's blood through an insistence on purity rituals.

Purity and Parturition

Le roman du comte d'Anjou begins with a father's incestuous desire. The wife of the Count of Anjou has died, and the devil inflames the count with a passion for his own daughter (she remains unnamed in this story). The daughter escapes her father's attentions by running away with her governess, and after a series of adventures they find lodging in the household of a castellan, earning their keep by teaching needlework to the castellan's daughters. The castellan's lord, the Count of Bourges, falls in love with the daughter of the Count of Anjou, and marries her without seeking to know her origins. The Count of Bourges's aunt, the Countess of Chartres, is deeply concerned about the unknown and presumably

nonnoble status of her nephew's wife, and about what her nephew's children will inherit from their mother.[20] When the daughter of the Count
of Anjou gives birth to a son while her husband is out of the country, the
Countess of Chartres intercepts a letter to the father announcing the birth
of a son and substitutes a letter announcing the birth of a monster, a "very
ugly figure, black and hairy, with the head of a bear or a dog or some
other animal."[21] When the count receives the news, he does not know
what to think, and he sends a response ordering that his wife and her
progeny should be kept safe until his return. The Countess of Chartres
intercepts this letter as well, and she substitutes instructions to execute
the new mother and her child immediately. The vassals charged with exe-
cuting this order take pity on the beautiful child, and release the mother
and child unharmed on the condition that they leave the country. The
countess travels with her newborn child to Estampes, then to Orleans,
where she finds shelter.

The incestuous desire of the father which sets this story into motion
is similar to that described in narratives like *La belle Hélène de Constantinople* or Philippe de Rémy's *Roman de la Manekine*, but in these stories
the father wants to marry his daughter because she looks like her mother,
not because the devil inspires the incestuous desire, as in *Le roman du
comte d'Anjou*. In *La belle Hélène* the daughter escapes before the marriage
can take place, and in *La Manekine* the daughter mutilates herself, chop-
ping off her own hand, in order to destroy the perfect resemblance to her
mother that provokes her father's desire. In *Le roman du comte d'Anjou*,
the father proposes seduction, not marriage, and the daughter avoids her
father's embrace by pleading an indisposition[22]:

"I will not oppose you any more; I will do whatever you wish. But please, if it
does not displease you, it cannot be tonight for I am a little indisposed. And
besides, I do not want anyone to notice or to speak about it with certainty."

("Ja plus ne vous contresterai:
Trestout vostre plesir ferai.
Mes, par amours, ne vous ennuit,
Ce ne porroit pas estre ennuit,
Que je sui un poi dehectie;
Et, avec ce, je ne veil mie
Que on s'en puist apercevoir
Ne qu'en en puist parler de voir." [*Le roman du comte d'Anjou*, ll. 473–80])

The daughter then asks her maids to prepare her bed and claiming to be ill with a fever, she orders them not to wake her the following morning by entering the chamber or knocking on its door.

The daughter's protest that she is indisposed and her claim to have a fever are both strategic lies. The first allows her to avoid her father's embraces, and the second hides her escape during the night. The fever is described in the language of illness and medicine ("I feel a great chill; and if Our Lord wills it, I will sweat a little and be healed without other cures. For I do not wish to put myself in the hands of doctors, who would make a big fuss out of it, if they knew of this little thing"[23]). However, the indisposition is described in vague terms ("je sui un poi dehectie"), and the count's daughter does not wish anyone to know about it. The father readily agrees to delay sleeping with his daughter because she is "a little indisposed," but what exactly does he understand her indisposition to be? The father is described as inspired by a demonic passion; it does not seem likely that he would be deterred from sleeping with his daughter just because she is not in perfect health. However, it is possible that the father's willingness to defer the seduction of his daughter may be explained by his reluctance to sleep with a menstruating woman; that is, the father may understand his daughter's "indisposition" as a reference to menstruation—she cannot sleep with him that night because she has her period.

There is no way to prove such a reading; indeed, it is suggested only by the reticence of the passage. But a Latin version of the story found in a fourteenth-century manuscript suggests its pertinence. In the Latin story, when the father announces his intention to take his daughter as his lover, the daughter initially refuses vehemently, then asks her father to delay his pleasure for four days because she suffers from a "feminine malady" ("infirmitas muliebris").[24]

In *Le comte d'Anjou* the daughter's "indisposition" might be read as part of the prominent attention paid to women's ritual purity and, implicitly, to women's blood in this romance. Throughout the story, the count's daughter is the object of an obsessive attention that focuses on the state of her body. When she is sent into exile with her new-born son, almost every character she encounters notices that she has failed to complete her *gesine*, the ritual lying-in period after childbirth.

The ritual isolation of postparturient women is inherited from Jewish purification laws, but has an ambivalent status in medieval culture. As early as the sixth century, Bede records a letter from Pope Gregory—the same letter about ritual pollution that I cited in Chapter 1—in which

Gregory redefines the blessing of the mother after the one-month post-partum seclusion ritual. Gregory claims that churching is not a purification ritual, it is a ritual of thanksgiving. Women may enter the church to give thanksgiving immediately after childbirth, he claims, and in his elimination of the mother's confinement after birth, he seems to disassociate the ritual from notions of purification. But as Dyan Elliott has noted, Gregory points to childbirth as linked to sin, in the act of pleasure that accompanies conception. More broadly conceived, the relationship between childbirth and sin is seen in women's pain in childbirth which is a legacy from Eve, and thus it is related to original sin. While childbirth is not a sin in itself, it is associated with the pollution of sin, and the logic of churching reflects that association, even though the ritual is often characterized as one of thanksgiving.[25]

Gregory's ambivalence about the impurity of childbirth was also typical of later medieval views of the ritual.[26] A woman who entered the church before completing her lying-in was subject to penance.[27] At the same time, however, the church continued to treat the ritual as one of thanksgiving, not of purification, though churching may have been perceived as a purification ritual by its practitioners and their families.[28] Or, as David Cressy has argued, "an alternative case can be made for the view that women normally looked forward to churching as an occasion of female social activity, in which the notion of 'purification' was uncontentious, minimal, or missing."[29] Gail Gibson has further suggested that the public liturgy of Candlemas, a yearly celebration that honors the purification of the virgin and the presentation of Christ in the temple, like the representation of Mary's churching in medieval plays, may have offered women viewers a spectacle "about the powerful centrality of Mary's female body in a preordained plan for salvation . . . a theater that celebrated the female body in both the fleshly and the corporate senses of the word."[30]

The lying-in period and the ritual blessing that concluded it suggest the contested values of the female body and its blood in medieval culture: Mary's churching may offer the spectacle of a celebrated maternal body, as Gibson suggests, whereas churching as a purification ritual points to the pollution of the bleeding maternal body. The representation of the lying-in period in medieval fiction is thus a narrative site in which it is possible to interrogate the values associated with women's blood. And unlike menstruation, which is almost never represented in medieval fiction, parturition and the lying-in do appear in narratives. In Chapter 3, I discussed the scene in *Jourdain de Blaye* where Oriabel states her intention to "lie in bed for nineteen or twenty full days, and then . . . go to mass, according to Christian custom, so that [her] body will not be impure," and a number of other stories refer to the lying-in.[31] But the *gesine* receives a curiously prominent representation in narratives about monstrous births. When the King of Scotland receives his mother's forged letter describing the monstrous child that his wife has produced in *La Manekine*, he replies in a letter asking that his wife be guarded safely in her *gesine*.[32] The king's mother has her scribe substitute an order to burn the new mother as soon as she rises from her lying-in.[33] In a dramatic version of the story from the thirteenth century, the mother is accused of giving birth to the three puppies that have been substituted for her three sons, and she will be imprisoned before she has completed her *gesine*.[34]

This attention to the lying-in period is represented with almost obsessive intensity in *Le roman du comte d'Anjou*. When the vassals charged with killing the mother and her new-born son release her unharmed, they counsel her to go to Estampes where she can complete her lying-in: "There you will be able to stay a week at the Hotel Dieu if you let it be known that you need to rest, for you have not lain in as long as necessary."[35] When the new mother reaches Estampes, the mayor's wife sees her nursing her baby in the church, notices from the child's age that the mother should still be in bed, and asks why she has not finished her lying-in (*gesine*).

The townswoman uncovers the child to see its face. When she sees that it is so young, she understands that the mother should still be lying in, if she had her rights. She takes pity on her and asks her courteously if she has given birth to the child and why she has not completed the number of days established for lying in.

(Lors le descuevre la bourjoise
Tant qu'elle a veü le visage.
Quant el voit de si jone aage
Bien voit qu'encor gesir deüst
La mere, se son droit eüst.
Pitié l'en prent et si li prie
Courtoisement qu'ele li die
Se cilz enfes est de li nez
Et pour quoi n'a touz terminéz
Les jours establiz a gesine. [*Le roman du comte d'Anjou*, ll, 4462–71])

This woman offers the count's daughter shelter, she bathes her and gives her food, but when her husband refuses to take on the expense of lodging the mother and child, the mayor's wife is forced to send the young mother to Orleans where the bishop dispenses alms to the poor. The bishop sees the young child, notices that he is not yet three weeks old, and asks why his mother is not in her lying-in.[36] The bishop sends her to the Hotel Dieu, where she is taken in and where she is eventually found by her penitent husband who has returned to Lorris, discovered his wife's absence and his aunt's treachery, and has abandoned his riches to travel as a poor man in search of his wife and child.

During his quest, the Count of Bourges identifies his wife by the recent birth. In Estampes, he tells the mayor's wife that he seeks his wife, who gave birth to a son only twelve days earlier,[37] and this lady recognizes the poor mother she tried to help: "a woman should be merciful toward another woman when she is poor and in need, especially when she has so recently been to bed to give birth."[38]

In *Le roman du comte d'Anjou*, the mother's recent experience of childbirth is noticed because her child is so young, not because of the mother's weakness. And she seems to need help because she has no resources, not because she is in ill health. Indeed, the emphasis in this text on the mother's failure to complete her lying-in seems much more focused on the incomplete ritual itself than on the needs of the mother's body. She has given birth and then completed an arduous journey—indeed her husband speaks a long lament about the hardships of the same journey, one that he undertook voluntarily and without the burden of a newborn child.[39] But the mother's body is never characterized as weak from childbirth or debilitated by the long journey; in fact, the mother's body is noticed for its beauty, not for its lack of strength or ill appearance.[40] Her premature exit from the birth-bed is deduced from the age of her child, and provokes an almost universal desire to care for her postpartum body.

It seems that care for the body and a concern for the mother's privacy are what motivate the desire to help her complete her *gesine*. And despite what seems to be a focused emphasis on the ritual confinement that follows childbirth, the postparturition lying-in period does not end in churching in *Le comte d'Anjou*: the mother does not go to mass, as does Oriabel in *Jourdain de Blaye*. Or at least the romance does not recount that she does— the end of the *gesine* is marked not by a religious ritual of reintegration, but by the new mother's reunion with her husband. The end of the lying-in takes the form of a symbolic restoration of the mother's purity in her husband's completion of his quest, his recognition of the mother's innocence, the restoration of her status, and the revelation of her own noble origins.[41]

The exaggerated attention to ritual purity in this romance might point to several concerns. Although I have suggested that the story does not stress the weakness of the postpartum body, the focus on the mother's failure to complete her lying-in period does point to the vulnerability of the mother and her child who are in exile, without resources and, at least initially, without allies. It also offers a representation of women caring intimately for other women, and identifies the care of the postpartum body as the domain of women. This segregation is endorsed by the bishop, who sends the new mother to the Hôtel Dieu, where she is cared for by another woman, the mistress of the hostel. Finally, the focus on postpartum ritual purity suggests an attention to mother's blood—to the blood of parturition, to the mother's bloodlines, and ultimately to the blood of menstruation. This focus is particularly apparent in the context of the Countess of Chartres's fears about what the mother of presumably nonnoble bloodlines will pass on to her children. It is further suggested by the way that recognition of the mother's postpartum body is consistently linked to nursing: characters in the story recognize that she has not completed her *gesine* when they see her nursing her newborn baby.

Breast milk not only nourishes a baby, it also transmits the mother's or the nursemaid's qualities to the child. According to Bernardino of Siena, "The child acquires certain of the customs of the one who suckles him. If the one who cares for him has evil customs or is of base condition, he will receive the impress of those customs because of having sucked her polluted blood."[42] According to Alfonso el Sabio's *Siete Partidas* the best wet-nurses are "well-mannered and healthy, and beautiful, and come from a good family."[43] The idea that mother's milk carries an essential identity from the breast to the child is demonstrated even further in stories about Jewish families who required that Christian wet-nurses express their milk into a latrine for three days after receiving the eucharist.[44] These stories are antisemitic fictions that promote the doctrine of transubstantiation, but they are based on the plausibility of the idea that breast-milk carries more than simple nourishment, that it can pass on the characteristics of the woman who nurses—even if she is not the mother of the child. And if breast-milk can pass on religious identity, it can also pass on sin: saints like Katarina of Sweden are said to have refused to nurse after their mothers had engaged in sexual relations.[45] Since intercourse was forbidden during lactation, the baby demonstrates its sanctity in avoiding the impurity of the mother's polluted body.

The story of Katarina of Sweden characterizes the maternal body as a site of danger and sin, and recalls Gregory's link between childbirth and the sinful pleasure of conception. And the impurity of the maternal body is demonstrated in its products: its monstrous offspring, its polluted milk, its dangerous blood.

Purity and Lineage

If narratives of sacrifice feature the father's relationship with his child as a blood relationship, narratives about monstrous births recognize that a child shares its mother's blood as well. This recognition is what motivates the Countess of Chartres's treacherous deception. Fearing that her nephew has "been deceived by a woman of lowly birth and origin whose children will be peasants,"[46] she destroys the seneschal's birth announcement to the father and replaces it with a letter that stresses the count's noble origins and the corruption of his lineage that results from his wife's disloyalty.[47] In the countess's view, the unknown origins of her nephew's wife signify a nonnoble origin, a status she equates with prostitution in the letter she forges in her nephew's voice.

"Castellan, since my departure I have understood with certainty that I was deceived because I did not know the identity of the woman I married before I gave her great honors. For I have been told that one could not find a woman more infamous, for she abandoned her body to all for money. So I have been told by those who found her in a brothel."

("Chastelain, puis mon partement,
J'ai entendu certainement
Que j'ai esté trop deceü
De ce que je n'ai pas seü
Quelle est la fame que j'ai prise,
Ainz que l'eüsse en honneur mise,
Quer on m'a bien fet assavoir
Que ne peüsse pas avoir
Fame qui tant fust diffamee,
Quer elle estoit habandonnee
De son cors a tous pour argent.
Ce m'a bien esté dit par gent
Qui bien l'ont au bourdel trouvee."
[*Le roman du comte d'Anjou*, ll. 3663–75])

In fact, whether or not the child is the ugly, black, and hairy animal-like progeny the countess falsely describes in her letter, it is still a monster in her eyes because of its unknown lineage.

The anxiety about lineage is stressed even more strongly in Chaucer's *Man of Law's Tale* and in Chaucer's source, Nicholas Trevet's *Cronicles*.[48] These versions of the story do not stress ritual purity; the mother's lying-in period is not mentioned in the narrative. Here, the story conflates royal lineage and religion in the marriage of a king to the unknown woman, here named Constance. The king converts to Christianity, and his mother, Donygild, resents both the corruption of the family line and the conversion, as Trevet recounts in *Les cronicles*.

At that time, the mother of King Alla was still alive, and she was a beautiful, proud woman, and she mortally hated Queen Constance. For she was angry that King Alla had abandoned his first religion, which all his ancestors had kept and observed, for the love of a foreign woman whose lineage he did not know.

(Vnquore a cel tenps estoit la mere le reis Alle en vie, bele dame e fere de corage, e que trop morteument hey Constaunce la reyne. Qar grant engayn auoyt que le reis Alle auoit pur lamour vne femme estraunge, e qi lynage lui nestoit pas conu, sa primere ley gwerpi, quele touz ses auncestres auoient leaulment e enterement gardes.)[49]

Like the Countess of Chartres in *Le roman du comte d'Anjou*, Donygild plots to get rid of Constance in her son's absence by announcing the birth of a monster, but she explains the monstrous birth not as a result of the mother's promiscuity, as in the Countess of Chartres's claim that she was a prostitute, but by claiming that Constance is a diabolical incarnation, not a woman at all.[50]

[She wrote] that Queen Constance, given into their care since the king's departure, had changed in manner and condition into another creature, for she was an evil spirit in the form of a woman, and the marvels that she had worked, which looked like miracles, were the deeds of the evil spirit in her body: "to which bears witness the child she has born, for it does not resemble the form of a man, but rather, it has a cursed hideous and shameful form."

(Escritz . . . qe la reyne Constaunce, bailee en lour garde puis le departir le rei, fu en manere e en condicioun chaungee, come en vne autre creature; qar ele fu maueise espirit en fourme de femme; dount les merueiles que ele fist, que sembleient miracles, furent fesaunces del mauueys espirit en soun corps: "a qey temoine lenfaunt de luy nee, que ne recemble pas a fourme de homme, mes a vne maladite fourme hidous e dolorouse." [Trevet, 173])

Chaucer repeats Trevet's emphasis on the supernatural explanation for the monstrous birth, but in *The Man of Law's Tale*, Constance is described not as an evil sprit, but as a fairy. Donygild claims that: "The mooder was an elf, by aventure / Ycomen, by charmes or by sorcerie" (*Man of Law's Tale*, ll. 754–55).[51]

The unknown origins of the mother are seen as a threat to lineage. This threat is explicitly a threat to noble status in all versions of the story, and the Trevet and Chaucer versions add the anxiety about conversion. The king's conversion intensifies the conflict between the Christian mother and her mother-in-law, and it is of course perfectly logical that a mother might resent her son's conversion and that she would hate the woman for whom he converted. Indeed, an Arabic chronicle that recounts just such a situation has been identified as the source for the story in Trevet's *Les Cronicles*.[52] But the story of the mother's resentment and treachery may also reveal a more general anxiety about intermarriage and impurity. That is, the English versions of the monstrous birth story and their source in Trevet's chronicle may reflect the anxious negotiation of intermarriage between Christians and Jews in legal discourses during the Middle Ages.

David Nirenberg has richly documented the prohibition of intercourse between people of different faiths in fourteenth-century Aragon, and he has emphasized the extent to which these prohibitions involve notions of purity and religious identity.[53] And while legal and religious practices in fourteenth-century Aragon do not necessarily apply to fourteenth-century England, they may suggest the ways intermarriage could provoke fears about the ritual purity of the bodies united in marriage. James Brundage has suggested that medieval regulations about intermarriage between Christians and Jews reveal concerns about ritual purity, about Christian fears of contracting impurity through intimate contact.[54] It may then be pertinent to think about Donygild's persecution of Constance not, or not only, as a resentful mother's vengeance on the woman who convinced her son to convert, but as the displaced enactment of Christian fears about intimate contact with nonchristians, and particularly Jews. In other words, when it is contextualized in a broader debate about intermarriage, Donygild's false accusation of a monstrous birth might be suggest the projection of an anxiety about ritual purity and intimate contact in which the locus of danger is the female body and its imagined products.

All the versions of the monstrous birth story focus on the mother's contribution to lineage, and all focus on the mother's bloodline. The desire to exclude the mother's blood from lineage motivates the deception that characterizes the mother's blood as the dangerous legacy of a prostitute whose contact with other men has corrupted her seed, or of a devil whose union with a man produces a monster, or of a fairy whose child is inhuman.[55]

Constance and the daughter of the Count of Anjou are, of course, not prostitutes, demons, or fairies, and in fact they are of noble lineage. And in the versions of the story by Trevet and Chaucer, King Alla's quest for his exiled wife, Constance, ends with Alla's recognition of his son, who "strongly resembles his mother," in the words of Trevet's *Chronicle*.[56] Carolyn Dinshaw has called this recognition "the patriarchal gaze" because it binds father and son through the woman's image.[57] But at the same time, this scene also clearly affirms the role of mother's blood in lineage. King Alla recognizes Constance in her son, a son who has a mother, but no father, as the senator explains in *The Man of Law's Tale*.[58]

This Alla kyng hath of this child greet wonder,
And to the senatour he seyde anon,
"Whos is that faire child that stondeth yonder?"
"I noot," quod he, "by God, and by Seint John!
A mooder he hath, but fader hath he noon
That I of woot" –and shortly, in a stounde,
He tolde Alla how that this child was founde. (*Man of Law's Tale*, ll. 1016–22)

The child resembles his mother perfectly ("Now was this child as lyk unto Custance / As possible is a creature to be" [*Man of Law's Tale*, ll. 1030–31]), and his resemblance to his mother leads to the reconciliation between his parents. And in all the versions of the story, the reconciliation restores a dynasty in which the son inherits not only his father's lands, but also the title and lands of his mother.

Stories about monstrous births imagine mother's blood as a contribution to lineage, and that contribution is noticed or made visible because it is seen as a threat. Although the husband is not concerned by his wife's unknown origins, his mother (or his aunt) is profoundly troubled by the prospect that nonnoble blood will contaminate her lineage. While the concern about the mother's unworthy bloodline is explicit in all the versions of the story I have discussed here, *Le roman du comte d'Anjou* makes an implicit connection between the blood of lineage and the blood of parturition in the emphasis on the mother's failure to complete her *gesine*, a postpartum purity ritual. And although the impurity of the mother's body is not stressed in the story, the function of the postpartum confinement as a liminal period in which the mother remains separate from her usual daily life is suggested in the way that the completion of this mother's *gesine* leads to the reunion with her husband and the restoration of her status as a pure wife and mother of a noble heir, and not the prostitute-mother of a monster. *Le roman du comte d'Anjou* suggests a conflation of the polluting blood of parturition and the supposedly non-noble blood of the mother that also pollutes because it produces monstrous offspring. And although the report of a monstrous birth is revealed to be a deception, the place of the mother's contribution to the conception of her child in the hierarchies of status and authority defined by active engendering remains somewhat uncertain in this story. While the mother clearly passes her likeness to her child, the significance of what a mother's blood might pass on to her child is obscured by the representation of contested lineage and of rituals that define the impurity of childbirth. The truths about mother's blood are, it appears, hidden in the prohibited scene of parturition.

5

The Scene of Parturition

THAT A CHILD SHARES its mother's blood is made vividly clear in birth: the umbilical cord offers striking evidence that the maternal relationship is a blood relationship. The blood of parturition further demonstrates a child's origins in its mother's blood, though the evidence of birth is often unacknowledged in symbolic representations of blood relationships, as anthropologist Brigitta Hanser-Schäublin emphasizes:

A flow of blood accompanies the delivery of the baby which is covered with its mother's fluids. It is followed by the afterbirth which is lifeless. In [modern] Western culture blood group factors give the impression that a child inherits its blood from either its father or its mother. But these factors blur the fact that a baby's blood as fluid originates exclusively from its mother.[1]

Medieval texts do not describe heredity in terms of blood group factors, though they do of course represent paternal relationships in terms of blood, as I have discussed in previous chapters. The relationship between mother and child was also explained in terms of blood: according to Pseudo-Albertus, who wrote in the late thirteenth or early fourteenth century, both father's blood (in the form of semen) and mother's blood (in the form of menses) are necessary for conception:

When a woman is having sexual intercourse with a man she releases her menses at the same time that the man releases sperm, and both seeds enter the *vulva* (vagina) simultaneously and are mixed together, and then the woman conceives. Conception is said to take place, therefore, when the two seeds are received in the womb in a place that nature has chosen. And after these seeds are received, the womb closes up like a purse on every side, so that nothing can fall out of it. After this happens, the woman no longer menstruates.[2]

Albert the Great, the Pseudo-Albert's teacher, offered a more Aristotelian view of conception: when he defined the generative properties of male

and female seed, he described the active faculty of the male and the passive faculty of the female.[3] The twelfth-century nun Hildegard of Bingen
offered a somewhat different explanation of male and female roles in generation in her medical writings, and one that contradicted classical ideas
about conception. Whereas Hildegard attributed seed only to the male,
she claimed that the woman's matter joined itself to the man's seed,
warming it and giving it form. However, like other medieval thinkers,
Hildegard believed that the strength of the man's semen determined the
sex of the child.[4]

Medical or scientific models of conception are not necessarily invoked in the representations of heredity in stories like *Le roman du comte
d'Anjou* or in *The Man of Law's Tale*. But these texts do offer a representation of a model of generation that valorizes the mother as a partner in
generation: the English versions of the monstrous birth story that recount
the son's resemblance to his mother suggest that the mother offers a significant contribution to his conception. So while narratives about sacrifice
valorize paternity in terms of the blood a child shares with its father, and
while medical models of reproduction identify the mother's blood as necessary for conception, but inferior to the father's engendering seed,
medieval fictions about monstrous conceptions recognize a mother's contribution to conception in their debates about the value of a mother's
blood in generation. The evil mother-in-law's story of corrupt maternal
lineage describes the mother's legacy as a dangerous one, whereas the
father's recognition of his wife in her son reunites the family and secures
lineage, status, and wealth.

The fact that a child shares its mother's blood would not seem to be
disputed: the scene of birth—although not explicitly described in these
stories—makes abundantly clear that the child literally shares its mother's
blood. But it is the *value* of the mother's blood that is in question in these
stories. If the mother's *menstruum* offers the material out of which the
child is formed, what essential identity is passed through the mother's
blood? This question is raised by the false accusation of monstrous birth:
the prostitute/demon/fairy mother is said to pass her monstrous nature to
her son. The value of a mother's contribution to conception is debated
further in a story in which the description of the mother offered by the
Donygild in her accusation of monstrous birth actually fits the woman
who gives birth.[5] In the story of Mélusine, maternal blood flows from a
fairy who gives birth to monstrous children.

Monstrous Birth

The late fourteenth-century *Roman de Mélusine* by Jean d'Arras recounts the foundation of the Lusignan dynasty, a family of important nobles from Poitou.[6] However, the story of Mélusine has an ambiguous status as a foundational narrative. It was not commissioned by the Lusignan family, but by subsequent owners of the lands and castles whose origins are attributed to Mélusine. And although Mélusine, la Mère Lusine, is identified as the matriarch whose heirs enjoy the territory she has acquired and the castles she has constructed, the story offers an ambiguous valorization of mother's blood in the lineage founded by Mélusine.[7]

The daughter of a human king and a fairy, Mélusine is a being who desires to be human, but cannot escape the fairy nature she inherits from her mother, the fairy Presine. Moreover, Mélusine herself is a mother whose own legacy to her children includes not only wealth and status, but physical deformities.[8]

Jean d'Arras begins his *Roman de Mélusine* with a discourse about fairies. Citing Gervaise of Tilbury as his authority, he describes fairies who take the form of women and impose various sorts of interdictions on the humans they marry.[9]

And [Gervaise] states further that these fairies took the form of very beautiful women, and several men took them as wives according to the promise that the fairies demanded: some that the husbands would never see them naked, others, that their husbands would not seek to know their whereabouts on Saturdays, and others, that if they had children, their husbands would never look on them during their lying-in. And as long as the husbands kept their promises, they enjoyed great esteem and prosperity. But as soon as they failed to keep their promise, they would lose their wives, and little by little all their happiness would disappear.

(Et [Gervaise] dit encores que les dictes faees se mettoient en forme de tres belles femmes, et en ont pluseurs hommes prinses pour moilliers, par my aucunes convenances qu'elles leur faisoient jurer, les uns qu'ilz ne les verroient jamais nues, les autres que le samedy n'enquerroient qu'elles seroient devenues, aucunes, se elles avoient enfans, que leurs maris ne les verroient jamais en leur gesine. Et tant qu'ilz leur tenoient leurs convenances, ilz estoient regnans en grant audicion et prosperité. Et si tost qu'ilz defailloient, ilz les perdoient et decheoient de tout leur bon eur petit a petit. [*Le roman de Mélusine*, 3–4])

Jean recounts this fairy lore to contextualize his own story—he does not attempt to account for other kinds of interdictions that might be imposed by fairies, like the promise not to speak of their relationship that the fairy in Marie de France's *Lanval* demands from her lover.[10] Jean's description represents the fairies' interdictions as taboos concerning the body. That the body in question is always a maternal body is suggested by the way that lineage is a central concern from the very beginning of his story: although Jean claims that he will recount "how the noble and strong fortress of Lusignan in Poitou was founded by a fairy,"[11] he begins his story not with Mélusine, but with her parents, the fairy Presine and King Helinas.[12]

King Helinas meets Presine at a fountain, he falls in love with her, and she agrees to marry him if Helinas will promise never to see his wife in her childbirth bed, in her *gesine*.

"If you wish to take me as your wife and you swear that if we have children, you will never try to see me in my childbirth bed, nor will you try in any way to see me, I will obey you as a loyal wife should obey her husband." And the king swore to it.

(Se vous me voulez prendre a femme et jurer que, se nous avons enfans ensemble, que vous ne mettrez ja peine de moy veoir en ma gesine, ne ne ferez par voye quel-conques tant que vous me voiez, je suiz celle qui obeiray a vous comme loyal moil-lier doit obeir a son espoux. Et le roy lui jura ainsi. [*Le roman de Mélusine*, 9])

The king agrees to Presine's demand and they are married. Presine be-comes pregnant, she gives birth to three daughters, and King Helinas for-gets his promise and goes to see the mother and children soon after birth. When the king enters the chamber where Presine is bathing her newborn daughters, she immediately accuses him of having broken his promise, takes the daughters, and disappears, never again to be seen in the land.

When Presine's daughters are fifteen years old, she tells them the story of their father's failure to honor the promise he made to her as a condition of marriage. Mélusine and her sisters decide to take vengeance on Helinas, and they imprison their father in a magic mountain. Presine still loves Helinas and, angered by her daughters' actions, she punishes them by revoking their father's heritage: Presine declares that Mélusine and her sisters will not become human like their father, they will remain fairies like their mother. Her curse negates the value of the father's blood and affirms the determining influence of the mother's nature, as she explains to Mélusine:

"The virtue of your father's seed would have given you and the others his human nature, and soon you would have left the customs of nymphs and fairies never to return. But now I give you the gift that on Saturdays you will be a serpent from the navel down. However, if you find a man who will take you as his wife and will promise never to see you on a Saturday, and never to seek to find you, and never to speak of it to anyone, you will live a natural life as a natural woman, and you will die a natural death. And a great and noble lineage will come from you, and your descendants will accomplish great and worthy feats. And if your husband betrays you, you will return to the earlier torment without end, as long as the High Judge holds his seat of judgment."

("La vertu du germe de ton pere toy et les autres eust attrait a sa nature humaine, et eussiés esté briefment hors des meurs, nimphes et faees, sans y retourner. Mais desormais je te donne le don que tu seras tous les samedis serpente du nombril en aval. Mais, se tu treuves homme qui te veuille prendre a espouse, que il te convenance que jamais le samedy ne te verra, non qu'il te descuevre, ne ne le die a personne, tu vivras cours naturel comme femme naturelle, et mourras naturelment. Et, non contretant, de toy ystra noble lignie moult grant, et qui feront de grans et haultes prouesces. Et se tu es dessevree de ton mary, saiches que tu retourneras ou tourment de devant, sans fin, tant que le Hault Juge tendra son siege." [*Le roman de Mélusine*, 12–13])

Mélusine's vengeance on her father for his transgression of Presine's interdiction leads to the negation of the father's legacy—his blood, his seed, or his *germe*—and to the affirmation of Mélusine's legacy from her mother: like Presine, she may marry only a man who promises to observe a taboo relating to her body.

Mélusine's first encounter with Raymondin, like the meeting of Presine and Helinas, takes place near a fountain. Mélusine reveals that she knows Raymondin's affairs and she promises to help him on two conditions. The first is that he marry her; the second is that he can never see her on a Saturday.

"You must swear upon all the oaths that a nobleman knows that you will never make an effort to see me or to know where I am on Saturdays. And I swear to you, on the peril of my soul, that on that day I will never do anything except that which adds to your honor."

("Vous me jurerez sur tous les seremens que preudoms doit faire, que le samedi vous ne mettrez jamais peine a moy veoir ne enquerre ou je seray. Et je vous jure, par le peril de l'ame de moy, que jamais cellui jour je ne feray ja chose qui vous puist estre atournee fors a toute honneur." [*Le roman de Mélusine*, 26])

Raymondin accepts Mélusine's help and acquiesces to the conditions she imposes: they marry and Raymondin promises never to try to see Mélusine on a Saturday. But after many years of marriage and after the births of ten children, Raymondin allows himself to be persuaded to transgress his wife's interdiction: when his brother accuses Mélusine of using her Saturdays for amorous dalliances, Raymondin decides to prove his brother wrong, and he pierces a hole in the door of his wife's chamber and sees her in her bath. He discovers that Mélusine is a woman from the waist up, but below the waist she has been transformed into a serpent. Still, he says nothing, and only later, when his son Geoffrey has burned a monastery and killed all the monks inside, including Geoffrey's own brother, does Raymondin erupt in anger and accuse Mélusine of being a monster: "Ha, false serpent, by God, neither you nor your deeds are anything but phantoms, and no heir you carried will come to a good end" ("Hee, tres faulse serpente, par Dieu, ne toy ne tes fais ne sont que fantosme, ne ja hoir que tu ayes porté ne vendra a bon chief en la fin").[13]

Curiously, Raymondin identifies only moral monstrosity in his children—Geoffrey acted monstrously in killing defenseless monks, among whom was his brother, Fromont. Raymondin does not seem to have noticed that his sons bear the mark of their mother's supernatural being on their bodies. One son has a single eye in the middle of his forehead; another has one ear bigger than the other, and yet another has lion's fur on his left cheek. Only the last two sons are exempt from the mother's marks.[14]

Le roman de Mélusine recounts the scenario imagined in narratives like Chaucer's *Man of Law's Tale* where a woman is accused of giving birth to a monster because of her fairy nature, yet the monstrous physical nature of Mélusine's sons is not even acknowledged by the other characters in the romance. Only moral monstrosity is chastised, in the case of Geoffrey, and eliminated, in the murder of Mélusine's son, Horrible, a murder sanctioned by Mélusine herself.[15] In other words, the monstrous deformations of Mélusine's children do not indicate any moral defect; although two of her children are characterized as moral monsters, their moral defect is not directly related to their physical deformities. The physical anomalies of Mélusine's sons are simply marks of their mother's "unnatural" origins that are not completely erased by their father's nature. Indeed, Gabrielle Spiegel has suggested that the deformities of Mélusine's sons point to a hybrid nature that is explained in medieval biological thinking by hybridization itself, a "mixing of semens" that is seen as a fundamental cause of monstrosity.[16]

Monstrous births are not limited to Mélusine, but—as Spiegel argues—also apply to Mélusine's mother, Presine, if we acknowledge the medieval notion, based on Aristotle, that twins are monsters. For Aristotle, twins are part of the category of the monstrous because of their rarity, but also because they confound the categories of human and animal: humans reproduce singly, animals in multiples.[17] And as Spiegel points out, in medieval reproductive theory, the responsibility for monstrosity lies with the mother; it is explained by an excess of material, of *menstruum*.[18]

Another possible medieval explanation for the birth of twins is that the children have two different fathers. In a fifteenth-century Italian version of the monstrous birth story, the wife gives birth to two sons, and a forged letter supposedly from her husband demands her death because the birth of twins proves her adultery.[19] However, this logic is usually represented in medieval fiction only to show that it is erroneous. Several stories, most famously perhaps Marie de France's *Fresne*, recount the story of a woman who calls her neighbor an adulteress because she has given birth to twins: only sex with two men will produce two children born at the same time. The accusing woman is inevitably punished in kind. She herself gives birth to twins, as in *Fresne*, or she gives birth to seven children, as in stories like *Le chevalier du cygne*, where an evil mother-in-law takes away the babies and substitutes seven puppies in their place, accusing the mother of having had sex with dogs.[20]

Mélusine's own monstrous birth is realized in her mother's revocation of the effect of her father's seed, his *germe*, and she will never be human unless her husband honors his promise never to see her on a Saturday. This interdiction would seem to be an arbitrary prohibition, similar to the many interdictions and taboos recorded in European folktales.[21] Yet the interdictions in the story of Mélusine are more than conventional indications of fairy identity. Folklorist Claude Gaignebet has suggested that the interdiction to see the wife in her bath, during her purifying ablutions, symbolically represents the interdiction that applies to women during menstruation in many cultures.[22] So if Mélusine in her bath is a (symbolically) menstruating woman, the interdiction to see the wife in the bath may be seen as a symbolic representation of taboos surrounding menstruation. Although as readers we know that Mélusine takes the form of a serpent in her Saturday bath, the interdiction to see Mélusine's bodily transformation may suggest or echo other prohibitions to see the functions of the female body. And this notion would seem to invite a similar reading of the interdiction that Mélusine's mother imposed on her father:

Presine's prohibition to her husband to see her in her childbirth bed might be seen as another interdiction to see women's blood, in this case, the blood of childbirth.

Seeing Birth

The interdiction to see the bed of parturition is related to fairy-lore in *Le roman de Mélusine*, and it is presented as a restriction that applies only to the father. Helinas is not present when Presine gives birth, but Mataquas, his son, seems to have been present at the birth, or to have seen the daughters soon after their birth, and he persuades his father to transgress Presine's interdiction in order to see his daughters.

Then it happened that [Presine] became pregnant with three daughters, and carried them to term and delivered them. The first-born was named Mélusine, the second, Melior, and the third, Palestine. King Helinas was not there at the time, but his son Mataquas was, and he saw the sisters who were marvelously beautiful. He came to his father the king and said to him, "My lady Queen Presine your wife has given you three of the most beautiful daughters that were ever seen. Sire, come see them." King Helinas did not remember the promise he had made to his wife Presine, and he said, "Beautiful son, I will." He went and without warning he entered the chamber where Presine was bathing her three daughters. And when he saw them he had great joy and said, "God bless the mother and the daughters." When Presine heard him, she responded horribly: "False king, you broke your covenant with me, and you will regret it, and you have lost me forever."

(Or advint qu'elle [Presine] fu enceinte de trois filles et les porta son terme et delivra au jour. La premiere nee ot nom Melusigne, la seconde Melior, la tierce Palestine. Le roy Elinas n'estoit pas pour lors au lieu, mais son filz Mataquas y estoit, et regarda ses trois sereurs qui furent tant belles qu'a merveilles. Il s'en vint devers le roy son pere, et lui dit: Ma dame la royne Presine, vostre femme, vous a apporté les trois plus belles filles qui oncques feussent veues. Sire, venez les veoir. Ly roys Elinas, a qui il ne souvenoit de la promesse qu'il avoit fait a Presine, sa femme, dist: Beau filz, si feray je. Et s'en vint despourveuement et entra en la chambre ou Presine baignoit ses trois filles. Et, quant il les vit, il ot grant joye et dist: Dieux beneye la mere et les filles. Quant Presine l'ouy, si respondi moult horriblement: Faulx roys, tu m'as failli de convenant, dont il te mesavenra, et m'as perdue a toujours mais. [*Le roman de Mélusine*, 9])

The interdiction to see the birth-bed does not apply to all men: Mataquas seems to have been free to go and see his newborn sisters. Presine's interdiction, like the one her daughter Mélusine will impose on her husband, is at least in part a test of his loyalty to his vow.

The interdiction does however resonate with other fictional representations of the childbirth bed as part of a restricted area that a father may not enter. The thirteenth-century French *Roman de Silence*, for example, recounts a father's entry into the birth chamber as an act that normally would cause him shame:

The count runs to the chamber to find out the news. He closes the door of the chamber behind him. His desire to know the truth takes away any shame that might prevent him from approaching the bed of the woman in childbirth. He touches her with his right hand and she feels great shame. However the count does not go away.

(Et li cuens en la cambre acort
Por l'estre savoir et enquere.
L'uis de la cambre apriés lui serre.
Le voloirs qu'a del voir savoir
Tolt qu'il ne puet vergoigne avoir
Qu'al lit ne voist de l'acolcie.
De sa main destre l'a tocie,
Et cele en a moult grant vergoigne.
Li cuens porquant ne s'en eslogne.")[23]

Gail Gibson has related this fictional representation to records of preparations for the childbirth of Margaret of Anjou, Henry IV's wife: all male servants and courtiers were to be excluded from the scene, and a curtain was to separate the birthing space from the royal apartments. The curtain was not to be opened until after the queen's lying-in period.[24]

In *Le roman de Silence*, as in the preparations for Margaret of Anjou's childbirth, the exclusion of the father from the scene of parturition has the status of a ritualized interdiction. But other fictional texts seem to offer a different view of the father's presence at the scene of childbirth. In the twelfth-century *Guillaume d'Angleterre* attributed to Chrétien de Troyes, Guillaume is alone with his wife in the forest when she goes into labor and, following his wife's instructions he helps deliver her children: "With great humility and courtliness, the king does everything she tells him to do (he does not disdain anything, nothing about it displeases him) until he has a beautiful son" ("Li rois par grant humilité / Et par grant deboinaireté / Fait quanques ele li enseigne / [Que riens a faire ne desdegne, / Nule cose ne li desplot] / Tant c'un vallet assés bel ot").[25] This story recounts an extreme situation—the woman who goes into labor in the wilderness and has no one to help her but her husband would not perhaps be governed by the same rituals of exclusion as the woman who gives birth in a bed attended by other women. But a comparison of the birth scene in *Guillaume d'Angleterre* with a similar episode in the story of Beves of Hampton suggests that an extreme situation does not necessarily negate the prohibition of a father's presence at the scene of birth.[26]

Beves of Hampton marries Josiane, a converted Saracen. They are exiled from England and while they wander in the wilderness with Thierry, their servant, the pregnant Josiane goes into labor. In the Anglo-Norman version of the story, Beves offers to help his wife, and she refuses, claiming that a husband is not allowed to see his wife in childbirth in any known law or religion:

Now the lady has pain in her stomach. Beves learns it, and does not take it lightly. "What will we do?" Beves asks Thierry. They get the lady off the mule, they make a shelter with their sharp swords, and put the worthy lady inside it. The pain takes her and she makes a great cry. "Lady," says Beves, "gentle and noble lady, I will stay with you to serve you and to help you, if you will agree. I can see your child[birth], never in my life will I hold it against you." "Sire, by faith, no! There is no religion or law that we have ever heard of that allows a man to see the child[birth] of a woman. Go away, hide yourself from this, and let God take care of me, Holy Mary will be at the delivery." They turn away sad and solemn. Josiane stays in the shelter and when the time is right she gives birth to two sons.

(Ore est la dame de mal de ventre pris;
Boves l'entent, n'out nul riz.
"Quey from nus?" dist Boves a Terriz.
De la mulete unt la dame avalis,
font un loge o lur brancs acerez,
leyns unt mis la dame de pris.
Le mal lui prent si getta ung grant cris.
"Dame," dist Boves, "franc femme e gentiz,
serra joe o vus pur vostre cors server,
pur vos aider, quant vus vent a pleiser?
Vostre enfant purray mult bien ver;
ja en ma vie ne vus averai le plus vil."
"Sire," dist ele, "ma foi, nanyl!
N'e dreit ne lei, ne nus ne avum oi.
K'enfant de femme dust home ver.
Alez vus en, celez vus de ci,
Si lessez damedeu convenr;
Sente Marie serra a le departer."

Il se turnent dolent e sanz riz.
Josian est en la loge remis;
ovre fu bon, si enfanta deus fiz.)[27]

In this version of the story, the pregnant woman sends her husband away, invoking the impropriety of a man seeing his wife's child, that is, the impropriety of a man seeing his wife in childbirth. And the wife appeals to a conventional ritual exclusion: "there is no religion or law that we have ever heard of that allows a man to see the child[birth] of a woman."

The English version of the story recounts a similar exclusion: when Beves offers "to help her in her need," Josiane sends him away, claiming that a man should not see a woman's private parts, her "pryute."[28] But this interdiction is represented differently in other versions of the story. In an Old French version of *Beves of Hampton*, it is not the mother who forbids the father to see her, but the father who refuses to see. Josiane goes into labor, she turns green with pain, and Beves takes her into a cave so that her cries will not be heard in the forest. Josiane pleads with Beves to help her, and here it is the father who refuses to be present: "Sister," says Beves, "I do not dare come to you, or see or look on your pains, or touch or contact you with my hands."[29] But in this version of the story, Josiane subverts the interdiction, and demands Beves's help with the delivery.

"Sire," she says, "cover your eyes, go around that which you cannot cross, the time is coming, I am close to delivery, but I am weak and cannot stay on my feet. "Lady," says Beves, "I cannot refuse. But by the lord who saves us all, I would rather enter the field to save my life against two men who hate me and want to cut off my head."

("Sire," dist ele, "faites vos ieus bender,
Rechevés chou que ne pöés fausser,
Li eure aproche, pres sui dou delivrer,
Mais si sui feble, ne puis sor piés ester."
"Dame," dist Bueves, "che ne puis je veer;
Par cel signor qui tout a a sauver,
Mieus ameroie en un camp a entrer
Contre deus homes por ma vie saver,
Qui me haïssent de la teste a coper.")[30]

Beves finally complies—he rips up his cloak and makes a blindfold, then hands out his children out of the cave to Thierry as Josiane gives birth.

The different versions of the story reveal different ideas about whether or not a father should attend the birth of his child. In an Italian version of the story and in another Old French version, there is no conflict at all. Like Guillaume in Chrétien's *Guillaume d'Angleterre*, Beves helps his wife with the birth "as well as he knows how," and no interdiction is ever mentioned.[31]

What exactly is the status of the scene of childbirth as a taboo scene? Although women giving birth were attended exclusively by women in the Middle Ages, fictional texts seem to offer a mixed reading of the exclusion of men or of fathers from the scene of childbirth.[32] To be sure, the stories that recount a father's participation in childbirth offer that representation as part of an extreme situation. As the narrator explains in *Guillaume d'Angleterre*, since there aren't any women around, the husband will have to suffice.[33] At the same time, though, these narratives offer different views of whether or not the father's participation transgresses some kind of taboo. In one version of the Beves story the interdiction to see the childbirth scene is represented as a law, in another as a custom that can be transgressed if necessary, and in another the interdiction is absent. And the taboo is upheld in one version by the mother, who refuses to allow her husband to help her, and in another it is the father who would rather do battle with "two knights who hate [him] and want to cut off his head" than to see his wife give birth. The disputed status of the prohibition to see the scene of childbirth identifies the prohibition itself as a site of anxiety. But why? How can we make sense of what seem to be conflicting representations of the prohibition of the childbirth scene in *Le roman de Mélusine* and in the *Beves of Hampton* stories?

There would in fact be many possible ways to explain the origins of the taboo against seeing childbirth. It could certainly be linked to the notions of impurity that give rise to the ritual of churching.[34] Or notions of modesty or privacy could dictate that only women should be present during a woman's labor. A husband could wish to be absent because he does not want to witness his wife's pain. Or childbirth could stand as a graphic and bloody reminder of the origins of all men. It would be possible to speculate about the forbidden scene of childbirth in many ways, but I want to question not the origin of the interdiction but what the interdiction *does* in medieval narratives.

The scene of parturition is not an isolated scene in medieval narratives, it is part of a story of lineage and it is part of a story about maternity. In medieval fiction, the prohibition of the childbirth scene also seems to appear as part of an anomalous situation: the gender of the child will be kept secret and scripted by its father, as in *Le roman de Silence*; the mother is alone with her husband, she does not have access to a midwife, as in *Guillaume d'Angleterre* and *Beves of Hampton*; or the mother is herself an anomalous creature, as in the Mélusine stories. In the normal course of events in medieval narratives, parturition takes place outside the narrative, and the fact that a childbirth scene is represented at all marks the episode as somewhat unusual. But what might these anomalous scenes tell us? What might the ambiguous prohibition to see the scene of childbirth suggest about the place of the maternal body in the construction of lineage, about the importance of mother's blood in naming a child's relationship to its parents?

There are at least two ways to understand the effect that the evidence of childbirth might have on the rhetoric of parental ties. On the one hand, the prohibited scene of childbirth constructs women's blood precisely as evidence, as a blood that offers concrete knowledge of the origin of the child—but also as a blood that is only evident, a blood that does not carry figural meaning. In other words, when medieval texts imagine father's blood, they imagine a metonymical relationship: a child is part of its father, a child shares its father's blood. And a father's blood relationship to his child is a figural relationship that also figures the world, since patriarchy is the model of medieval cultural order. By contrast, when medieval texts imagine mother's blood, they imagine matter, the material of conception and birth that acquires form only when inspired by a father's blood or semen. So ultimately, the value of mother's blood is a material value and only a material value, and the opposition between father's blood and mother's blood corresponds to the traditional and conventional association of women with the body and of men with the spirit. Mother's blood is formless matter, father's blood figures the higher goods of lineage, covenant, honor, and worth. While a mother may participate in the conception of a child, even determine the child's nature, mother's blood cannot provide access to higher values and higher goods. Mélusine's legacy from her mother would seem to confirm this exclusion: when Presine negates the value of her father's seed, his *germe*, her daughters lose the possibility of becoming human, and humanity is represented in this text as access to mortality and salvation.

But there is another way to think about how the difference between mother's blood and father's blood might be constructed in birth scenes. The prohibition to see childbirth may figure a narrative reluctance to acknowledge the bloody evidence of the maternal act. That is, the blood of birth demonstrates not only the child's origin in and dependence on its mother's blood, it also demonstrates that the essential metonymy that describes paternal lineage and right (a child is part of its father, a child shares its father's blood) can only have figural status. In other words, the knowledge that parturition offers is the visible evidence, the visible truth of a mother's contribution to lineage—and the anxious negotiation of the scene of birth as a forbidden scene shows that truth to be an uneasy one.

Stories that include false rumors of monstrous births represent the mother's contribution to lineage as a threat to the father's bloodline, or, in the Mélusine story, as a threat to the father's seed, his *germe*. In these stories mother's blood explains something about descent or about lineage. And the concern about the value of a mother's blood is part of an anxious negotiation of the rhetoric of parental ties and parental privilege. Or to put this another way, stories about monstrous birth debate the figural or explanatory value of mother's blood.

Birth offers visible evidence of the importance of mother's blood in lineage—the blood of parturition demonstrates the child's ties to its mother's blood and recalls the blood of menstruation that provides the matter out of which the child is formed, according to medieval reproductive theory.[35] In birth, as Elaine Scarry has suggested, "a baby not only emerges out of the interior of the body but itself represents the interior of the parental body."[36] In scenes that scrutinize the birthing body and constitute it as a forbidden scene, the body whose interior is made visible is the maternal body, and knowledge about birth is represented as knowledge about the mother's body.

The concrete, visible evidence of mother's blood may be perceived to diminish the value of paternal blood ties which must remain figural. The child shares its father's blood, but that sharing is always a metonymy, it is always a rhetorical sharing whose demonstration is constructed through rituals: through baptism, through naming, through a father's legal right to dispose of his child. In other words, stories about monstrous birth debate the relative values of seeing and describing parental relationships: the tension between what is seen and what is reported is certainly at stake in the false accusation of a monstrous birth, in the broken promise not to see the fairy wife in her lying-in or in her bath, and in the negotiation of the law that forbids a husband to see his wife in childbirth. It is no accident that this conflict is played out on the birthing body of the mother. The narratives I have discussed construct childbirth as the site of a dangerous knowledge—they suggest that the evidence of parturition offers a truth about origins, and they expose the fragility of the figural values associated with paternity. Medieval stories about unknown maternal bloodlines and forbidden birth scenes suggest that because it challenges the rhetoric of paternal blood ties, the scene of birth is always monstrous.

Ultimately, the scene of birth may be seen as a site in which the literal and figural meanings of blood are in conflict. In Chapter 6, I turn to the scene of the eucharist, a site in which the literal and figural meanings of blood are collapsed into the paradox of the visible truth of transubstantiation.

6

The Grail and Its Hosts

THIS STUDY HAS FOCUSED primarily on the metaphorical or figural meanings of blood in medieval fictions—on the valorization of men's public bloodshed in contrast to the private and hidden bloodshed of women in the construction of military heroism, and on the way that parental relationships are described with respect to blood. I have argued that the symbolic meanings of blood depend on a valorization of masculine bloodshed that assumes the inability of women's blood to signify beyond the body.

Nowhere in medieval culture do the literal and figural meanings of blood come together in a more potent combination than in the eucharistic ritual. The miracle of the wine that becomes the sacrificial blood of Christ and the bread that becomes his flesh introduces intense debates not only about the literal transformation of the wine and the bread into actual blood and flesh, but also about literal and figural meanings in the eucharistic ritual. The medieval development of the doctrine of transubstantiation has been well studied by such scholars as Miri Rubin.[1] Fictional representations of the eucharist have also received critical attention.[2] These are found most prominently in grail romances, particularly thirteenth-century examples, where the holy grail is a eucharistic vessel, and where the eucharistic ritual is described as a blood sacrifice: the figure of the bleeding crucified Christ appears in the chalice.

Christ's blood is not the only blood associated with the grail, however. The holy vessel is usually found in the care of a wounded man, the grail king who is "wounded between both thighs," in the terms of one of the earliest grail romances, Chrétien de Troyes's twelfth-century *Conte du graal*.[3] In some thirteenth-century narratives, this wound will not stop bleeding.[4] Two kinds of blood are intimately associated with the grail: the blood of the wounded Christ who appears in the grail, and the blood of the wounded man who is charged with keeping the grail. Romances about the holy grail thus represent and even juxtapose two models of wounded masculinity: the crucified Christ and the castrated king.[5]

Holy Blood

In medieval romances, the grail is identified as the vessel used by Joseph of Arimathea to collect the blood of the crucified Christ, and it later comes to hold the body of Christ in eucharistic visions such as those in the thirteenth-century *Perlesvaus*. In an early episode in this romance, King Arthur sees a woman kiss her baby and address him as her son, her father, and her lord. She hands the baby to a priest, who places him on an altar and begins the mass. Arthur then sees the priest holding in his hands the bleeding body of the crucified Christ, which changes into the shape of an infant, who is called an "offering" (*Perlesvaus*, 35–37). Miri Rubin has described this kind of imagery as bringing together what she calls "two strains in Eucharistic symbolism, one which stresses the presence of a real human, suffering body, a historic Christ born to a Virgin, and the other [which] stresses redemption through sacrifice."[6]

Grail romances certainly participate in early thirteenth-century debates about transubstantiation—the *Perlesvaus*, like several other grail stories, prominently represents the True Presence, that is, it describes the host transformed into the actual body of Christ. However, grail romances are not primarily theological texts, and although representations of the eucharist as a crucified body take part in cultural thinking about the nature of the eucharistic ritual, this is not all that these representations do. After all, the eucharistic miracles viewed by Arthur and his knights are miracles associated with the grail, an object that is subsumed into Christian symbolism, but which also remains apart, strange, magical, and *fictional* despite its association with Christian forms.[7] And fictional accounts of the eucharist stress its mystical character: knights who observe the ritual are rendered incapable of speech and movement, or they gaze in wonder at the vision, and sometimes they understand its significance only later in the story.

Eucharistic miracles are spectacles in the *Perlesvaus* and they take place as part of the grail procession. The literal transformation of the eucharist into the flesh and blood of Christ is observed by knights who are unworthy to participate in the ritual. In the following passage in which Gauvain sees the grail procession, the spectacle renders him powerless to move:

Sir Gauvain looks at the Grail, and he thinks he sees a candle inside it. . . . He sees the point of the lance from which the red blood falls, and he thinks he sees two angels carrying two golden candelabras filled with candles. The maidens pass in front of Sir Gauvain and go into another chapel. . . . Then the two maidens come back out of the chapel and pass again in front of Sir Gauvain . . . He thinks he sees the form of a child inside the Grail. . . . Then the two maidens come back and pass in front of the table, and it seems to Sir Gauvain that there are three of them, and he looks up and it seems to him that the Grail is raised in the air. And he thinks he sees above it a man crucified on a cross, with a lance thrust in his side.

(Messire Gavains esgarda le Graal, et li senble q'il voie une chandoile dedenz . . . et voit la pointe de la lance donc li sans vermauz chiét, et li senble qu'il voit .ii. angres qui portent .ii. changelabres d'or espris de changoiles. Les damoiseles passent par devant Monsaignor Gavin et vont en une autre chapele. . . . Atant es vos les .ii. damoiseles ou il issent de la chapele et revienent par devant Monsaignor Gavain . . . et il senble q'il voit enmi le Graal la forme d'un enfant. . . . Atant es vos les .ii. damoiselles qui revienent par devant la table, et senble a Monsaignor Gavain q'il en i ait trois; et esgarde contremont et li senble que le Graax soit tot en l'air. Et voit, ce li est avis, par deseure un home cloufichié en une croiz, et li estoit le glaive fichié eu costé. [*Perlesvaus*, 1: 119])

The grail procession is clearly linked to the celebration of the eucharist by the appearance of the Christ child and the crucified Christ in the grail chalice, and Gauvain sees the miraculous transformation but does not partake of the ritual meal, and he does not ask whom the grail serves.

The spectacular nature of the eucharistic sacrifice is stressed even more pointedly in the description of the ritual in the thirteenth-century *Estoire del saint graal*, and in this episode, those who observe the trans-formation of the host into a body do participate in the ritual.[8] The *Estoire* describes Josephus's first celebration of the eucharistic sacrament among his people. He begins the ritual with the repetition of Jesus's words to his disciples, "Take, eat, for this is my body, which for you and for others will be delivered unto torments . . . Take and drink, for this is the blood of the new law, my own blood which will be shed for the remission of your sins," and the bread becomes flesh and the wine, blood.

And then Josephus clearly saw that he held between his two hands a body like that of a child, and it seemed to him that the blood he saw in the chalice had fallen from the child's body. . . . Then Our Lord said to him, "Josephus, you must dis-member that which you hold, so that there are three pieces." And Josephus responded to him, "Ah, Lord, have pity on your servant, for my heart cannot bear to dismember such a beautiful figure!" And Our Lord said to him, "If you do not follow my commandments, you will have no part in my inheritance."

Then Josephus took the body, and put the head to one side and severed it from the rest as easily as if the child's flesh had been cooked. . . . After that he fear-fully made two parts of the rest, sighing deeply and crying. And as he started to separate the body, the angels who were there came before the alter and knelt beside him until Our Lord said to Josephus, "What are you waiting for? Receive that which is before you and take it, for it is your salvation." And Josephus fell to his knees and began to strike his chest and cry for mercy for his sins.

And when he had risen, he saw before him on the plate only what looked like a piece of bread and he took it, raised it, and when he had thanked his Creator, he opened his mouth and wanted to put it inside. And he looked, and saw that it was an entire body. And when he wants to draw it back, he cannot, and he feels the whole thing being put into his mouth before he can close it. And when he had taken it, he felt all the sweetnesses and pleasures that one can name enter into his body. Afterwards he received the holy sacred drink that was in the chalice. . . . And [all the people] thought that when the morsel that looked like bread was placed in their mouths, they saw a complete child enter their mouths.

(Et lor vit Josephés tout apiertement ke il tenoit entre ses .II. mains un cors autresi comme d'un enfant et li sanbloit ke chil sans qu'il veoit el calisce fust cheüs del cors a l'enfant. . . . Lors li dist Nostre Sires: "Josephé, il te convient desmenbrer chou ke tu tiens, si ke il i ait trois pieches." Et Josephé li respondi: "Ha! Sire, aiés pitié de vostre serf, car mes cuers ne porroit souffrir a desmembrer si biele figure!" Et Nostre Sires li dist: "Se tu ne fais mes commandemens, tu n'aras point de part en mon hyretage."

Lors prist Josephés le cors, si mist la teste a une part et dessevra del bu tout autresi legierement comme se la chars de l'enfant fust toute quite. . . . Aprés chou fist .II. parties du remanant a mout grant paour, comme chil qui mout durement souspiroit et plouroit. Ensi com il commencha a faire les parties, si chaïrent tout li angele qui laiens estoient devant l'autel a terre et furent tout a coutes et a genous tant ke Nostre Sires dist a Josephé: "Quel chose atens tu? Rechoif chou qui est devant toi et si l'use, car che est tes sauvements." Et Josephés se mist a genous et bati son pis et cria merchi en plourant de tous ses pechiés.

Et quant il fu redrechiés, si ne vit devant soi sour la platine ke une pieche en samblanche de pain et si le prist, se le leva en haut et, quant il eut rendu grasces a son Creatour, si ouvri la bouche et vaut metre dedens. Et il regarde, si voit ke che restoit uns cors tous entiers. Et quant il le vaut traire arriere, si ne paut, ains sentoit c'on li metoit tout dedens la bouche, anchois qu'il le peüst clore. Et quant il l'eut usé, si li fu avis ke toutes les douchours et les suatumes ke on porroit nomer de langue li fuissent entrees el cors. Aprés rechut une partie del saint boire sacré qui estoit el calise. . . . [I]l estoit a chascun avis, quant on li metoit en la bouche la pieche en samblanche de pain, ke il veïst entrer en sa bouche un enfant tout fourmé. [*Estoire*, 86–88])

This strange and strangely beautiful passage illustrates in startlingly specific terms the transformation of the eucharist into the actual body of Christ, here in the form of the Christ child, and the wine into the "holy sacred drink" that is the blood of Christ.

The romance in which this episode is found recounts the prehistory of the grail—its origins and its arrival in England before King Arthur's knights undertake the grail quest. The main protagonist of the *Estoire* is Joseph of Arimathea, and the romance describes how Joseph collects the blood of the crucified Christ in the vessel used by Christ at the Last Supper, and later known as the grail.[9] It then recounts the imprisonment of Joseph by the Romans, his miraculous liberation, and his subsequent mission to convert the pagans in the East, and then in Britain, at which point the guardianship of the grail is passed from Joseph to his son, Josephus, who—as in the passage cited above—is not only the grail's guardian, but also serves a priestly function in the eucharistic ritual.[10]

The *Estoire* is explicitly a story about conquest and conversion, and it repeatedly describes conversion in terms of embodiment: the human body is the site on which conversion is demonstrated and proved. In particular, the text stresses the link between conversion and sexual purity, and between proper religion and proper sex: converts must give up concubines, seek marriage with Christians, and, in one extraordinary episode, a converted king must give up an image, a sort of big doll (*une poupee*) that he loves and with which he has carnal relations.[11]

In fact, in the *Estoire del saint graal* conversion itself is described as a sex act: the mission to convert the pagans is described in terms of procreation. God commands Joseph, the guardian of the grail, to spread his seed (*semenche*) throughout the world.

Joseph dreamed that Jesus Christ came to him and said, "Joseph, the time has come for you to go and preach my name, and for my sake you must leave this rich land, and you will never return. Your seed will be spread in lands so far away that you cannot imagine or believe in them, for I have elected to fill foreign lands with your seed, but not from that which you will engender, for from Josephus, your son, there will be no carnal fruit, for he has promised to remain chaste forever.

(si li vint une avisions, ke Jhesucris venoit devant lui, si li disoit: "Joseph, li termes est venus ke tu t'en iras preechier mon non, et si te convenra laissier pour moi toute la terriene rikeche, ne jamais en cheste terre ne retourneras, anchois sera ta semenche espandue en si lontaignes terres ke tu ne le porroies penser ne quidier, car j'ai esleü a emplir les estranges terres de ta semenche, ne mie de cheli ke tu engenras, car de Josephés, ton fil, n'istra jamais carneus fruis, car il m'a promise pardurable chaasté. [*Estoire*, 37–38])

In this context *semenche*, or seed, describes procreation in a metaphorical sense (the Christian lineage that Joseph will found), in contrast to a biological sense (Joseph's lineage, his descendants, his sons). At the same time, the text valorizes chastity: Joseph's lineage will not continue through his son, Josephus, because the son has vowed himself to eternal chastity, and Joseph himself preserves his privileged relationship with God by refusing sexual desire. Only when God commands him to produce another son does he have sex with his wife, and even then they manage to conceive without desire.

[Joseph and his wife] did not lie together as lustful people do, but as religious people, for they did not sleep together after the time they left their country according to the commandment of Jesus Christ. . . . [T]hey engendered Galahad, their last child, according to the commandment of our Lord, who commanded [Joseph] to prepare a new fruit with his seed, and with this fruit He would fill the new land where He wanted to lead them. And by this commandment Galahad was engendered, and when he was engendered they did not come together out of desire, for they had no lust, but in order to accomplish the commandment of their Lord, who had demanded Joseph's seed.

(Mais il ne gisoient mie ensamble a guise de gent luxurieuse, mais comme gens plains de religion, car il ne jurent onques tant ensamble entre aus deus, puis chele eure ke il issirent hors de lor païs par le commandement Jhesucrist. . . . [I]l engenrerent Galaad, lor daerrain enfant, par le commandement Nostre Signeur, qui le commanda que il li apparillast de sa semenche un noviel fruit de quoi il empliroit en avant la terre ou il les voloit mener: par chelui commandement fu engenrés Galaad, et, quant il fu engenrés, n'assemblerent il mie par couvoitise que il eurent de nule luxure, mais pour acomplir le commandement de lor Signour, qui semenche avoit demandé a Joseph. [*Estoire*, 68–69])

The *Estoire* offers the portrait of a chaste father, the patriarch who reproduces without desire. Joseph and his eldest son, Josephus, found a lineage of chaste guardians of the grail and of the Christian faith, and their spiritual purity is demonstrated as a bodily purity, a purity defined by a lack of sexual desire. In other words, religious devotion is a spiritual condition demonstrated on the body, and dedication to God is equated with embodied purity. This is not surprising, of course, since the purity of the body dedicated to God is a prominent idea in Christianity and in many other religions. It is represented in most grail narratives by the chaste knights who are destined to succeed in the quest for the holy grail because of their purity.

But the body's purity is almost always a contested virtue in grail romances. Stories that recount the quest for the grail represent the chastity of the grail knights as a sexual purity constantly under siege by demons who would corrupt the knights' chastity and render them unworthy to see the grail.[12] And the knights prove their chastity, purity, and worthiness to attain the grail by resisting the devil's seductions. In the *Estoire*, the assault on bodies takes a different form. Alongside the valorization of virginity in this romance, we find a proliferation of "wounds in the thigh."

When King Mordrain converts to Christianity he orders all those in his kingdom who will not receive baptism into exile, and as they leave the country a devil smites the unconverted people with a bloody sword—they die or are wounded in the arm or the thigh. The devil's castrating sword underscores the fecundity of Christian conversion, of the Christian *semenche* that brings life. But when Josephus learns of the devil's punishment, he stops baptizing the converted and goes to try to save those fleeing from harm. An angel then takes a lance and wounds Josephus in the thigh because he was more concerned with those who rejected baptism than with those who wished to convert.

The angel came to him and loosed the lance he carried and struck Josephus in the right thigh so hard that the iron hit the bone. As soon as the he had struck him, the angel let the lance fall without pulling it out and said to Josephus: "This is the witness of my people whom you stopped baptizing to help those who despise my law. You will carry this reproach all the days of your life, and if you expiate it elsewhere, do not be surprised." And with that, the angel departed.

(li angeles s'aproche de lui et lait aler une lanche ke il tenoit, si l'en fiert parmi la destre cuisse si durement ke li fiers hurta en l'os et, tout maintenant ke il l'en ot feru, si laissa la lanche chaoir sans metre hors et si li dist: "Che est li tesmoins de mon pule ke tu a laissié a baptisier pour rescoure les despiseurs de ma loy: chis reprueches te dura a tous les jours de ton eage, et, se tu le comperes ailleurs, si ne t'en mervelle mie." Atant s'en tourna li angeles. [*Estoire*, 159])

Josephus's wound will not stop bleeding ("ne laissa ele onques a sainier" [*Estoire*, 160]), and later the angel returns to cure it with blood from the lance. The angel strikes Josephus again with the lance, withdraws the iron from his wound, and then puts the iron of the lance into a white box he carries. The blood that drips from the iron fills the box, and when the angel washes Josephus's wound in the thigh with the blood, it is healed without a scar.[13]

This episode demonstrates God's severe mercy toward his people: "After my great vengeance, my great remedy," declares a voice from within the arc where the grail is kept ("Aprés ma grant venjanche, ma grant medechine!" [166]). And after the angel heals Josephus, he announces the meaning of the lance that wounded, then healed him.

This is the beginning of the marvelous adventures that will take place in the land where God has told you he will lead you. Great marvelous things will happen there, and great prowess will be demonstrated, and true chivalry will be discovered. Then the false will be separated from the true, for terrestrial chivalry will become celestial chivalry. None shall know of these adventures nor be certain of their end before that time that they shall happen, but at the time they should begin it will happen that this lance will offer blood, just as you have seen it offer now, and ever before has a drop of blood fallen from it before the adventures you have heard about should begin. . . . And this lance which wounded you will strike only one more man, and he will be a king, and a descendant of your lineage, and he will be the last of the good men. He will be struck between both thighs and will not be healed until the marvels of the grail are discovered by he who will be full of all the goodness you have heard me name.

(Che est li commenchemens des mervilleuses aventures qui avenront en la terre ou Diex a proposé qu'il te menra. Illuec avenront les grans mervelles, et les grans proueches i seront demostrees, et lors seront les vraies chevaleries descouvertes; lors se departiront li faus de la compaignie as vrais, car les chevaleries terrienes devenront chelestiaus. Ne nus ne sera ja asenés de ches aventures ne chertains du termine ou eles avenront devant ichelui terme ke eles deveront avenir, mais au tans ke eles deveront commenchier avenra que cheste lanche rendra sanc tout autresi come tu as veü ke ele l'a orendroit rendu, ne jamais des ore en avant nule goute de sanc n'en kerra devant ichele eure que les aventures deveront avenir ensi come tu as oï. . . . Et de cheste lanche dont tu as esté ferus ne sera jamais ferus ke uns seus hom, et chil sera rois et descendera de ton lignaige, si sera li daerrains des boins. Chil en sera ferus parmi les cuisses ambedeus ne ja n'en garira jusc'atant ke les mervelles del Graal seront descouvertes a chelui qui sera plains de toutes les bontés ke tu m'as oï nomer. [*Estoire*, 167–68])

Most grail romances include the figure of the wounded king—the guardian of the grail, often called the Fisher King, is wounded in the thigh or between the two thighs. In all of the grail romances, this king has lost the use of his members and he cannot move without help. He will be healed only when the good knight arrives and asks whom the grail serves. Although the grail king's wound is explicitly described as a genital wound only in Wolfram von Eschenbach's *Parzival*, the king's wound is always linked to sterility and to a general political and economic devastation that can only be repaired by the chaste knight's discovery of the grail secrets.

And the sterility symbolized by the wound, along with the emphasis on sexual purity in grail romances, suggests that the grail king's wound might be seen as a sexual wound. This identification of the wound is further suggested in romances like Wolfram's, where the wound is identified as a punishment for a sexual transgression. In *Parzival*, the wound is a punishment for sexual promiscuity, and the grail king, Anfortas, is struck "through the scrotum" with a wound that will not stop bleeding.[14] In *Sone de Nausay*, a thirteenth-century romance that includes the story of the grail, the wound is a punishment for a sexual and religious transgression, the king's marriage to an unconverted woman.[15] In the *Elucidation*, a prologue to Chrétien's *Conte du graal*, the general devastation linked to the wound is explained as the result of a sexual transgression, a rape.[16]

In this study, I have focused on the definition of sexual difference through biology and blood, and through the identification of blood as specifically male and female blood. And in the construction of the heroic values of war and the prerogatives of warriors, as in the representation of parental bonds and the privileges they define, it seems that literary texts, like other kinds of cultural discourses (medicine, law, theology), insist on the difference between men's blood and women's blood, a difference that is mapped onto biology in the opposition of the public, voluntary bloodshed of men and the private, involuntary bloodshed of women. But the representation of the bleeding wound between the thighs in grail romances might be seen to disrupt the categories that we have thus far seen to gender bloodshed. The grail guardian's wound will not stop bleeding, and it bleeds from between the thighs.[17] Whether or not the wound is a genital wound, the blood that continues to flow is similar to genital bleeding. But although genital bleeding is often considered a polluting blood (we've seen examples in other chapters), the grail guardian's bleeding wound does not identify his body as unworthy of access to holy relics. In fact, it does quite the opposite: the wound marks the body of the divinely ordained guardian of a holy relic. The wound that will not stop bleeding is represented as a purifying wound in the representation of Josephus in the *Estoire del saint graal*. That is, the wound in the thigh is called a punishment, but it is also an act of grace—it marks the body of God's chosen servant. In the *Estoire*, the blood of the wound is like sacrificial blood in that it purifies the sinful body that waits for the final healing and redemption that the good knight will bring. And this purifying blood is available only to men.

Women's Blood

Women's blood is represented in the *Estoire* in the story of a woman cured of a blood flux. During his mission to convert pagans, Josephus encounters a woman who is already a Christian—she converted with her mother who sought to be cured of what the text calls a woman's disease ("une enfermeté ke nus ne seufre se feme non" [136]).[18] When the suffering woman converted, God cured her, and she regained "the strength of her body and all its members" ("la forche du cors et de tous les membres" [138]). This episode recalls the biblical account of Jesus' healing of a woman with a blood flux, and although it offers the only example of women's blood in the story (in contrast to the many episodes in which men are wounded in the thigh or between the thighs), as a biblical citation, it has a particular authority in the text.

In this episode the woman's bleeding does not have the sacrificial status of men's bleeding, it does not bring her purity in suffering—her suffering is abject and miserable, and her excessive blood loss is a sign of her impurity and her nonchristian identity. Moreover, the woman's blood hemorrhage is not a wound, it is an illness—or even a natural condition to the extent that what the text calls a "woman's disease" recalls menstruation. In the *Estoire*, women's bleeding would seem to be represented as the abject opposite of men's bleeding: women's bleeding is an illness to be cured by conversion, whereas men's bleeding represents a sacrificial wound that is inscribed within a heroic economy of conversion and procreation. At the same time, though, the man's bleeding wound and the woman's bleeding body share one similarity: Josephus's wound that will not stop bleeding is cured, just like the woman's blood flux, by a divine intervention.

The woman with the blood flux in the *Estoire* is healed when she converts. In fact, she converts in order to be healed, as she tells the hermit whom she asks how she can be relieved of her condition: "There is nothing in this world that I would not do, if you tell me to do it, in order to be cured of this great suffering" ("il n'est nule riens en chest monde, se vous le me commandés, ke je ne fache, par covent ke je garisse de cheste grant dolour" [*L'estoire*, 137]). As a metaphor for her pagan status, the blood flux is an illness that marks this woman's damnation. The representation of women's blood as pagan's blood may be influenced by the ideas of blood pollution implicit in the ritual isolation of women after childbirth,

and by the vestiges of the belief that menstruating women should not participate in the eucharistic ritual, but the pollution of women's blood
seems less important here than the proliferation of blood—the woman's
illness consists in the inability to stop bleeding.

The biblical example of the woman with the blood flux is one cultural model for conversion and for the figural association of a purifying
blood, the blood of Christ, that redeems those who live with impure
blood, the blood of the unconverted. But the association of excess blood
and nonchristian identity is also found in another medieval representation: Jews, too, are thought to bleed in excessive amounts from the anus.
Women, then, are not the only group whose exclusion from Christian
salvation is figured through blood.

Jewish Blood

Bleeding Jewish bodies are not represented in the *Estoire del saint graal*.
Jews appear only in the story of the crucifixion recounted at the beginning
of the romance. Nor are Jews the target of Joseph's holy mission: he
converts pagans ("Saracens"), not Jews. The *Estoire* distinguishes between
pagans and Jews when the narrator identifies Jews as the murderers of
Christ, and pagans (like the converted emperor Vaspasien who burns the
Jews responsible for the crucifixion), as those who avenge Christ's murder:

This example shows the disloyalty of the Jews, for those that he had called "dogs"
were the pagans, who did him more honor than those he called "his sons," that is
to say, the Jews, for the Jews had crucified him and the pagans avenged it.

(Et che fu pour example moustrer de la desloiauté des Juis, car chil qui il avoit
apielé "kiens", che furent li paien, ki li fisent plus d'oneur ke chil qui il apieloit "ses
fiex", che furent li Juif, car li Juif l'avoient cruchefiiet et li paien le vengoient.
[*Estoire*, 37])

The view of the Jews as the enemies of Christ is a commonplace of
medieval theology,[19] and medieval antisemitism finds one of its most
potent forms in blood symbolism, and particularly in the claim that Jewish men suffer from a blood flux: the notion that Jewish males experience
a flow of blood annually on Good Friday was a widespread conviction
among thirteenth-century Christian writers.[20]

The earliest descriptions of Jewish male blood flux seem to derive from a motif found in Christian texts as early as late antiquity, the belief that the bad man is punished by God with a bleeding anus. As Willis Johnson explains:

The nature of this man's crime is variously understood in different periods. First, it is a crime of betrayal of God, heresy; and it is imputed to the paradigmatic enemies of God in each successive age: Judas, Arians/heretics, and Jews. This idea may well have originated when the heresiarch Arius died by prolapse—the herniated extrusion of the intestines—in a public toilet in Alexandria. This death was interpreted by his contemporaries as a divine condemnation of Arius's teachings regarding the physical body of Christ, and exegetically equated with the mysterious bursting of Judas's belly (Acts 1: 18) when he hanged himself. As symbolic betrayers of Christ, Jews were exegetically linked with Judas and Arius in many texts through the early middle ages.[21]

The theological explanation of Jewish male bleeding is complemented by a medical explanation. Jewish men, the explanation goes, have a melancholic complexion, and because of an excess of cold, wet humors, they have hemorrhoids.[22] Bleeding from hemorrhoids, like menstrual bleeding, was considered to be a natural process through which the body rid itself of excess blood. In fact, menstrual and hemorrhoidal bleeding were seen as interchangeable by the thirteenth-century physician Arnold of Villanova:

There are five haemorrhoidal veins at the opening of the rectum. Some men have these small veins hanging out—some only three, some only one. Others have them inside the rectum. Many men are purged [of bad humours] via these small veins (just as women are by their menses) and preserved from diverse illnesses when they flow in the appropriate amount. But when they flow immoderately, this can give men tubercular fever or dropsy, and cause them to fall ill with many other illnesses. Hence these men who have such immoderate haemorrhage—should they know how to preserve themselves by provoking the haemorrhoids to haemorrhage, or by stanching them, as is appropriate—would live in wondrous health and be healed of their illnesses. . . . Every flow of blood, as Galen said, is unhealthy, except for a moderate flow of blood from haemorrhoids, nosebleeds, and menses. Such moderate bleeding should not be restrained.[23]

Women may also suffer from hemorrhoids, and physician Bernard de Gordon claimed that menstrual blood is sometimes purged through hemorrhoidal bleeding when menses are retained, although Johnson points out that Aristotle thought women had neither hemorrhoids nor nosebleeds, precisely because they menstruate.[24]

In thirteenth-century texts, then, the bleeding body of the Jew can be described in medical terms as a body that purges excess blood through hemorrhoidal bleeding, or in terms of Christian polemics as a body punished by God with an annual blood flux. At least one thirteenth-century source describes this blood flux as a monthly, not an annual flow. Jacques de Vitry claimed that the Jews "have become unwarlike and weak even as women, and it is said that they have a flux of blood every month."[25] By the early fourteenth century the medical, theological, and popular traditions had merged into the claim that Jewish men menstruated: Jewish men, like women, were subject to the curse of Eve.

Jewish male bleeding, like the bleeding of the woman with the blood flux in the *Estoire del saint graal*, represents an excessive bleeding, a bleeding that cannot be controlled. In this it is different from the examples of male "menstruation" that I discussed in Chapter 1. The ritual wounding of the male genitals as a controlled affirmation of masculinity is different from the periodic blood flux that cannot be controlled and is seen to debilitate the body. The blood flux of Jewish men is represented in the thirteenth-century accounts as an illness rather than a natural condition, and this bleeding is closely associated with blood libel and ritual murder: only Christian blood could remedy the blood loss of the Jews cursed by God.[26] And the bleeding can only be stopped by Christian salvation.

I do not claim that the author of the *Estoire* indirectly represented Jewish bleeding in the figure of the converted woman cured of a blood flux, though it is possible, if not likely, that the belief that Jewish men bled regularly and excessively could have been a cultural model, along with the biblical story of the woman healed by Christ, for the representation of conversion as the staunching of blood. That is, although the bleeding woman is cured of an illness—in this her story is like many miracle stories—the excessive bleeding that results from her illness could in itself be a mark of the unconverted, those who are marked by impure blood in medieval Christian thought: Jews and women.

In the *Estoire*, converted people are those whose blood is spilled by God through a sacred wounding, or used in the service of God, as in Joseph's spreading of his *semenche* in the creation of a new chosen people whose privileged relationship with God is demonstrated in their possession of the grail and by Josephus's access to the intimate secrets of his Lord ("les privetés de son Signour" [164]). And in the identification of the grail as a eucharistic vessel, the *Estoire* emphasizes the priestly function of the grail's guardian. Whereas in the twelfth-century *Conte du graal*, the grail is a mystical object carried by a young woman and associated vaguely with the Christian faith, in the thirteenth-century *Estoire del saint graal*, the grail is clearly incorporated into Christian devotional practice. It is a eucharistic vessel containing a host which is transformed into the Christ child and which is distributed by the man marked as guardian of the grail by the wound in his thigh. This evolution is part of the progressive Christianization of the grail story, but it is also part of a progressive gendering of sacred space and of sacred bodies as male. Dyan Elliott has shown how ecclesiastical reforms in the Middle Ages, and particularly the demand for a celibate clergy, demonized women as dangerous to the ritual purity of the priesthood.[27] Grail stories certainly perpetuate that association—Susan Aronstein has shown how women are marginalized from eucharistic devotion in the grail quest, and in the thirteenth-century *Queste del saint graal* demons transform into women in attempts to seduce the chaste knights Perceval and Bors so that their sexual purity will be corrupted and they will no longer be able to attain the grail.[28]

Female religious figures are not absent from grail stories—there are nuns, recluses, and holy women scattered about the forest in which the grail quest takes place. And in the *Estoire*, converted Saracen women are incorporated into the grail guardians' lineage.[29] But when the grail is imagined as an explicitly eucharistic vessel, only men handle it. And grail romances promote the purity of the men who care for holy objects through contrast with what they represent as women's inability to attain that purity: this gendered hierarchy of values is seen most clearly in the complete exclusion of women from the grail quest. It is worth stressing that a particular literary tradition is at stake here—I am leaving aside the many and varied expressions of women's spirituality found in other kinds of texts and traditions during this period in order to focus on the way that grail romances offer a progressive gendering of sacred space and of access to sacred objects: as the grail becomes more explicitly associated with eucharistic ritual, its access is increasingly restricted to men.

Access to holy objects is not restricted only according to gender—the *Estoire* recounts several episodes in which men are punished for approaching too closely to the grail. This story identifies a priesthood whose access to God's body is authorized by God himself, and whose privileged position in marked by sexual purity and, sometimes, by a wound between the thighs. But women never approach the grail in this story, and unlike other grail romances, the *Estoire* never represents a woman or a maiden carrying the grail. In the *Estoire* access to the grail has become uniquely the privilege of men, and this gendering of access to the sacred vessel clearly corresponds to the explicitly eucharistic function of the grail and to the ritual role of the priest in celebrating the eucharist. That is, the romance imagines the eucharistic ritual as "a male cleric handling the body of a male God," in Elliott's words.[30] And it imagines the gendering of sacred space and of access to sacred objects through the unlikely analogy of the blood of Christ and the blood of castration. The bleeding wound in the thigh marks God's chosen servants, it is a wound to be suffered, not an illness to be healed, like the woman's disease or the Jew's disease represented by the blood flux. The blood of castration, like the blood of crucifixion, is a salvific blood, it punishes and saves the converted. It is also, of course, men's blood. It marks ritual devotional practice as the practice of men, and devotional objects as the province of men. But that gendering may not be as secure as it initially appears in the *Estoire*.

Bleeding Wounds

One difference between Josephus's wounded body and the bleeding bodies of women and Jews is located precisely in the fact that Josephus bleeds from a wound, whereas the pagan woman and Jews bleed because of an illness which is seen as a curse from God.[31] The wound inflicted by an angel is a wound that marks God's chosen servant, as I have argued above, and the wound received in battle—here a spiritual battle—is part of the heroic exchange of bloodshed in war, as I have argued in earlier chapters.

But a wound may have other meanings, as I find suggested in a modern rewriting of Wolfram von Eschenbach's *Parzival*. When Richard Wagner rewrites Wolfram's story, he transforms Wolfram's explanation of the wound as the inability not to desire and makes it into the sign of "the fevered blood of sin . . . ever renewed from the fount of longing that no repentance can ever still."[32] Wagner represents Amfortas's wound in the flesh as a metaphor whose force Parsifal can also share. When Kundry kisses Parsifal, the hero describes his initiation into desire (and his awakening to the possibility of sin) as an experience of Amfortas's wound: "Amfortas! The wound! the wound! It burns within my heart. . . . I saw the wound bleeding; now it bleeds in me!"[33] In other words, the most important moment in Wagner's story—the moment in which Parsifal resists sexual temptation and proves his worthiness to take Amfortas's place—is one described in terms of blood: the blood of the wounding sin, which is Amfortas's blood, and the blood of redemption, which is Christ's blood. And in Parsifal's awakening to desire and to sin, they are imagined as the same blood.

The conflation of the blood of Christ and the blood of the wounded grail king, and the similarity between the wounds of Christ and the wound of the grail king is suggested in grail romances by the juxtaposition of the wounded guardian of the grail and the wounded body of Christ in the eucharistic ritual. This equation is rendered visually in Hans-Jürgen Syberberg's 1982 film version of Wagner's *Parsifal*.[34] Syberberg represents the wound as external to the body: it is displayed on a platter and carried in the grail procession. And the bleeding wound looks like a vagina.[35] Slavoj Žižek describes Syberberg's depiction of the wound "in the form of a vaginalike partial object out of which blood is dripping in a continuous flow (as, *vulgari eloquentia*, a vagina in an unending period)."[36] Syberberg's representation of the wound also looks like medieval illustrations of the wound of Christ.

The feminization of the body of Christ in medieval expressions of piety has been richly documented by Caroline Walker Bynum. She shows how twelfth-century Cistercian monks conceived of God as a female parent, and how the nurturing terms in which female mystics described Christ's body position Christ as a maternal figure and as a body that nurtures and feeds.[37] Karma Lochrie has extended the consideration of the feminizing of Christ's body to include what she calls "the sacred wound's polysemy." Lochrie discusses the way that erotic language characterizes descriptions of mystics' devotion to Christ's wound, and she cites the *Stimulus Amoris* of James of Milan, a text in which critic Wolfgang Riehle identifies a "typical and quite consciously intended analogy between this wound of Christ and the female pudenda."[38] As Lochrie points out, this analogy is rendered visually in late medieval devotional imagery: Christ's wound is represented as detached from his side and dramatically enlarged in illustrations that vividly recall a vagina or vulva. Lochrie's characterization of this imagery might also apply to the grail king's wound, particularly when seen through Syberberg's eyes: "The polymorphousness of Christ's body, with its feminine genital wound and its simultaneous masculine properties, introduces confusion at a very foundational level of religious language and, therefore, of religious devotion."[39]

I have strayed rather far from the thirteenth-century Old French *Estoire del saint graal*. Syberberg's imagination of the wound as a relic is a twentieth-century interpretation of a nineteenth-century opera based on a thirteenth-century German grail romance. Even the images of Christ's wound that suggest its resemblance to the female vulva are late medieval images and would not have been known to the author of the *Estoire*. Yet the nexus of images offered in the rhetorical and the visual, the modern and the medieval, the devotional and the fictional representations of wounds, offers a perspective that may be useful for thinking about how the values of blood contribute to the gendering of religious space and privilege in the *Estoire del saint graal*.

The *Estoire* establishes a masculine lineage that is also a masculine priesthood marked by a bleeding wound, and the story suggests the sanctifying function of this wound in the implicit juxtaposition of the wounded body of Christ and the wounded body of the grail's guardian. But the bleeding wound between the thighs may also be seen to trouble gender identity at the same time that it defines gender in terms of conversion and ethnicity: God's servant bleeds from a wound, the unconverted (women and, perhaps implicitly, Jews) bleed because of an illness. And although the *Estoire* describes the woman's blood flux as different from the bleeding wound of Josephus and the future grail kings, it also invites a comparison of the two kinds of blood and suggests that the difference between sanctified men's blood and unconverted women's blood might not be as well-defined as it would seem.

If indeed the *Estoire* invites the questioning of the difference between men's blood and women's blood, what might that questioning suggest? One thing it points to is that the difference between men's blood and women's blood is a constructed difference, even when it appeals to the authority of biological explanation. And to the extent that masculine identity and priestly identity are marked by blood, by the wound between the thighs that defines masculine and priestly privilege, it suggests the fragility of the gendering of the priesthood. This romance gives priestly functions to the grail's guardian, and although it represents eucharistic miracles in startling detail, it remains a fiction about the grail, not a treatise about priests or about the clergy. So the *Estoire* does not necessarily constitute a challenge to a masculine clergy, but it does reveal the potential fragility of the symbolic system on which the gendering of sacred space is grounded in the story.

As a story about origins, about the conversion of the west and the Christianization of Europe, the *Estoire* recounts the origins of rituals and their evolving forms, and it genders those rituals through a focus on the gendered values of blood. And in the story of origins in the *Estoire*, the values of blood come from the gendered bodies that shed it as well as from the divine cause of bloodshed. At the same time, though, the strange and repeated representation of the grail king's genital bleeding suggests not only the inherent uncertainty in essentializing representations of gendered blood, but also the occasional inadequacy of gendered categories to describe bodies and their blood.

Conclusion:
Bleeding for Love

IN THE PRECEDING CHAPTERS, I have identified a number of medieval narratives in which blood plays an important role in defining the gendered values that structure the stories they recount. And I have argued that in these representations blood itself comes to be gendered, and to naturalize gendered cultural values. I have examined a range of texts, but this survey has been rather selective; every reader will surely know of at least one prominent representation of blood that I have neglected to discuss. My goal has not been to offer a comprehensive account of the ways in which medieval literary texts describe blood, but rather, to examine in some detail a selection of texts in which blood can be seen to participate in the definition of cultural values that in turn define status and authority in medieval culture. I have tried to suggest the ways in which the "natural" is used to ground the "cultural," and to explore the ways in which the negative values associated with women's bleeding come to define the positive values associated with men's bleeding. And I have suggested that despite historical variations in definitions of the functions and nature of blood, the values associated with women's blood and men's blood are surprisingly consistent across centuries and across regions. Although menstruation is no longer called "the curse of Eve," as in Abelard's formulation, it is still widely called "the curse," and I have noted some of the enduring qualities associated with gendered blood, even while focusing on medieval understandings of the values of blood.[1]

Medieval people inherited ideas about blood from popular beliefs about bodies and blood, from religious discourses about blood, and from medical definitions of the functions and nature of blood. And as I have argued throughout this study, literary texts also contribute to the definition of what blood means in medieval culture. I've suggested that stories about chivalric heroism and war describe the bloodshed of men as a public act that establishes and maintains social order, an order defined in part by the exchange and sexual possession of women. By contrast, women's blood-shed is associated with hidden blood, the blood of menstruation and childbirth, which is defined in terms of pollution and containment. Values are assigned to the visible physiological differences between women's bodies and men's bodies (women menstruate and give birth to children, men do not), and those perceived differences between women's bodies and men's bodies also define less visible differences. This is seen perhaps most clearly in the medieval practice of bloodletting, or phlebotomy.

Phlebotomy is an ancient procedure, and it was based on the notion that bloodletting allowed corrupt matter to drain from the body.[2] In the Middle Ages, phlebotomy was thought to ensure the balance of the body's four humors, as defined by Galen and others.[3] That is, health depends on the proper harmonization of the body's humors: yellow bile, which is hot and dry; blood, which is hot and damp; phlegm, which is cold and damp; and black bile, which is cold and dry.[4] In Galen's theory of the necessary balance of the body's humors, balance may be upset by excess, and a super-fluity of blood, called a *plethos* or *plethora*, is one of the principal indications for bloodletting.[5]

According to Galen, women are much less likely to suffer from *plethos* than men, since women regularly expel excess blood:

Does not [Nature] evacuate all women every month, by pouring forth the superfluity of the blood? It is necessary, in my opinion, that the female sex, who stay indoors, neither engaging in strenuous labour nor exposing themselves to direct sunlight—both factors conducive to the development of plethos—should have a natural remedy by which it is evacuated. This is one of the ways in which nature operates in these conditions; another is the cleansing that follows child-birth, although indeed the conceptus itself is also an evacuation, since it is nour-ished from the blood of the uterus; and the development of milk in the breasts after delivery is itself also an important factor in eliminating the plethos.[6]

Because of their natural evacuations, women do not normally need to be bled, and descriptions of the therapeutic value of phlebotomy focus largely on men's bodies.

Phlebotomy was used both as a cure and as a preventive measure. Nancy Sirasi cites a letter written in the twelfth century by Abbot Peter the Venerable to his doctor, in which Peter complained that he had become ill because he had to forgo his regular bimonthly bloodletting.[7] The abbot's practice of regular phlebotomy is echoed in a literary text from a few decades later in the century. In Marie de France's *Equitan*, King Equitan uses the pretext of preventive bloodletting to find time alone with his lover, the wife of his seneschal.

When King Equitan falls in love with his seneschal's wife, he recognizes that he would betray his seneschal if he seduced his wife, but he justifies the betrayal of his vassal in terms of the lady's well-being and his own—it is better for his seneschal to suffer from betrayal than for the king to suffer from love:

> "Alas," he said, "what destiny brought me to this region? Because of this lady I have seen, my heart has been overwhelmed by a pain so great that my whole body trembles. I think I have no option but to love her. Yet, if I did love her, I should be acting wrongly, as she is the seneschal's wife. I ought to keep faith with him and love him, just as I want him to do with me. If he managed somehow to find out about the love, I know full well it would grieve him. But nevertheless, it would be far worse if I were to be laid low because of her. How sad if such a beautiful woman were not in love or had no lover! How could she be a true courtly lady, if she had no true love? There is no man on earth who would not benefit greatly, if she loved him.[8]

> ("Allas! fet il, queils destinee
> M'amenat en ceste cuntree?
> Pur ceste dame qu'ai veüe
> M'est une anguisse al quor ferue,
> Ki tut le cors me fet trembler:
> Jeo quit que mei l'estuet amer.
> E si jo l'aim, jeo ferai mal:
> Ceo est la femme al seneschal;
> Garder li dei amur e fei
> Si cum jeo voil k'il face a mei.
> Si par nul engin le saveit,
> Bien sai que mut l'en pesereit.
> Mes nepurquant pis iert asez
> Que pur li seië afolez.
> Si bele dame tant mar fust,
> S'ele n'amast de druërie?
> Suz ciel n'ad humme, s'el l'amast,
> Ki durement n'en amendast. [ll. 65–84])[9]

Equitan's therapeutic logic also governs the seduction scene: the king goes out to hunt but comes back early, claiming that he is ill, and he goes to his room to lie down ("Then he rose and set off on his hunt. But he soon turned back, saying how ill he was, and returned to his chamber to lie down" [p. 57]; "Il est levez, si vet chacier, / Mes tost se mist el repeirier / E dit que mut est deshaitiez; / Es chambres vet, si s'est cuchiez" [ll. 103–6]). The seneschal believes that his lord has fallen ill, and the king sends for the seneschal's wife and he tells her that he is dying of his love for her.[10] Equitan pleads so eloquently for her love that the lady gives it to him.

Their love lasts a long time, and is made possible by another therapeutic ruse by the king: he claims that he must be alone while he is bled, and he uses this privacy to meet his lover.

When they had arranged to meet and speak with each other, the king told his followers he was to be bled in private. The doors of the bedchamber were closed. Never would anyone have dared to enter without the king's summons. (59)

(As termes de lur assembler,
Quant ensemble durent parler,
Li reis feseit dire a sa gent
Que seignez iert priveement.
Li us des chambres furent clos;
Ne troveissez humme si os,
Si li reis pur lui n'enveiast,
Ja une feiz dedenz entrast. [ll. 187–94])

The lai describes a private space of love-making as a private space of bleeding, and this is curious. The king's desire to bleed in private would seem to disrupt some of the most prominently gendered categories defined by blood in medieval texts—men bleed in public places, women bleed in private. Even the blood Lancelot shed in Guenevere's bed during an intimate encounter with the queen becomes public when it is taken as evidence of Guenevere's adultery with Sir Kay and leads to a battle in which Lancelot defeats the queen's accuser. A medical procedure is different from a battle, of course, especially if it masks an intimate encounter, and it may be that phlebotomy was seen as a procedure that should be hidden from the court. But a medical procedure would seem to involve a medical practitioner, and if the king's ruse is meant to allow him to be alone with the lady, it is not likely that he would be accompanied by a doctor or a surgeon. Perhaps the lady herself is meant to bleed the king?

The king's use of bloodletting as a pretext for private encounters with his lover is even more curious when read in the context of a phlebotomy procedure that actually does take place in the story: the lady grows impatient with her status as the king's secret lover and demands that he marry her. The king and his lover then plot to kill the seneschal: the lady suggests that the king arrange to be bled together with her husband, after which the two men will bathe together, and the lady will prepare arrange for her husband to die:

"Lord," she said, "please come hunting in the forest in the region where I live. Stay in my husband's castle, be bled there and take a bath on the third day. My husband will be bled and take a bath with you. Make sure you tell him to keep you company. I shall have the baths heated and the two tubs brought in. The water in his bath will be so boiling hot that no mortal man could escape scalding or destruction, before he has settled down in it. When he has been scalded to death, summon your vassals and his. Show them how he died suddenly in the bath." (59)

("Sire, fet ele, si vus plest,
Venez chacier en la forest
En la cuntree u jeo sujur.
Dedenz le chastel mon seignur
Sujurnez; si serez seignez
E al tierz jur si vus baignez.
Mis sire od vus se seignera
E avoec vus se baignera.
Dites li bien, nel lessiez mie,
Que il vus tienge cumpainie!
E jeo ferai les bains temprer
E les deus cuves aporter;
Sun bain ferai chaut e buillant:
Suz ciel nen ad humme vivant
Ne fust escaudez e malmis
Einz que dedenz se feust asis.
Quant morz serat e escaudez
Vos hummes e les soens mandez,
Si lur mustrez cumfaitement
Est morz al bain sudeinement." [ll. 241–60])

The plan to murder the lady's husband proceeds: the king is bled along with his seneschal, then three days later announces that they will bathe together. The lady has the tubs brought into the king's chamber, but instead of leaving him alone to wait for his vassal's arrival, she joins the king in his bed, where they are discovered by the seneschal. To hide his shame, Equitan leaps into the scalding bath and is killed; the seneschal forces his wife head first into the same bath, and she too is killed.[11]

Marie ends the story with a moralizing conclusion: "Evil can easily rebound on him who seeks another's misfortune" (60). "Evil" and "misfortune" both translate the Old French *li mals* (which may also be spelled *li maus*, or, when an object of the verb, *le mal*): "Tels purcace *le mal* d'autrui / Dunt tuz *li mals* revert sur lui" (ll. 309–10).[12] "Li mals" is also used to describe the lovesickness that afflicts the king when he first meets his seneschal's wife, and which the seneschal cannot understand: "The seneschal is grieved by this, not realizing the cause of the illness [*li maus*] or why the king was feverish" (57); "Dolenz en est li senescaus; / Il ne seit pas queils est *li maus* / De quei li reis sent les friçuns" (ll. 107–9). It is also the word used to describe the therapeutic effect of bleeding: "He had himself bled together with his seneschal, as a precaution against illness (*mal*)" (60); "Seiner se fet cuntre sun *mal*, / Ensemble od lui sun senescal" (ll. 265–66). In *Equitan*, "li mals" has both a moral and a medical meaning; it describes evil and misfortune, and it describes sickness.

Marie's attention to homophony and word play has been amply described by critics like R. Howard Bloch.[13] Here, Marie's repeated use of the word "mals" (evil/illness) may suggest the way that moral transgression and therapeutic action are brought together in the act of bleeding—and in the act of loving.[14] But is bleeding gendered in Marie's lai?

The privacy associated with bleeding in *Equitan* stands in opposition to the public display of men's blood recounted in other narratives, as I suggested above. It may also suggest a privacy usually associated with women's blood. In this reversal the representation of blood and privacy in Marie's lai could echo the gender reversal that some critics have noted in the story: the lady, who is ruled by the ideals of courtly love, dominates the king, who should be ruled by the bonds of fealty to his seneschal, as the king himself recognizes when he first falls in love with the seneschal's wife, though he easily forgets feudal loyalty in the pursuit of his vassal's wife.[15] However, the privacy demanded by the bloodletting procedure is emphasized only when the king uses it as an excuse to meet his lover; when the king and the seneschal are bled together, the text does not mention any requirement of privacy. Indeed, even though the shared therapeutic procedure is staged as part of a plot to gain the seneschal's trust before killing him, it still emphasizes the intimacy between the two men that is defined by the bond (and perhaps by the lady's body) they share.

The representation of bleeding in *Equitan* reflects the conflict that structures the story from the beginning: the demands of feudal loyalty oppose the desires of courtly love. The association of bleeding with both sides of the opposition also points to the way that the opposition between love and fealty is conceived of in gendered terms. Of course, it is no surprise that the bonds of love are shared by the king and his lady, and the bonds of fealty are shared by the king and his vassal, but the way that both relationships are described in relation to bleeding underscores the conflict between the king's two relationships and gives value to the relationship between the king and his seneschal. The public (or at least, not explicitly private) bloodshed shared by the two men contrasts with the private bleeding that hides the love affair, and underscores the virtues of men's shared, public bloodshed in opposition to the secrecy of the king's liaison with his lover, a secrecy that is enabled by a fiction about private bleeding that may recall the deleterious effects associated with women's blood and women's wastes. This is not to say that the king's relationship with the seneschal is valorized because it is public and his relationship with his lover is condemned in the narrative because of its secrecy, but rather, that the values of the public and the private are defined by the values associated with blood, with men's public bloodshed and women's private bleeding.

In *Equitan,* only men bleed, and even though the bond that the king and his seneschal share and demonstrate by being bled together has already been broken, the ritualized bleeding and bathing is intended to demonstrate their mutual love and loyalty. The gendering of bleeding in the lai not only reflects the condemnation and punishment of betrayal that the story recounts, it valorizes the story's outcome by suggesting that the rituals shared by men are ultimately more important, and certainly more symbolically effective, than the private pleasures that a man shares with a woman. At the same time, though, through the descriptions of the king's bloodletting rituals, the lai emphasizes not the wife's betrayal of her husband, but the king's betrayal of his vassal. Although it is the lady who suggests the plot to kill her husband and although she too dies at the end of the story, the focus on bloodletting and on the valorization of feudal bonds that it enacts and betrays points to the king's treachery as the evil (*li mals*) of the story.

If blood is gendered in medieval literature, that gendering is accomplished through the representation of culturally defined truths about bodies and their functions. But the gendering of blood in literature does not simply reflect medical, religious, or popular views of sexual difference. Rather, in their appropriation and modification of cultural views about men's blood and women's blood, literary texts expose the gender systems that these views construct. The gender of blood, as I have tried to show throughout this study, is not an essential quality; it is part of a broader system of cultural values in which men's blood is celebrated in public displays but women's blood as characterized as dangerous, as polluting, and as a bleeding that should not be seen. Literature intervenes in this system to recognize the gendered hierarchies that it promotes and, sometimes, to question their legitimacy and the values they promote.

Notes

Preface

1. *The Trotula: An English Translation of the Medieval Compendium of Women's Medicine*, ed. and trans. Monica H. Green (Philadelphia: University of Pennsylvania Press, 2001), 19–22; Joan Cadden, *Meanings of Sex Difference in the Middle Ages: Medicine, Science, and Culture* (Cambridge: Cambridge University Press, 1993), 173–74, 177; Danielle Jacquart and Claude Thomasset, *Sexuality and Medicine in the Middle Ages*, trans. Matthew Adamson (Princeton, N.J.: Princeton University Press, 1988), 77.

2. As Buckley and Gottlieb note, "the 'menstrual taboo' is at once nearly universal and has meanings that are ambiguous and often multivalent." Thomas Buckley and Alma Gottlieb, "A Critical Appraisal of Theories of Menstrual Symbolism," in *Blood Magic: The Anthropology of Menstruation*, ed. Buckley and Gottlieb (Berkeley: University of California Press, 1988), 7. "Curse of Eve" is from Abelard's letter to Heloise in "The Personal Letters Between Abelard and Heloise," ed. J. T. Muckle, *Mediaeval Studies* 15 (1953): 90–91; translation in Betty Radice, *The Letters of Abelard and Heloise* (New York: Penguin, 1974), 150.

3. Charles T. Wood has suggested that "In the Middle Ages as at other times, the nature of menstruation provided a curious meeting ground for religious thought, scientific theory, practical physiology, and popular prejudice; and in that conjunction one can gain remarkable insight . . . into the medieval value system." "The Doctors' Dilemma: Sin, Salvation, and the Menstrual Cycle in Medieval Thought," *Speculum* 56 (1981): 711.

4. Howard Eilberg-Schwartz, *The Savage in Judaism: An Anthropology of Israelite Religion and Ancient Judaism* (Bloomington: Indiana University Press, 1990), 91. Eilberg-Schwartz responds to critiques of comparative inquiry, 93–102.

5. "La fin d'un tabou? L'interdiction de communier pour la femme menstruée au moyen âge. Le cas du XIIe siècle," in *Le sang au moyen âge*, ed. Marcel Faure, Cahiers du CRISMA 4 (Montpellier: CRISMA, 1999), 180–81.

Chapter 1. Only Women Bleed

1. Alice Cooper, *Welcome to My Nightmare* (Atlantic Recording Corporation, 1975).

2. Anne Berthelot argues convincingly that this identification, which attaches Perceval's sister to the larger context of the grail miracles in *La queste*,

actually modifies an older and widespread belief that leprosy can be cured with a virgin's blood. "Sang et lèpre, sang et feu," in *Le sang au moyen âge*, ed. Marcel Faure, Cahiers du CRISMA 4 (Montpellier: CRISMA, 1999), 31. Andrew Lynch shows how Malory's version of this episode stresses royal lineage as an essential quality of Perceval's sister's blood, and Martin B. Shichtman points to the way that she is positioned as a potential bride: the spilled blood symbolizes a sexual consummation, and the virgin dies during a symbolic marriage and deflowering. Lynch, *Malory's Book of Arms: The Narrative of Combat in Le Morte Darthur*, Arthurian Studies 30 (Cambridge: D.S. Brewer, 1997), 71; Shichtman, "Perceval's Sister: Genealogy, Virginity, and Blood," *Arthuriana* 9, 2 (1999): 11–20. Hartmann von Aue's *Der arme Heinrich* is probably the best-known literary treatment of the blood cure for leprosy.

3. However, the blood of martyrs is not quite as abundant in their stories as is conventionally thought, at least in the thirteenth- and fourteenth-century prose vernacular *vitae* studied by Jean-Pierre Perrot in "Du sang au lait: l'imaginaire du sang et ses logiques dans les passions de martyrs," in *Le sang au moyen âge*, 459–70.

4. Caroline Walker Bynum, *Holy Feast and Holy Fast: The Religious Significance of Food to Medieval Women* (Berkeley: University of California Press, 1987), 394, n. 105. William of Saliceto insisted on the importance of distinguishing between the blood shed by a virgin at her first intercourse and the blood of menstruation (lest men be fooled). The blood of virginity is less abundant and lighter in color, and exits the body with greater force than menstrual blood. Helen Rodnite Lemay, "William of Saliceto on Human Sexuality," *Viator* 12 (1981): 175.

5. It is not irrelevant here to mention another belief of Hildegard's: that menstrual blood is a cure for leprosy. I will come back to the question of the healing qualities of blood below.

6. On twelfth- and thirteenth-century debates about the Virgin Mary and menstruation, see Charles T. Wood, "The Doctors' Dilemma: Sin, Salvation, and the Menstrual Cycle in Medieval Thought," *Speculum* 56 (1981): 710–27; and for pre-twelfth-century debates, Paulette L'Hermite-Leclercq, "Le sang et le lait de la vierge," in *Le sang au moyen âge*, 145–62.

7. In the following paragraphs I offer a very general overview in order to describe the broad contours of medieval ideas about menstruation. For a warning about reduction in accounts of medieval menstrual taboos and for a detailed analysis of twelfth-century attitudes toward menstruation, see Charles de Miramon, "La fin d'un tabou? L'interdiction de communier pour la femme menstruée au moyen âge. Le cas du XIIe siècle," in *Le sang au moyen âge*, 163–81.

8. Cited by Wood, "The Doctors' Dilemma," 714. See also Dyan Elliott, *Fallen Bodies: Pollution, Sexuality, and Demonology in the Middle Ages* (Philadelphia: University of Pennsylvania Press, 1999), 6–7, 28–19, 108, 109; Peter Brown, *The Body and Society: Men, Women, and Sexual Renunciation in Early Christianity* (New York: Columbia University Press, 1988), 145–46, 433–34; Miramon, "La fin d'un tabou?" 166–74; and Shaye J. D. Cohen, "Menstruants and the Sacred in Judaism and Christianity," in *Women's History and Ancient History*, ed.

Sarah B. Pomeroy (Chapel Hill: University of North Carolina Press, 1991), 273–99, esp. 287–91 on Christianity.

9. Wood, "The Doctors' Dilemma," 714.

10. Joan Cadden, *Meanings of Sex Difference in the Middle Ages: Medicine, Science, and Culture* (Cambridge: Cambridge University Press, 1993), 23; Wood, "The Doctors' Dilemma," 715.

11. Jocelyn Wogan-Browne, "Chaste Bodies: Frames and Experiences," in *Framing Medieval Bodies*, ed. Sarah Kay and Miri Rubin (Manchester: Manchester University Press, 1994), 24, and 27–30 for further discussion of bodily fluids and the body as boundary.

12. Aline Rousselle, *Porneia: On Desire and the Body in Antiquity*, trans. Felicia Pheasant (Cambridge, Mass: Basil Blackwell, 1988), esp. 5–23; and see Elliott's study of theological discussions of nocturnal emissions and her analysis of the way that they betray anxieties about gender in *Fallen Bodies*, 14–34.

13. Brown, *The Body and Society*, xviii; Bynum, *Holy Feast and Holy Fast*, 122, 138, 148, 211. See also Dyan Elliott, "The Physiology of Rapture and Female Spirituality," in *Medieval Theology and the Natural Body*, ed. Peter Biller and A. J. Minnis (York: York Medieval Press, 1997), 168.

14. Francesca Canadé Sautman, *La religion du quotidien: Rites et croyances populaires de la fin du moyen âge* (Florence: Olchki, 1995), 85.

15. "The Letter of Heloise on Religious Life and Abelard's Reply," ed. J. T. Muckle, *Mediaeval Studies* 17 (1955): 246; trans. Betty Radice in *The Letters of Abelard and Heloise* (New York: Penguin, 1974), 166. See my discussion in "The Curse of Eve: Female Bodies and Christian Bodies in Heloise's Third Letter," in *Listening to Heloise: The Voice of a Twelfth-Century Woman*, ed. Bonnie Wheeler (New York: St. Martin's Press, 2000), 217–31. On the ambivalent status of menstruation as polluting and healing in another culture, see Alma Gottlieb, "Rethinking Female Pollution: The Beng Case (Côte d'Ivoire)," in *Beyond the Second Sex: New Directions in the Anthropology of Gender*, ed. Peggy Reeves Sanday and Ruth Gallagher Goodenough (Philadelphia: University of Pennsylvania Press, 1990), 115–38.

16. Mary Douglas, *Purity and Danger: An Analysis of the Concepts of Pollution and Taboo* (London: Routledge and Kegan Paul, 1966). For a summary and critique of Douglas's influence on studies of menstruation, see Thomas Buckley and Alma Gottlieb, "A Critical Appraisal of Theories of Menstrual Symbolism," in *Blood Magic: The Anthropology of Menstruation*, ed. Buckley and Gottlieb (Berkeley: University of California Press, 1988), 26.

17. Mary Douglas, "Self Evidence: The Henry Myers Lectures," in Douglas, *Implicit Meanings* (London: Routledge and Kegan Paul, 1975). Buckley and Gottlieb further explain that "in the vast majority of the world's societies, men have a virtual monopoly on routine or ritual forms of bloodletting: hunting, butchering, warfare, rituals involving sacrifice, mutilation, and scarification alike. Thus the fact that menstruation may be the only act in which women normatively and routinely let blood may, depending on the culture, constitute a symbolic anomaly." "A Critical Appraisal," 27.

18. Buckley and Gottlieb, "A Critical Appraisal," 30. Howard Eilberg-

Schwartz has emphasized that pollution systems also create the oppositions from which they draw their symbolic meaning. *The Savage in Judaism: An Anthropology of Israelite Religion and Ancient Judaism* (Bloomington: Indiana University Press, 1990), 195–99.

19. Lawrence A. Hoffman, *Covenant of Blood: Gender and Circumcision in Rabbinic Judaism* (Chicago: University of Chicago Press, 1996), 135.

20. Hoffman, *Covenant of Blood*, 154. See also Eilberg-Schwartz, *The Savage in Judaism*, 187–88.

21. Ian Hogbin, *The Island of Menstruating Men: Religion in Wogeo, New Guinea* (Scranton, Pa.: Chandler, 1970), 88.

22. Donald Tuzin, "Discourse, Intercourse, and the Excluded Middle: Anthropology and the Problem of Sexual Experience," in *Sexual Nature, Sexual Culture*, ed. Paul R. Abramson and Steven D. Pinkerton (Chicago: University of Chicago Press, 1995), 266.

23. Brigitta Hauser-Schäublin, "Blood: Cultural Effectiveness of Biological Conditions," in *Sex and Gender Hierarchies*, ed. Barbara Diane Miller (Cambridge: Cambridge University Press, 1993), 95.

24. Eilberg-Schwartz notes that in Israelite religion the ritual mixture used to cleanse a person from impure contact with a corpse is called "waters of *niddah*," and that "niddah" also describes the impure state of a menstruating woman. He suggests that "while women's menstrual blood, which flows uncontrollably, contaminates all sorts of other things, men's 'menstrual fluid,' which is intentionally produced, has the power to reverse the contamination of death, the worst form of impurity." *The Savage in Judaism*, 188.

25. Bruno Bettelheim, *Symbolic Wounds: Puberty Rites and the Envious Male* (Glencoe, Ill.: Free Press, 1954), 101–2, 112. Bettelheim's study contrasts with William N. Stephens's claim that castration anxiety explains menstrual taboos. "A Cross-Cultural Study of Menstrual Taboos," *Genetic Psychology Monographs* 64 (1961): 385–416.

26. Bettelheim, *Symbolic Wounds*, 105ff.

27. For the Middle Ages, the control of semen, a form of blood, and the way in which nocturnal emissions are seen to corrupt the pure body would also participate in this competitive symbolic act. For an early modern study that focuses on the gendered control/lack of control of bodily fluids, see Gail Kern Paster, *The Body Embarrassed: Drama and the Disciplines of Shame in Early Modern Culture* (Ithaca, N.Y.: Cornell University Press, 1993), 23–112, esp. 83–84.

28. *La queste del saint graal*, ed. Albert Pauphilet (Paris: Champion, 1923), 240. My translation.

29. Susan Aronstein sees Perceval's sister's voluntary death as an "ultimate *imitatio Christi*" that is undermined in the narrative by her death. "Rewriting Perceval's Sister: Eucharistic Vision and Typological Destiny in the *Queste del San Graal*," *Women's Studies* 21 (1992): 218–19.

30. Because the knights are saved, Philippa Beckerling suggests that the sacrifice is ultimately effective, since it ends the practice of taking innocent lives. "Perceval's Sister: Aspects of the Virgin in *The Quest of the Holy Grail* and

Malory's *Sankgreal*," in *Constructing Gender: Feminism and Literary Studies*, ed. Hilary Fraser and R. S. White (Nedlands: University of Western Australia Press, 1994), 50.

31. *Malory's Book of Arms*, 60. Laurie A. Finke and Martin B. Shichtman claim that in Malory's *Morte d'Arthur*, "violence often has a structure, one that is oriented toward a purpose, in this case the construction of a hegemonic masculinity based on martial prowess." "No Pain, No Gain: Violence as Symbolic Capital in Malory's *Morte d'Arthur*," *Arthuriana* 8, 2 (1998): 118. I suggest that Malory finds this ethos, though perhaps in a less exaggerated form, in his French sources.

32. On the structure of the exchange of women within courtly love, see Christiane Marchello-Nizia, "Amour courtois, société masculine et figures du pouvoir," *Annales: Economies, sociétés, civilisations* 36, 6 (1981): 969–82; Roberta L. Krueger, *Women Readers and the Ideology of Gender in Old French Verse Romance* (Cambridge: Cambridge University Press, 1993), 128–55; and my *The Romance of Adultery: Queenship and Sexual Transgression in Old French Literature* (Philadelphia: University of Pennsylvania Press, 1998), 84–118.

33. On the bloody sheets episode in *Tristan*, see Jean-Charles Huchet, *Tristan et le sang de l'écriture* (Paris: PUF, 1990), 56–76. Sarah Melhado White notes that Béroul's King Mark and Chrétien's Méléagant use the same words to describe the "true signs" offered by the blood: "veraie enseigne" (Béroul, l. 778) and "ansaignes bien veraies" (Chrétien, l. 4774). "Lancelot's Beds: Styles of Courtly Intimacy," in *The Sower and His Seed: Essays on Chrétien de Troyes*, ed. Rupert T. Pickens (Lexington, Ky.: French Forum, 1983), 123.

34. Chrétien de Troyes, *Le chevalier de la charrete*, ed. Mario Roques (Paris: Champion, 1958), ll. 4775–84; trans. David Staines in *The Complete Romances of Chrétien de Troyes* (Bloomington: Indiana University Press, 1990), 228.

35. "Par mon chief, fet Meleaganz, / quanque vos dites est neanz." *Le chevalier de la charrete*, ll. 4785–86.

36. *Theory and the Premodern Text* (Minneapolis: University of Minnesota Press, 2000), 213. Strohm analyzes Malory's retelling of the bloody sheets episode in light of Freud's theory of the primal scene, suggesting that Mellyagant "is 'infantile' as a result of his regressive reduction to confusion and passive spectatorship within the presuppositions of the primal scenario" (212), but also suggests that "the blood in Guinevere's bed may be read as another kind of symptom altogether: as a symptom of woman's secrets, the obscurity and terror of her gynecological functions, the inevitable and unknowable character of her private space" (213).

37. However, as Francis Gingras points out, the notion that the queen was menstruating during the sexual encounter doubles the knight's transgression: "non content d'étreindre la femme de son seigneur, le chevalier a pu s'unir à une femme impure, prohibition suprême dans le calendrier de la continence judéo-chrétienne." "Le sang de l'amour dans le récit médiéval (XIIe–XIIIe siècle)," in *Le sang au moyen âge*, 211. I explore literary echoes of the prohibition of intercourse during a woman's menstruation in Chapter 4.

38. Freud's view of the relationship between the nose and the genitals is

best illustrated in his correspondence with Fliess on the case of Emma Eckstein, Freud's patient who experienced menstrual difficulties. Freud invited Fliess to do surgery on Eckstein's nose in recognition of Fliess's theory that nasal therapy could relieve certain menstrual problems. For a detailed discussion of this case and of the critical commentary on it, see Mary Jane Lupton, *Menstruation and Psychoanalysis* (Urbana: University of Illinois Press, 1993), 17–38. For a reading of the nosebleed as a symbol of menstruation in medieval literature, see Michel Zink, ed., *Le roman d'Appolonius de Tyr* (Paris: Union Générale d'Editions, 1982), 14.

39. Patricia Crawford, "Attitudes to Menstruation in Seventeenth-Century England," *Past and Present* 91 (1981): 56.

40. Bleeding hemorrhoids might be another source of blood that does not come from a wound, one that is associated with menstruation in antisemitic claims that Jewish men experience a periodic blood flux. For a detailed examination of medieval texts that describe Jewish male bleeding, see Willis Johnson, "The Myth of Jewish Male Menses," *Journal of Medieval History* 24, 3 (1998): 173–95. I return to this subject in Chapter 6.

41. For a discussion of this characterization, see Karma Lochrie, *Margery Kempe and Translations of the Flesh* (Philadelphia: University of Pennsylvania Press, 1991), 23–27.

42. This romance is a reworking of *La chanson de Florence de Rome*. Only one copy is extant and it is found in a fifteenth-century manuscript, though the form of the story is considered to be much earlier. *Florence de Rome*, ed. A. Wallensköld, 2 vols. (Paris: Firmin-Didot, 1909), 1: 5–8. Analogues include *Le roman de la Violette*, *La chanson de Florence de Rome*, *Le Bone Florence of Rome*, and Chaucer's *Man of Law's Tale*. On the somewhat confused generic classifications of stories like *Florence*, see Sarah Kay, *The* Chansons de geste *in the Age of Romance: Political Fictions* (Oxford: Clarendon Press, 1995), 7.

43. "Le roman de Florence de Rome," ll. 3533–59, in *Florence de Rome*, ed. Wallensköld, 1: 246–47. My translation.

44. *Le roman de Florence de Rome* is the version of the story that most emphasizes the discovery of the bloody sheets; in other versions the discovery focuses on the bloody knife. A newly edited fifteenth-century version of *Florence de Rome*, emphasizes the blood in the bed along with the knife: . . . le lit tout plain de sang du corps de leur fille" (LXXXI. 15). I am very grateful to Sarah Crisler for sharing passages from this text before its publication as "Flourence de Rome: A Critical Edition and Literary Analysis," dissertation, University of Texas, 2000.

45. *Le Haut Livre du Graal, Perlesvaus*, ed. William A. Nitze and T. Atkinson Jenkins, 2 vols. (Chicago: University of Chicago Press, 1932), 1: 74. My translation.

46. Nitze notes that while the "Lady in the Water story" may have its source in earlier analogues, the killing of the wife and the escape of her murderer are original in the *Perlesvaus*. *Perlesvaus*, 2: 239.

47. I have discussed this episode in relation to the romance economy of sacrifice in "The Poetics of Sacrifice: Allegory and Myth in the Grail Quest," *Yale French Studies* 95 (1999): 152–68.

48. Margaret Schlauch relates representations of the Old Law and the New in the *Perlesvaus* to contemporary church literature on the Synagogue and the Church, however she does not treat this episode in the romance. "The Allegory of Church and Synagogue," *Speculum* 14 (1939): 448–64. Rosemund Tuve discusses the ways in which the *Perlesvaus* resists a sustained allegorical reading. This resistance renders both the event and its explanation all the more surprising. *Allegorical Imagery: Some Medieval Books and Their Posterity* (Princeton, N.J.: Princeton University Press, 1966), 402–10.

Chapter 2. The Amenorrhea of War

1. And when military women are killed in combat situations their deaths seem to solicit a particular horror. Linda Bird Francke describes reactions to the death of Major Marie Rossi, killed in Iraq in the first wave of the Allied ground offensive in 1991: "At the Port Mortuary in Dover, Delaware, where all fatalities from the Gulf were processed for identification, the young male 'body handlers' had fallen apart when Rossi's body and other female remains came through. Servicemen were supposed to die in war, not servicewomen. 'The guys were grief-stricken,' says Lieutenant Colonel 'Happy' McGuire, a twenty-year veteran of the Mortuary Affairs unit. 'They didn't feel women should die that way.'" *Ground Zero: The Gender Wars in the Military* (New York: Simon and Schuster, 1997), 17.

2. The exclusion policies are cited by Jeff M. Tuten in "The Argument Against Female Combatants," in *Female Soldiers: Combatants or Noncombatants?*, ed. Nancy Loring Goldman (Westport, Conn.: Greenwood Press, 1982), 237–65, esp. 255–59.

3. M. C. Devilbiss, "Women in Combat: A Quick Summary of the Arguments on Both Sides," *MINERVA: Quarterly Report on Women and the Military* 8, 1 (1990): 29–33. For historical perspectives on women and war, see Linda Grant De Pauw, *Battle Cries and Lullabies: Women in War from Prehistory to the Present* (Norman: University of Oklahoma Press, 1998); Barton C. Hacker, "Women and Military Institutions in Early Modern Europe: A Reconnaissance," *Signs: Journal of Women in Culture and Society* 6, 4 (1981): 643–71; and Megan McLaughlin, "The Woman Warrior: Gender, Warfare and Society in Medieval Europe" *Women's Studies* 17 (1990): 193–209. I return to McLaughlin's study below.

4. See, for example, James H. Webb, "Women Can't Fight," *Washingtonian* (November 1979): 144–48, 273–82; Niel L. Golightly, "No Right to Fight," *U.S. Naval Institute Proceedings* (December 1987): 46–49; Jeff M. Tuten, "The Argument Against Female Combatants"; Brian Mitchell, *Women in the Military: Flirting with Disaster* (Washington, D.C.: Regnery, 1998); Paul E. Roush, "Combat Exclusion: Military Necessity or Another Name for Bigotry?" *MINERVA: Quarterly Report on Women and the Military* 8, 3 (1990): 1–8; Mady Wechsler Segal, "The Argument for Female Combatants," in *Female Soldiers*, 267–90; Francke, *Ground Zero*.

5. *G.I. Jane*, dir. Ridley Scott, 1997.

6. Segal, "The Argument for Female Combatants," 273.

7. Tuten, "The Argument Against Female Combatants," 239.

8. Rudolf Thurneysen has suggested that the story may have been recorded as early as the mid-seventh century. *Die irisch Helden- und Königsage* (Halle: Niemeyer, 1921), 112. Myles Dillon notes that the Ulster cycle reflects a culture older than that of any other vernacular literature, and sees the story as describing "a life much like the life of the Gauls as the ancients have described it." *Early Irish Literature* (Chicago: University of Chicago Press, 1948), 2–3, on the *Táin*, 3–4. James Carney argues strongly for the literate, written composition of the *Táin* and sees the traditional elements as a nucleus around which medieval clerics fashioned stories. *Studies in Irish Literature and History* (Dublin: Dublin Institute for Advanced Studies, 1955), 276–323. For an introduction to the text and to its three recensions, see Cecile O'Rahilly's introduction to her edition and translation. *Táin Bó Cúalnge from the Book of Leinster*, Irish Text Society 49 (Dublin: Dublin Institute for Advanced Study, 1967), ix–lv. Many thanks to Caroline Jewers, who first brought this story to my attention.

9. *Táin Bó Cúalnge*, 139.

10. *Táin Bó Cúalnge*, 133–34; 269–70.

11. *Dictionary of the Irish Language based mainly on Old and Middle Irish Materials*, 4 vols. (Dublin: Royal Irish Academy, 1913–76). On the etymology of "fúal," see J. Loth, "Notes étymologiques et lexicographiques," *Revue celtique* 45 (1928): 180. I am very grateful to Thomas N. Hall for help with the Old Irish in this passage. See also Thomas Kinsella's translation in *The Táin from the Irish Epic Táin Bó Cuailnge* (Oxford: Oxford University Press, 1969), 250: "Then Medb got her gush of blood."

12. Charles Bowen, "Great-Bladdered Medb: Mythology and Invention in the Táin Bó Cuailgne," *Eire-Ireland* 10, 4 (1975): 33.

13. For a discussion of the linguistic echoes of menstruation as sickness in the context of battle, see Patricia Kelly, "The Táin as Literature," in *Aspects of the Táin*, ed. J. P. Mallory (Belfast: December Publications, 1992), 82. Kelly sees Medb as representing a failed challenge to male sovereignty (77–84); I am interested here in the way that the failure is specifically identified with biology.

14. Kinsella, *Táin*, 7–8 and n. 6. This text is edited by Ernst Windisch, "Uber die irishce Sage Noinden Ulad," *Berichte über die Verhandlungen der Königlich Sächsichen Gesellschaft der Wissenschaften zu Leipzig: Philologisch-Historische Classe* 36 (1884).

15. Carol Clover has suggested the Old Norse sex-gender system seems to allow daughters to take on the role of sons when they have no brothers, and that sagas imagine this substitution in the figures of warrior maidens, often young women who are their fathers' only heirs. "Maiden Warriors and Other Sons," *Journal of English and Germanic Philology* 85 (1986): 35–49. She further explores the flexibility of gender categories in what she identifies as the one-sex, one-gender model in medieval Icelandic society. "Regardless of Sex: Men, Women, and Power in Early Northern Europe," *Speculum* 68, 2 (1993): 363–87.

16. Jenny Jochens, *Old Norse Images of Women* (Philadelphia: University of Pennsylvania Press, 1996), 105.

17. ". . . ok var sterk sem karlar, ok pegar hon mátti sér nojjytm tanðisk hon mier við skot ok skjold ok sverð en við sauma eða borða." *Saga Heiðreks konungs ins vitra/The Saga of King Heidrek the Wise*, ed. and trans. Christopher Tolkien (London: Thomas Nelson, 1960), 10.

18. Clover, "Maiden Warriors," 48–49; Jochens, *Old Norse Images of Women*, 110–12.

19. Judith Jesch, *Women in the Viking Age* (Woodbridge: Boydell, 1991), 21–22.

20. Jesch discusses Saxo's women warriors and their relation to the women warriors of Old Norse literature in *Women in the Viking Age*, 176–202.

21. *Saxo Grammaticus: The History of the Danes*, ed. and trans. Peter Fisher and Hilda Ellis Davidson, 2 vols. (Cambridge: D.S. Brewer, 1979), 1: 212; *Saxonis Gesta Danorum*, ed. C. Knabe and Paul Herrmann, rev. Jørgen Olrik and H. Raeder (Copenhagen: Levin and Munksgaard, 1931), 7: 6.

22. *Eneas, roman du XIIe siècle*, ed. J.-J. Salverda de Grave, 2 vols. (Paris: Champion, 1925–29), ll. 7076–77.

23. "'Se je fusse hons': les guerrières dans *Ansëys de Mes*," in *Charlemagne in the North: Proceedings of the Twelfth International Conference of the Société Rencesvals*, ed. Philip E. Bennett, Anne Elizabeth Cobby, and Graham A. Runnals (London: Grant and Cutler, 1993), 293.

24. Ibid., 294; Aimé Petit, "Le traitement courtois du thème des Amazones d'après trois romans antiques: *Enéas, Troie* et *Alexandre*," *Le Moyen Age* 89 (1983): 76–77.

25. "Petit parolent amont de donoier
Que en tote Flandre n'a a paines moillier.
En Angleterre font querre et envoier. . .
Dusqu'a Verdun ne remest franc princier
Que il ne facent belle fame envoier
Por le païs peupler et enrangier."
Ansëys de Mes According to Ms. N [Bibliothèque de l'Arsenal 3143], ed. Herman J. Green (Paris: Les Presses Modernes, 1939), ll. 8895–8904.

26. Heldris de Cornäuille, *Le roman de Silence*, ed. Lewis Thorpe (Cambridge: Heffer, 1972); Huon de Bordeaux, *Esclarmonde, Clarisse et Florent, Yde et Olive: Drei Fortsetzungen der Chanson von Huon de Bordeaux*, ed. Max Schweigel (Marburg: Elwert, 1889). See my "'The Boy Who Was a Girl': Reading Gender in the *Roman de Silence*," *Romanic Review* 85 (1994): 517–36; Christiane Marchello-Nizia, "Travesties et transexuelles: Yde, Silence, Grisandole, Blanchandine," *Romance Notes* 24 (1985): 328–40. For a reading that suggests how normative sexuality may be disrupted in the romance, see Kathleen Blumreich, "Lesbian Desire in the Old French *Roman de Silence*," *Arthuriana* 7, 2 (1997): 47–62.

27. A number of scholars have discussed the gender subversions enacted by cross-dressing, though not explicitly in the context of war. See Marjorie B. Garber, *Vested Interests: Cross-Dressing and Cultural Anxiety* (New York: Routledge, 1992), Vern L. Bullough and Bonnie Bullough, *Cross Dressing, Sex, and Gender* (Philadelphia: University of Pennsylvania Press, 1993), Valerie R. Hotchkiss,

Clothes Make the Man: Female Cross Dressing in Medieval Europe (New York: Garland, 1996), and my "'The Boy Who Was a Girl.'"

28. Francke, *Ground Zero*, 218. For the "menstrual" logic that keeps women pilots out of combat, see 254–55. For menstruation in modern debates about women in the military, see also Segal, "The Argument for Female Combatants," 273–74; Golightly, "No Right to Fight," 49.

29. For a detailed account of Joan's military career, see Kelly DeVries, *Joan of Arc: A Military Leader* (Phoenix Mill: Sutton Publishing, 1999). On medieval women and war, see McLaughlin, "The Woman Warrior."

30. *Procès de condamnation et de réhabilitation de Jeanne d'Arc dite la Pucelle*, ed. Jules Quicherat (Paris: Renouard, 1845), 3: 219. Françoise Michaud-Fréjaville notes that Jean d'Aulon also reported that Joan could not support the sight of blood, and Michaud-Fréjaville wonders if the horror of spilling blood may have manifested itself in amenorrhea. "L'effusion de sang dans les procès et les traités concernant Jeanne d'Arc (1430–1456)," in *Le sang au moyen âge*, ed. Marcel Faure, Cahiers du CRISMA 4 (Montpellier: CRISMA, 1999), 339. I am grateful to Ruth Mazo Karras for suggesting that I think about Joan's amenorrhea and to Nadia Magolis for generous help with sources.

31. Marina Warner sees amenorrhea primarily as a sign of Joan's purity, but she also mentions that amenorrhea may be associated with women of extraordinary strength. *Joan of Arc: The Image of Female Heroism* (Berkeley: University of California Press, 1981), 19–22. On the heat of the virago's body and the suspension of menstruation, see Marie-Christine Ponchelle, "L'hybride," *Nouvelle revue de psychanalyse* 7 (1973): 53–54. On the amenorrhea of mystics and saints, see Peter Brown, *The Body and Society: Men, Women, and Sexual Renunciation in Early Christianity* (New York: Columbia University Press, 1988), xviii; Caroline Walker Bynum, *Holy Feast and Holy Fast: The Religious Significance of Food to Medieval Women* (Berkeley: University of California Press, 1987), 122, 138, 148, 211; Dyan Elliott, "The Physiology of Rapture and Female Spirituality," in *Medieval Theology and the Natural Body*, ed. Peter Billar and A.J. Minnis (York: York Medieval Press, 1997), 168; and on the Virgin Mary and menstruation, see Charles T. Wood, "The Doctors' Dilemma: Sin, Salvation, and the Menstrual Cycle in Medieval Thought," *Speculum* 56 (1981): 710–27; and Paulette L'Hermite-Leclercq, "Le sang et le lait de la vierge," in *Le sang au moyen âge*, 145–62. Françoise Meltzer attributes Joan's amenorrhea to her practice of fasting. *For Fear of the Fire: Joan of Arc and the Limits of Subjectivity* (Chicago: University of Chicago Press, 2001), 94–95.

32. *Almanach de Gotha* (1822), 63, cited by Warner, *Joan of Arc: The Image of Female Heroism*, 19.

33. For the debate about Joan's claim to divine inspiration, see Deborah A. Fraioli, *Joan of Arc: The Early Debate* (Woodbridge: Boydell, 2000). For a reading of the heresy trial transcripts that argues for the importance of the interrogation itself in shaping Joan's testimony as a dialogue between the inquisitors and Joan herself, see Karen Sullivan, *The Interrogation of Joan of Arc* (Minneapolis: University of Minnesota Press, 1999).

34. Susan Schibanoff demonstrates the essential relationship between

Joan's transvestism and the charge of idolatry. "True Lies: Transvestism and Idolatry in the Trial of Joan of Arc," in *Fresh Verdicts on Joan of Arc*, ed. Bonnie Wheeler and Charles T. Wood (New York: Garland, 1996), 31–60. Susan Crane convincingly argues that Joan's transvestism cannot be read only as a military choice or necessity and must be read in relation to Joan's sexuality. "Clothing and Gender Definition: Joan of Arc," *Journal of Medieval and Early Modern Studies* 26, 2 (1996): 297–320.

35. Shakespeare's sources are mainly sixteenth-century chronicles, primarily Holinshead's *Chronicles of England, Scotland and Ireland* (2nd ed., 1576) and Edward Hall's *The Union of the Two Noble and Illustre Famelies of Lancastre & Yorke* (1548). For a discussion of the historical project of Shakespeare's early plays, see Phyllis Rackin, *Stages of History: Shakespeare's English Chronicles* (Ithaca, N.Y.: Cornell University Press, 1990). Dominique Goy-Blanquet suggests that some details in the plays may indicate that Shakespeare knew of rumors circulating in France about Joan. *Le roi mis à nu: L'histoire d'Henri VI de Hall à Shakespeare* (Paris: Didier, 1986), 76–77.

The authenticity of this play as a work of Shakespeare has been questioned. Although it is now accepted as Shakespeare's play, Leah S. Marcus notes that when the play was reinstated in the Shakespeare canon, the one element that continued to be seen as a composite work was the portrayal of Joan la Pucelle: "The exposure of the sublime Maid of Orleans as a witch and strumpet was a low gesture that had to be separated from Shakespeare, lest both idealized figures fall together." *Puzzling Shakespeare: Local Reading and Its Discontents* (Berkeley: University of California Press, 1998), 52.

36. References to Shakespeare refer to *The Norton Shakespeare*, gen. ed. Stephen Greenblatt (New York: Norton, 1997). Gabriele Bernhard Jackson discusses Shakespeare's Joan in the context of early modern representations of Amazons in "Topical Ideology: Witches, Amazons, and Shakespeare's Joan of Arc," *English Literary Renaissance* 18 (1988): 40–65. In *Tough Love: Amazon Encounters in the English Renaissance* (Durham, N.C.: Duke University Press, 2000), Kathryn Schwarz offers a broader study of Joan as Amazon in her exploration of the figure of the Amazon in early modern English literature (80–91). On the relationship between Shakespeare's portrait of Joan and Elizabeth I's self-presentation as an Amazon at Tilbury in 1588, see Jackson, "Topical Ideology," 55–58; on Joan as a distorted image of Elizabeth, see Marcus, *Puzzling Shakespeare*, 66–83.

37. McLaughlin, "The Woman Warrior," 194.

38. Jesch, *Women in the Viking Age*, 21–22.

39. McLaughlin, "The Woman Warrior," 196–99.

40. McLaughlin, "The Woman Warrior," 202–3.

41. McLaughlin, "The Woman Warrior," 195.

42. Kelly DeVries, "A Woman as Leader of Men: Joan of Arc's Military Career," in *Fresh Verdicts on Joan of Arc*, 4.

43. Régine Pernoud and Marie-Véronique Clin, *Joan of Arc: Her Story*, trans. and rev. Jeremy DuQuesne Adams (New York: St. Martin's Press, 1999), 33; *Procès en nullité de la condamnation de Jeanne d'Arc*, ed. Pierre Duparc (Paris:

Klincksieck, 1977), 1: 370. The testimony of Jean d'Aulon concurs: "Dit outre que, non obstant ce qu'elle feust jeune fille, belle et bien formée, et que par plusieurs foiz, tant en aidant à icelle armer que aultrement, il luy ait veu les tetins, et aucunes foiz les jambes toutes nues, en la faisant apareiller de ses plaies; et que d'elle approuchoit souventesfoiz, et aussi qu'il feust fort, jeune et en sa bonne puissance: toutesfoiz oncques, pour quelque veue ou atouchement qu'il eust vers ladicte Pucelle, ne s'esmeut son corps à nul chanel désir vers elle, ne pareillement ne faisoit nul autre quelconque de ses gens et escuiers, ainsi qu'il qui parle leur a oy dire et relater par plusieurs foiz" (*Procès*, ed. Quicherat, 3: 219).

44. DeVries, "A Woman as Leader of Men," 4–5, citation 5.

45. Charles T. Wood, "Joan of Arc's Mission and the Lost Record of her Interrogation at Poitiers," in *Fresh Verdicts on Joan of Arc*, 22.

46. Fraioli, *Joan of Arc: The Early Debate*, 8.

47. Jean E. Howard and Phyllis Rackin, *Engendering a Nation: A Feminist Account of Shakespeare's English Histories* (New York: Routledge, 1997), 54, 57–58.

48. Françoise Meltzer argues for the importance of Joan's viriginity as a crucially important site of Joan's challenge to authority. *For Fear of the Fire*, 53–118, esp. 58–68. On virgin's blood and mother's blood in Greek tragedy, see Nicole Loraux, *Tragic Ways of Killing a Woman*, trans. Anthony Forster (Cambridge, Mass.: Harvard University Press, 1987). Loraux argues that the values of blood are established through the ways in which women (mothers, wives, virgins) die.

49. Pernoud and Clin, *Joan of Arc*, 46–47, 77.

50. Howard and Rackin suggest that "the gendered opposition between Joan and Talbot defines the meaning of the conflict between France and England." *Engendering a Nation*, 54. See also Jackson, "Topical Ideology," 40–42.

51. Joanna Bourke, *An Intimate History of Killing: Face to Face Killing in Twentieth-Century Warfare* (New York: Basic Books, 1999), xiii.

52. Michaud-Fréjavaille, "L'effusion de sang," 331–34.

53. Michaud-Fréjaville cites Martin Berryuer and Jean de Montigny, and Jean d'Aulon. "L'effusion de sang," 336, 339.

54. Michaud-Fréjaville, "L'effusion de sang," 336.

55. Michaud-Fréjaville, "L'effusion de sang," 334.

56. Webb, "Women Can't Fight," 147–48; Tuten, "The Argument Against Female Combatants," 252–55.

57. For a discussion of this attitude in World War II, see Bourke, *An Intimate History*, 309–12.

58. Bourke, *An Intimate History*, 327.

Chapter 3. The Gender of Sacrifice

1. The romance is edited by Anne Berthelot in Chrétien de Troyes, *Oeuvres complètes*, gen. ed. Daniel Poirion (Paris, Gallimard, 1994), 917–52. The only extant form of the twelfth-century romance is found as part of the *Ovide moralisé*,

composed around 1328. For a summary of the authorship debate and an affirmation of Chrétien's authorship, see Elisabeth Schulze-Busacker, "Philomena: Une révision de l'attribution de l'oeuvre," *Romania* 107 (1986): 459–85. For the idea that Chrétien supplemented Ovid with Hyginus's *Fabulae*, see Edith Joyce Benkov, "Hyginus' Contribution to Chrétien's *Philomena*," *Romance Philology* 36, 3 (1983): 403–6.

2. Marylène Possamaï-Perez, "Chrétien de Troyes au début du XIVe siècle: *Philomena* "moralisé," in *L'oeuvre de Chrétien de Troyes dans la littérature française; Réminiscences, résurgences et réécritures*, ed. Claude Lachet (Lyon: Université Jean Moulin, 1997), 173–74. Possamaï-Perez argues that Chrétien's moralization of the characters is what explains the incorporation of his version of the Philomela story in the *Ovide moralisé*.

3. "Soon afterwards Gudrun killed her two sons and had goblets made out of their skulls with silver and gold. Then a funeral was held for the Niflungs. At this feast Gudrun had mead served to King Atli in these goblets, and it was mixed with the boys' blood, and she had their hearts cooked and given to the king to eat. And when this had been done, she told him of it to his face with many unsavoury words." Snorri Sturluson, *Edda*, trans. Anthony Faulkes (London: Dent, 1987), 104. See also "The Greenlandish Lay of Atli" (Atlamál hin groenlenzku) in *The Poetic Edda*, trans. Lee M. Hollander (Austin: University of Texas Press, 1962), 294–310, esp. 305–6.

4. *The Nibelungenlied*, trans. A. T. Hatto (London: Penguin, 1965), 236, 243, and for the episode in the *Thiðrejssaga*, 302–303.

5. Medieval rewritings of Medea are studied by Ruth Morse, *The Medieval Medea* (Cambridge: Cambridge University Press, 1996), and Joel N. Feimer, "The Figure of Medea in Medieval Literature: A Thematic Metamorphosis," dissertation, City University of New York, 1983.

6. Natalie Grinnell, "Medea's Humanity and John Gower's Romance," *Medieval Perspectives* 14 (1999): 70–83; Carole M. Meale, "Legends of Good Women in the European Middle Ages," *Archiv für das Studium der Neueren Sprachen und Literaturen* 229,1 (1992): 55–70; Joel N. Feimer, "Jason and Medea in Benoit de Sainte-Maure's *Le roman de Troie*: Classical Theme and Medieval Context," in *Voices in Translation: The Authority of "Olde Bookes" in Medieval Literature*, ed. Deborah M. Sinnreich-Levi et al. (New York: AMS, 1992), 35–51; John Jay Thompson, "Medea in Christine de Pizan's *Mutacion de Fortune*, or How to be a Better Mother," *Forum for Modern Language Studies* 35 (1999): 158–74; Joel N. Feimer, "Medea in Ovid's *Metamorphoses* and the *Ovide moralisé*: Translation as Transmission," *Florilegium* 8 (1986): 40–55.

7. Barbara Newman, "'Crueel Corage': Child Sacrifice and the Maternal Martyr in Hagiography and Romance," in Newman, *From Virile Woman to WomanChrist: Studies in Medieval Religion and Literature* (Philadelphia: University of Pennsylvania Press, 1995), 77.

8. This distinction corresponds to the distinctions of priestly sacrifice, where an individual or a group brings a sacrificial offering to a priest who kills the victim and performs the ritual offering. The first is the sacrifier (*sacrifiant*), and the second, the sacrificer (*sacrificateur*), in the terminology of Henri Hubert

and Marcel Mauss, *Sacrifice: Its Nature and Function*, trans. W. D. Halls (1898; reprint Chicago: University of Chicago Press, 1964).

9. "Opposition between sacrifice and childbirth, or between sacrifice and childbearing women, that is, mothers or potential mothers, is present in countless different sacrificial traditions. . . . It is a common feature of unrelated traditions that only adult males—fathers, real and metaphorical—may perform sacrifice. Where women are reported as performing sacrifice it is never as mothers, but almost always in some specifically non-childbearing role: as virgins (or dressed as if they were virgins), as consecrated unmarried women, or as post-menopausal women." Nancy Jay, *Throughout Your Generations Forever: Sacrifice, Religion, and Paternity* (Chicago: University of Chicago Press, 1992), xxiii.

10. Jay, *Throughout Your Generations Forever*, 37. On sacrifice and symbolic childbirth, see also Mary Douglas, *Leviticus as Literature* (Oxford: Oxford University Press, 1999), 68.

11. Bruce Lincoln, *Death, War, and Sacrifice: Studies in Ideology and Practice* (Chicago: University of Chicago Press, 1991), 204–5.

12. I am concerned here with the gendered representation of sacrifice. I do not attempt to account for the practice of infanticide in the Middle Ages, nor do I attempt to speculate about parental affection for children in medieval culture or about what the emotional nature of familial bonds might have been like for medieval parents or children. On infanticide, see Y.-B. Brissaud, "L'infanticide à la fin du moyen âge: Ses motivations psychologiques et sa répression," *Revue historique de droit français et étranger* 50 (1972): 229–56; and see John Boswell's discussion of infanticide in various contexts in *The Kindness of Strangers: The Abandonment of Children in Western Europe from Late Antiquity to the Renaissance* (New York: Pantheon, 1988); and Carol Clover, "The Politics of Scarcity: Notes on the Sex Ratio in Early Scandinavia," *Scandinavian Studies* 60 (1988): 147–88. On parental affection and the representation of familial attachments in literature, see James A. Schultz, *The Knowledge of Childhood in the German Middle Ages, 1100–1350* (Philadelphia: University of Pennsylvania Press, 1995), 2–4, 106–42.

13. Actually, the sacrifice is not interrupted in all versions of the Abraham story. In Rabbi Ephraim of Bonn's twelfth-century *Me-Aggadot ha-Akedah*, Abraham slaughters Isaac twice before a ram is substituted for the burnt offering. For the text and a discussion of this tradition, see Shalom Spiegel, *The Last Trial: On the Legends and Lore of the Command to Abraham to Offer Isaac as a Sacrifice: The Akedah*, trans. Judah Goldin (Woodstock, Vt.: Jewish Lights, 1993), 28–37, 148–49. See also Jon D. Levenson, *The Death and Resurrection of the Beloved Son: The Transformation of Child Sacrifice in Judaism and Christianity* (New Haven, Conn.: Yale University Press, 1993), 180–81, 192–99; and Jeremy Cohen, "Philosophical Exegesis in Historical Perspective: The Case of the Binding of Isaac," in *Divine Omniscience and Omnipotence in Medieval Philosophy: Islamic, Jewish and Christian Perspectives*, ed. Tamar Rudavsky (Dordrecht: D. Reidel, 1985), 137–38.

14. Dramatic representations of Abraham's sacrifice are found in the four fifteenth-century English Corpus Christi cycle plays that have survived, as well

as in two independent plays, the Northampton *Abraham* and the Brome *Abraham*. *The Chester Mystery Cycle*, ed. R. M. Lumiansky and David Mills, 2 vols., EETS s.s. 3, 6 (London: Oxford University Press, 1974–86); *The Towneley Plays*, ed. George England with Alfred W. Pollard, EETS e.s. 71 (London: Oxford University Press, 1987); *The York Plays*, ed. Richard Beadle (London: Edward Arnold, 1982); and *The N-Town Play*, ed. Stephen Spector, 2 vols, EETS s.s. 11, 12 (London: Oxford University Press, 1991). The Northampton and Brome plays are edited in *Non-Cycle Plays and Fragments*, ed. Norman Davis, EETS s.s. 1 (London: Oxford University Press, 1970). The story of Abraham and Isaac is also dramatized in the fifteenth-century *Mistére du Viel Testament*, ed. James de Rothschild, 6 vols. (Paris: Firmin-Didot, 1878). This text is about 50,000 verses long; its editor estimates that a performance of the entire compilation would have taken around twenty-five days (1: xv, n. 1). However, individual plays from the compilation, including "The Sacrifice of Abraham," were printed separately and were most certainly performed alone (1: xviii–xxx; 2: i–iv).

15. Mieke Bal calls the sacrifice of Jephthah's daughter "the only fully explicit human sacrifice in the Bible." *Death and Dissymmetry: The Politics of Coherence in the Book of Judges* (Chicago: University of Chicago Press, 1988), 41. Bal's provocative analysis focuses on the daughter, the father's sacrifice, and the gendered concept of virginity. I am interested in interrogating the gender of the sacrificer: the sacrificed daughter is still a father's sacrifice, not a mother's.

16. *The Riverside Chaucer*, gen. ed. Larry D. Benson, 3rd ed. (Boston: Houghton Mifflin, 1987), 192–93, ll. 2338–41. Anne Lancashire discusses Chaucer's tale in relation to biblical models of sacrifice in "Chaucer and the Sacrifice of Isaac," *Chaucer Review* 9, 4 (1975): 320–26.

17. Newman points out that the following chapter in Genesis begins with the death of Sarah, and both Jewish and Christian commentaries on Genesis 22 inscribe Sarah into the scene of sacrifice, though not as the sacrificer of her son. Newman cites rabbinic midrashim where "Satan tempts Sarah and it is said that she died of grief (or alternatively, of joy when she learned that Isaac had been spared after all)" ("'Crueel Corage,'" 78).

18. *The Chester Mystery Cycle*, 1: 70, ll. 297–300. Also in the Brome play, *Non-Cycle Plays*, 48, ll. 176–77.

19. *Non-Cycle Plays*, 37, ll. 198–99.

20. *Non-Cycle Plays*, 49, ll. 205–6.

21. *The Towneley Plays*, 47, ll. 225–28.

22. Sarah is mentioned only briefly in the York play, and not at all in the N-Town play.

23. Newman notes that in the French play, Sarah is associated with human affection and Abraham, with the "higher" good of the love of God ("'Crueel Corage,'" 78).

24. *Abraham on Trial: The Social Legacy of Biblical Myth* (Princeton, N.J.: Princeton University Press, 1998), 109. See also Newman, "'Crueel Corage,'" 77.

25. Jody Enders discusses the way that mnemonics structures the rhetorico-dramatic function of the play, particularly in the *Procès du Paradis* that frames the individual plays, and she notes that the story of the *engendrement* of

Isaac "exemplifies the dramatic and exegetical engenderments that will soon be revealed." *Rhetoric and the Origins of Medieval Drama* (Ithaca, N.Y.: Cornell University Press, 1992), 196; see also 193–94.

26. Delaney, *Abraham on Trial*, 7–8, 27–34.

27. The earliest extant version of the story is found in a late eleventh-century epistle by Rodulfus Tortarius, monk of Fleury, who tells the story as an exemplum of friendship. *Rodulfi Tortarii Carmina*, ed. Marbury B. Oble and Dorothy M. Schullian, Papers and Monographs of the American Academy in Rome 8 (Rome: American Academy in Rome, 1933), 256–67. I will discuss the thirteenth-century Old French *Ami et Amile, chanson de geste*, ed. Peter F. Dembowski (Paris: Champion, 1969), and the roughly contemporaneous Anglo-Norman *Amis e Amilun* in *Amis and Amiloun*, ed. Eugen Kölbing (Heilbronn: Henninger, 1884), 109–87. Translations of these texts are mine.

28. Critics have made the intriguing suggestion that the story is modeled on a historical case: the friendship between counts Guillaume III of Poitou (Duke Guillaume V of Aquitaine) and Guillaume Taillefer II of Angoulême. See Francis Bar, *Les épitres latines de Raoul le Tourtier (1065?–1114?): Etude de sources, La légende d'Ami et Amile* (Paris: Droz, 1937), 65–74. The friendship between the two fictional knights has been seen as problematic by some critics. François Suard emphasizes that they are not to be seen as an amorous couple. "Le merveilleux et le religieux dans 'Ami et Amile,'" in *De l'étranger à l'étrange ou la conjointure de la merveille (en hommage à M. Rossi et P. Bancourt)*, Senefiance 25 (Aix-en-Provence: CUERMA, 1988), 451–62. Whereas the text does not overtly eroticize the relationship between the two knights, neither does it entirely suppress the possible erotic aspects of the friendship. This seems particularly evident in the Anglo-Norman poem, where the love between the two men is subsumed in a model of courtly love: the poet introduces the knights as courtly lovers (*fyns amaunz*) and goes on to say that they found loyal love and suffered from it (Kölbing, 111, manuscript C).

29. William Calin sees the friendship as part of a larger exploration of the dialectic of goodness in relation to evil and to reality. *The Epic Quest: Studies in Four Old French* Chansons de Geste (Baltimore: Johns Hopkins University Press, 1966), 95–96. My goal is to interrogate how the narrative of child sacrifice represents a father's right to sacrifice his children as a right and as an example of "goodness."

30. Hugette Legros, "Le vocabulaire de l'amitié, son évolution sémantique au cours du XIIe siècle," *Cahiers de civilisation médiévale* 23 (1980): 131–39. C. Stephen Jaeger discusses the vocabulary of love in nonerotic relationships in *Ennobling Love: In Search of a Lost Sensibility* (Philadelphia: University of Pennsylvania Press, 1999), see 73–74 on the Amicus and Amelius legend. For an astute analysis of the woman as object of exchange and as subject of seduction, see Sarah Kay, "Seduction and Suppression in 'Ami et Amile,'" *French Studies* 44 (1990): 129–42.

31. Ojars Kratins insists on the spiritual and sacrificial nature of the leprosy in "The Middle English *Amis and Amiloun*: Chivalric Romance or Secular Hagiography?" *PMLA* 81 (1966): 352–53.

32. Although curiously, as Micheline de Comarieu du Grès notes, when Amile hesitates and prays to God before killing his children, he does not acknowledge the fact that God himself has sanctioned the sacrifice. "Une extrême amitié," in *Ami et Amile: Une chanson de geste de l'amitié*, ed. Jean Dufournet (Paris: Champion-Slatkine, 1987), 26. In the earliest version of the story, by Radulfus Tortarius, the cure for leprosy is announced not by an angel, but by doctors who claim that the disease can be cured with the blood of children (*Rodulfi Tortarii Carmina*, 266, ll. 34–36).

33. Amile's decision to take his friend's place in the judicial battle is a decision to sacrifice the truth to friendship, and despite the narrative justification of the deception in the insistence on the treachery of Hardré, the substitution undermines legal truth. Emanuel Mickel discusses the story in the context of medieval legal systems in "The Question of Guilt in *Ami et Amile*," *Romania* 106 (1985): 19–35.

34. Calin sees a "progression in sacrifice" in the story (*Epic Quest*, 95–96), but the terms in which Amile agrees to sacrifice his children insist on reciprocity rather than on escalation.

35. This "alikeness" has been explored in various ways. For example, Alice Planche proposes that the two friends represent two halves of a complete self. "Ami et Amile ou le même et l'autre," *Beiträge zum romanischen Mittelalter*, ed. Kurt Baldinger (Tübingen: Niemeyer, 1977), 269. Sarah Kay offers an analysis of the epic friendship in relation to Luce Irigaray's work on sexual identity and *hommosexualité* ("Seduction and Suppression," 139–42). I am insisting on the way that resemblance is defined and redefined through blood.

36. Leach sees the friendship as representing a last manifestation of an earlier institution of *compagnonage* (*Amis and Amiloun*, lxvi–lxviii).

37. Planche notes that "la résurrection attribue en quelque sorte à Ami les fils de son compagnon," but she sees Ami's new paternity as a sign of the nature he shares with his friend, rather than as a redefinition of paternal lineage to include a second father in place of the mother ("Ami et Amile ou le même et l'autre," 262).

38. I do not mean to suggest that the friendship has the same value in all of the versions of the story. As Susan Dannenbaum [Crane] has pointed out, the religious context of the Middle English poem transforms the representation of friendship as "the unquestionable arbiter of right and wrong" in the Anglo-Norman poem. "Insular Tradition in the Story of Amis and Amiloun," *Neophilologus* 67 (1983): 618. Yet I do want to suggest that the idea that friendship is a higher good that merits sacrifice is consistent in all the versions of the story of Amicus and Amelius.

39. *Amis e Amilun* in *Amis and Amiloun*, ed. Kölbing, 167, ms. C, ll. 78–87.

40. Samuel N. Rosenberg notes that it is as if Belissant had married both men: her marriage is not only an alliance with Amile, but a ratification of the friendship, and when her husband meets her with the newly-healed Ami she cannot tell the two men apart. "Lire *Ami et Amile*, le regard sur les personnages féminins," in *Ami et Amile: Une chanson de geste de l'amitié*, 75.

41. Yet as Dannenbaum [Crane] notes in her study of the Middle English and Anglo-Norman versions of the story, "the superficial association of an act of

friendship with Christian piety denies the possibility that Ami's sons might have a claim to his protection equal to the claim of friendship" ("Insular Tradition in the Story of Amis and Amiloun," 618).

42. *Amis e Amilun* in *Amis and Amiloun*, ed. Kölbing, 183, ll. 1126–32. My translation. The names are reversed in this version of the story, Amilun is the knight with leprosy.

43. Newman, "'Crueel Corage,'" 76–107, esp. 96, 103.

44. For a recent example of the retelling of the Abraham story, see Neil Gordon, *The Sacrifice of Isaac* (New York: Random House, 1995); and for a recent fictional exploration of the pathological explanations of maternal murder, see Caleb Carr, *The Angel of Darkness* (New York: Random House, 1997).

45. Ovid says only that: "Then Procne tore from her shoulders the robe gleaming with a broad golden border and put on black weeds; she built also a cenotaph in honor of her sister, brought pious offerings to her imagined spirit, and mourned her sister's fate, not meet so to be mourned" ("velamina Procne / deripit ex umeris auro fulgentia lato / induiturque atras vestes et inane sepul-crum / constituit falsisque piacula manibus infert / et luget non sic lugendae fata sororis"). *Metamorphoses*, trans. Frank Justus Miller, rev. G. P. Goold (Cambridge, Mass.: Harvard University Press, 1977), 328–29, ll. 565–70. Raymond Cormier notes that the pagan text is Christianized in Procne's sacrifice to Pluto for the repose of her sister's soul. *Three Ovidian Tales of Love* (New York: Garland, 1986), 186. The extended scene of sacrifice is not included in Chaucer's version of the story, though according to John Livingstone Lowes, he knew and used the Old French *Philomena*. "Chaucer and the *Ovide moralisé*," *PMLA* 33 (1918): 302–25.

46. Cormier discusses the sacrifice and suggests it may be modeled on the representation of ritual sacrifice in the Medea episode of Ovid's text (*Three Ovidian Tales of Love*, 189).

47. I am inspired here by E. Jane Burns's study of *Philomena*, where she shows how the rape and the murder may be read as parallel narratives of seduction, abduction, and silencing. *Bodytalk: When Women Speak in Old French Literature* (Philadelphia: University of Pennsylvania Press, 1993), 117.

48. And the cannibalism is a tragedy, not a triumph of love that "remembers" the dismembered male lover's body in a perfect union with his lady, as Helen Solterer has described eaten heart episode in *Le roman du châtelain de Couci*. "Dismembering, Remembering the Châtelain de Couci," *Romance Philology* 46 (1992): 116. Madelaine Jeay suggests that a reading of eaten heart stories in the context of *Philomena* exposes the violence that is normalized in these stories. "Consuming Passions: Variations on the Eaten Heart Theme," *Violence Against Women in Medieval Texts*, ed. Anna Roberts (Gainesville: University Press of Florida, 1998), 75–96. See also Milad Doueihi, *A Perverse History of the Human Heart* (Cambridge, Mass.: Harvard University Press, 1997).

49. "Si com requiert drois et nature / De toute humaine creature, / Et si com pitiez le desfent, / Que mere ne doit son enfent / Ne ocirre ne desmembrer . . . . Si com la tenoit acolee / Li petis enfes par chierté, / Par dÿablie et par fierté,/ Que dÿables li amonneste, / A a l'enfant copé la teste" (*Philomena*, ll.

1315–32). Burns points to the way that the categories of "natural" and "unnatural" in this judgement reveal less about female sentiments than about the construction of cultural values (*Bodytalk*, 142).

50. *Abraham on Trial*, 22–23. See also Carol Delaney, "The Meaning of Paternity and the Virgin Birth Debate," *Man* n.s. 21 (1986): 494–513.

51. *Non-Cycle Plays*, 38, ll. 242–43.

52. "Abraham fera ung autel, / Sus lequel, de couraige franc, / De son seul filz et propre sang / Me vouldra faire sacrifice" (*Le mistére du Viel Testament*, 2: 16, ll. 9680–83).

53. The equation between bloodline and resemblance is not represented only in the child's resemblance to its father. In fourteenth-century stories like *Le roman du comte d'Anjou* or Chaucer's *Man of Law's Tale*, the child's resemblance to its mother is emphasized. I discuss these stories and their representation of mother's blood in Chapter 4.

54. *Jourdain de Blaye* and *Ami et Amile* form what Peter Dembowski has called the short epic cycle of Blaye. *Jourdain de Blaye*, ed. Peter F. Dembowski (Paris: Champion, 1991), xi.

55. "Il s'est navréz el bras de maintenant, / N'avoit autre arme dont il se fust aidant. / Por ce le fist, gel voz di et creant: / Mers ne puet sanc souffrir ne tant ne quant" (*Jourdain de Blaye*, ll. 1260–63).

56. "Lor est cist maus de la mer avenus, / Que mers ne sueffre arme qui navré fust / Qui en cors soit ne navrés ne ferus, / Ansois le giete conme fondres qui bruit / Que tex est sa nature" (*Jourdain de Blaye*, ll. 2156–60).

57. Maurice Delbouille, "Apollonius de Tyr et les débuts du roman français," in *Mélanges offerts à Rita Lejeune* (Grembloux: J. Duculot, 1969), 1193–96; Peter F. Dembowski, "Autour de Jourdain de Blayes, aspects structuraux et problèmes connexes," *Neophilologus* 51 (1967): 238–45; D. J. A. Ross, "Blood in the Sea: An Episode in 'Jourdain de Blaivies,'" *Modern Language Review* 66 (1971): 532–41.

58. Ross notes that "pechié" could mean simply misfortune rather than sin, but that a meaning like sin seems to emerge from the context ("Blood in the Sea," 533).

59. Other literary examples of women who observe ritual purification after childbirth are found in "Le dit du buef" ("La dame après son mois est à confesse alee"), in *Nouveau recueil de contes, dits, fabliaux et autres pièces inédites des XIIIe, XIVe et XVe siècles*, ed. Achille Jubinal, 2 vols. (Paris: Edouard Pannier, 1839), 1: 52; *La manekine* ("Quant ele ot jeü tout son mois, / On li fist faire tous ses drois. / Honerablement se leva, / Et a son droit se releva . . ."), in *Oeuvres poétiques de Philippe de Remi, Sire de Beaumanoir*, ed. Hermann Suchier, 2 vols. (Paris: Firmin-Didot, 1884–85), 1: ll. 3621–24; and *Bliocadran* ("La dame a son termine fu / Tant que tans fu de relever"), in *Bliocadran: A Prologue to the Perceval of Chrétien de Troyes*, ed. Leonora D. Wolfgang (Tübingen: Niemeyer, 1976), ll. 312–13. Kathryn Gravdal has discussed the unusual attention paid to the female pregnant body in the first two of these texts, which are also incest narratives. "Confessing Incests: Legal Erasures and Literary Celebrations in Medieval France," *Comparative Literature Studies* 32 (1995): 280–95, esp. 284. I will discuss postpartum purification rituals in Chapter 4.

60. Dyan Elliott discusses menstrual pollution and purity rituals surrounding parturition as part of her study of the persistence and increasing interconnectedness of ideas about women, ritual pollution, sexual regulation, and the status of the demonic in the high and later Middle Ages. *Fallen Bodies: Pollution, Sexuality, and Demonology in the Middle Ages* (Philadelphia: University of Pennsylvania Press, 1999), esp. 3–6, 108–9. Other studies of women's blood in medieval thought include Charles T. Wood, "The Doctors' Dilemma: Sin, Salvation, and the Menstrual Cycle in Medieval Thought," *Speculum* 56 (1981): 710–27; Peter Brown, *The Body and Society: Men, Women, and Sexual Renunciation in Early Christianity* (New York: Columbia University Press, 1988), 145–46, 433–34; and Shaye J. D. Cohen, "Menstruants and the Sacred in Judaism and Christianity," in *Women's History and Ancient History*, ed. Sarah B. Pomeroy (Chapel Hill: University of North Carolina Press, 1991), 273–99, esp. 287–91.

61. Howard Eilberg-Schwartz notes that "Israelite religion never makes what could have been a positive metaphoric association between menstrual bleeding and the flow of blood from a sacrifice. Had such an association occurred, perhaps Israelites would have sprinkled menstrual blood on the altar." *The Savage in Judaism: An Anthropology of Israelite Religion and Ancient Judaism* (Bloomington: Indiana University Press, 1990), 181.

62. *Riverside Chaucer*, 88, ll. 72–74. In *The Legend of Good Women*, Chaucer does not recount Medea's infanticide (*Riverside Chaucer*, 617).

63. See note 32 above.

64. "Crueel Corage," 96, 103.

65. "Mar voz portai neuf mois en mon costel" (*Jourdain de Blaye*, l. 654).

66. "Noz sommez vostre, de vostre engenrement," says Amile's eldest son to his father. *Ami et Amile*, l. 3003.

Chapter 4. Menstruation and Monstrous Birth

1. "Blut und Glauben: Uber Judisch-christliche Symbiose," in *Wissensbilder: Strategien der Uberlieferung*, ed. Ulrich Raulff and Gary Smith (Berlin: Akamedie Verlag, 1999), 145–68. I am indebted to David Biale for the description of the text and for the translation.

2. *Sefer Nizzahon Yashan*, in David Berger, *The Jewish-Christian Polemic in the Middle Ages* (Philadelphia: Jewish Publication Society of America, 1979), 224, no. 237. For an overview of the laws of family purity governing the *niddah* (menstruation, or menstruating woman) and *miqveh* (ritual dipping or cleansing), see Rahel R. Wasserfall, "Introduction: Menstrual Blood into Jewish Blood," in *Women and Water: Menstruation in Jewish Life and Law*, ed. Wasserfall (Hanover, N.H.: Brandeis University Press and University Press of New England, 1999), 1–18; Rachel Biale, *Women and Jewish Law* (New York: Schocken Books, 1984), 147–74; and Charlotte Elisheva Fonrobert, *Menstrual Purity: Rabbinic and Christian Reconstructions of Biblical Gender* (Stanford, Calif.: Stanford University Press, 2000), 15–39.

3. On the use of the Abraham story as a model of sacrifice in Hebrew

chronicles of the crusades, see Shalom Spiegel, *The Last Trial: On the Legends and Lore of the Command to Abraham to Offer Isaac as a Sacrifice: The Akedah*, trans. Judah Goldin (Woodstock, Vt.: Jewish Lights, 1993), 17–27.

4. "Chronicle of Solomon bar Simson," in Shlomo Eidelberg, trans. and ed., *The Jews and the Crusaders: The Hebrew Chronicles of the First and Second Crusade* (Hoboken, N.J.: KTAV Publishing, 1996), 32. Eidelberg notes that the narrator's derogatory characterizations of Christ and his mother were influenced by earlier Jewish polemical literature (144, n. 10).

5. James A. Brundage, *Law, Sex, and Christian Society in Medieval Europe* (Chicago: University of Chicago Press, 1987), 91–92, 156–57, 198–99, 242, 283, 451, 508. The earliest Christian references to the separation of menstruating women are from the third century; for a discussion of these texts, see Shaye J. D. Cohen, "Menstruants and the Sacred in Judaism and Christianity," in *Women's History and Ancient History*, ed. Sarah B. Pomeroy (Chapel Hill: University of North Carolina Press, 1991), 287–91. See also D. L. D'Avray and M. Tausche, "Marriage Sermons in *Ad Statis* Collections of the Central Middle Ages," *Archives d'histoire doctrinale et littéraire du moyen âge* 48 (1979): 78–80.

6. Brundage suggests that this notion may originate with Christian writers, since it does not appear in Jewish sources. *Law, Sex, and Christian Society*, 155–56.

7. Brundage, *Law, Sex, and Christian Society*, 451, 508.

8. See Helen Rodnite Lemay's introduction to *Women's Secrets: A Translation of Pseudo-Albertus Magnus, De Secretis Mulierum with Commentaries*, trans. Lemay (Albany, N.Y.: SUNY Press, 1992), 37. Lemay suggests that "the shift toward censure of the female because of her impure biological nature" is seen most clearly in the writings of Albertus Magnus (47).

9. Examples include: Pseudo-Albertus, *Women's Secrets*, 77, 129; 130–31; Innocent III in *Lotharii Cardinalis (Innocent III) De Miseria Humane Conditionis*, ed. Michele Maccarrone (Lugano: Thesaurus Mundi, 1955), 11–12; bk. 1: 4; Thomas Aquinas in *Summa theologica*, trans. Fathers of the English Dominican Province, 19 vols. (London: Burns Oates and Washbourne; New York: Benziger, 1911–22), 17: 316–18; q. 64, art. 3–4. For the evolution of the notion in the sixteenth century (and for its survival in modern popular views of reproduction), see Ottavia Niccoli, "'Menstrum Quais Monstruum': Monstrous Births and Menstrual Taboo in the Sixteenth Century," trans. Mary M. Gallucci, in *Sex and Gender in Historical Perspective: Selections from Quaderni Storici*, ed. Edward Muir and Guido Ruggiero (Baltimore: Johns Hopkins University Press, 1990), 1–25. New medical knowledge in the thirteenth century also influences discussions of impurity, as Dyan Elliott points out. See her discussion of William of Auvergne in *Fallen Bodies: Pollution, Sexuality, and Demonology in the Middle Ages* (Philadelphia: University of Pennsylvania Press, 1999), 6.

10. Lemay dates the text to the late thirteenth or early fourteenth century. *Women's Secrets*, 1.

11. Pseudo-Albertus, *Women's Secrets*, 129–31. Albertus Magnus explains abnormal births with reference to the imbalance of female matter and male sperm, to the imprint of imagination, and to astrological influences. Luke Demaitre and Anthony A. Travill, "Human Embryology and Development in

the Works of Albertus Magnus," in *Albertus Magnus and the Sciences; Commemorative Essays 1980*, ed. James A. Weisheipl, Studies and Texts 49 (Toronto: Pontifical Institute of Medieval Studies, 1980), 433–39.

12. For a discussion of how medieval thinkers could have conceived the idea that disease might be transmitted through menstrual blood or through the blood of parturition, see Danielle Jacquart and Claude Thomasset, *Sexuality and Medicine in the Middle Ages*, trans. Matthew Adamson (Princeton, N.J.: Princeton University Press, 1988 [1985]), 186–88.

13. Pseudo-Albertus, *Women's Secrets*, 112–14. "I have heard tell that a man who was lying sideways on top of the woman during sexual intercourse caused the woman to produce a child with a curved spine and a lame foot, and the deformity was attributed to the irregular position" (114).

14. See Lemay's discussion of the evolution of ideas about women from Pseudo-Albertus to the *Malleus Maleficarum*, 49–58. This is also a focus of Dyan Elliott's more extended argument in *Fallen Bodies*. Elliott also points to the way that the relaxation of pollution concerns generates its own anxieties, and she shows that notions of impurity continued to resurface in new and covert ways in medieval culture. She demonstrates the intimate and usually overlooked relationship between concerns about clerical purity, the rise of the cult of the virgin, and the promotion of the doctrine of transubstantiation, and she shows how images of pollution, sexuality, and demonology, repeated in different and shifting contexts, contributed toward the materialization of the figure of the witch (*Fallen Bodies*, esp. 6–13, 157–63). Medieval fiction certainly reimagines concerns about impurity in relation to the sacred—I will explore one example of that relationship as it is represented in grail narratives. But here I focus on another way that medieval texts interrogate impurity, and that is in relation to lineage, as part of a debate about the value of mother's blood and bloodlines.

15. However, a scene in the fourteenth-century *Siete Infantes de Lara* may symbolically refer to intercourse during menstruation. John R. Burt has suggested that when Doña Lambra throws a cucumber covered with blood at Gonzalo, she "shows him [how much she values him] subconsciously by conceiving an insult that expresses fully the depth and extent of her passion for him. She desires him so much that she would commit for him and with him the double sin of having an adulterous sexual relations with him while menstruating." "The Bloody Cucumber and Related Matters in the *Siete Infantes de Lara*," *Hispanic Review* 50 (1982): 350–51. But for a different view of this episode, see Carolyn Bluestine, "The Power of Blood in the *Siete Infantes de Lara*," *Hispanic Review* 50 (1982): 201–17. My thanks to Enrique Garcia Santo-Tomás for these references.

16. Jean Maillart, *Le roman du comte d'Anjou*, ed. Mario Roques (Paris: Champion, 1931), 104, ll. 3408–10. All translations of this romance are mine.

17. Analogues include: Geoffrey Chaucer, *The Man of Law's Tale*, in *The Riverside Chaucer*, gen. ed. Larry D. Benson (Boston: Houghton Mifflin, 1987), 89–103; Nicholas Trevet's *Cronicles*, in "Trivet's [Trevet's] Life of Constance," ed. Margaret Schlauch in *Sources and Analogues of Chaucer's Canterbury Tales*, ed. William Frank Bryan (Chicago: University of Chicago Press, 1941), 165–81; John Gower, *Confessio amantis* in *The English Works of John Gower*, ed. G. C. Macaulay,

2 vols., EETS e.s. 81, 82 (London: Oxford University Press, 1900–1901; reprint 1969), 1: 146–73; *La Manekine*, in *Oeuvres poétiques de Philippe de Rémi, Sire de Beaumanoir*, ed. Hermann Sucher, vol. 1 (Paris: Firmin Didot, 1884); *La belle Hélène de Constantinople*, ed. Claude Roussel (Geneva: Droz, 1995); a Catalan tale, "La istoria de la filla de l'emperador Contasti," ed. Hermann Suchier, *Romania* 30 (1901): 519–38; a fourteenth-century Latin tale, "Ystoria regis franchorum et filie in qua adulterium comitere voluit," ed. Hermann Suchier, *Romania* 39 (1910): 61–76. For an extended discussion of the story in its many forms, see Margaret Schlauch, *Chaucer's Constance and Accused Queens* (New York: New York University Press, 1927); and Alexandre Haggerty Krappe, "La belle Hélène de Constantinople," *Romania* 63 (1939): 324–53.

18. In these stories, the accusation of a monstrous birth is always described as evidence of the mother's corrupt bloodlines, not as a portent or as an omen. On monstrous births as portents in the ancient and medieval worlds, see John Block Friedman, *The Monstrous Races in Medieval Art and Thought* (Cambridge, Mass.: Harvard University Press, 1981), 108–15, 178–81. See also Jean Céard, *La nature et les prodiges: L'insolite au XVIe siècle, en France* (Geneva: Droz, 1977), 33–34.

19. In fact, it is the beauty of the child that saves him and his mother. In several versions of the story, the servants ordered to execute the mother and her child cannot bear to kill the beautiful laughing baby. See, for example, *Le comte d'Anjou*, ll. 4257–78.

20. Focusing on Chaucer's version of this story in *The Man of Law's Tale*, Carolyn Dinshaw reads the mother-in-law's jealousy (in *Le comte d'Anjou*, the aunt's jealousy) as a representation of the potentially incestuous desires of mothers for their sons. *Chaucer's Sexual Politics* (Madison: University of Wisconsin Press, 1989). Dinshaw is undoubtedly right, but I am interested here in exploring how the text's explanation for the enmity—the concern about lineage—leads to the accusation of monstrous birth.

21. See note 16.

22. In the representation of a desired seduction rather than a desired marriage, *Le comte d'Anjou* is like *Le roman d'Apollonius de Tyre*, though in *Apollonius* the daughter does not escape her father's attentions, and is associated in somewhat ambiguous ways to his desire. *Le roman d'Apollonius de Tyr*, ed. Michel Zink (Paris: Union Générale d'Editions, 1982), 17–37.

23. "Quer une trop grant frichon sent; / Et, se Nostre Sire consent / Que je puisse un petit süer, / Gueirie serai sanz müer, / Que ja n'en serai es lïens / Ne es mainz de fusicïens, / Qui une grant chose en feroient, / Se ce tentet de mal savoient" (*Le roman du comte d'Anjou*, ll. 601–8).

24. "Ystoria regis franchorum et filie in qua adulterium comitere voluit," 65.

25. As Elliott describes Gregory's position: "woman, even though free of personal sin, nevertheless becomes a compelling image for original sin and the fallen condition of the human body—an image of woman that would remain available throughout the Middle Ages" (*Fallen Bodies*, 4).

26. According to Charles de Miramon, the ritual is revived at the end of the eleventh century, and becomes widespread in Western Europe by around

1150. "Déconstruction et reconstruction du tabou de la femme menstruée (XII–XIIIe siècle)" in *Kontinuitäten und Zäsuren in der Europäischen Rechtsgeschichte: Europäisches Forum Junger Rechtshistorikerinnen und Rechtshistoriker, Müchen 22–24 Juli 1998* (New York: Peter Lang, 1999), 86.

27. Elliott, *Fallen Bodies*, 5.

28. David Cressy, "Purification, Thanksgiving, and the Churching of Women in Post-Reformation England," *Past and Present* 141 (1993): 108–9. However, see Peter Rushton's study of the popular notions of purification associated with the ritual in "Purification or Social Control? Ideologies of Reproduction and the Churching of Women After Childbirth," in *The Public and the Private*, ed. Eva Gamarnikow et al. (London: Heinemann, 1983), 127–31.

29. Cressy, "Purification," 110.

30. Gail McMurray Gibson, "Blessings from Sun and Moon: Churching as Women's Theater," in *Bodies and Disciplines: Intersections of Literature and History in Fifteenth-Century England*, ed. Barbara A. Hanawalt and David Wallace (Minneapolis: University of Minnesota Press, 1996), 147.

31. See Chapter 3, p. 58. For other literary examples of women who observe ritual purification after childbirth, see Chapter 3, n. 59.

The *gesine* seems to be an attribute of femaleness in the thirteenth-century *Aucassin et Nicolette*, where, in the gender-reversed world of Torelore, the queen goes off to fight a war after giving birth, while her husband lies in the childbirth bed: "Dist li rois: 'Je gis d'un fil; / quant mes mois sera conplis / et je sarai bien garis, / don't irai le messe oïr, / si com mes ancestre fist.'" *Aucassin et Nicolette; chantefable du XIIIe siècle*, ed. Mario Roques (Paris: Champion, 1925), 30.

32. "Li rois d'Escoce mande et prie / As trois qui il laissa s'amie, / Qu'en sa gesine soit gardee / Cele qui il a tant amee" (*La Manekine*, ll. 3295–98).

33. "Et les paroles li escrit / Li mauvais clers, qui a escrit, / Que li rois au senescal mande / Que il ja mais jour ne l'atende, / Se ardoir ne fait s'espousee / Si tost comme ele ert relevee" (*La manekine*, ll. 3445–50).

34. "*La mere au roy*. Osanne, n'arez pas un mois / Pour vous efforcier de jesine. / Maintenant, sanz plus de termine, / Ne sanz vous plus ici tenir, / Vous fault en autre lieu venir / Où vous menray." *Un miracle de Nostre-Dame*, in *Théatre français au moyen-age*, ed. L. J. N. Monmerqué et Francisque Michel (Paris: H. Delloye and Firmin Didot, 1839), 557.

35. "La porréz sejourner quinzaine / A l'Ostel Dieu, se savoir fectes / Que de gesir aiez souffrectes, / Quer vous n'avéz pas tant geü / Comme mestier vous a eü" (*Le roman du comte d'Anjou*, ll. 4390–94).

36. "Et du petit enfant demande / S'il est sienz. 'Certes, oïl, sire.' / —Comment, fet il, l'osez tu dire? / Il n'a pas encor trois semaines / Qu'il fu nez, et ainsi te maines? / S'il fust tienz, gesir en deüsses, / Encore lever ne peüssez. / —Sire, dit elle, or escoutéz: / Li enfez est mienz, n'en doutéz, / Mez par force m'estuet lever, / Combien qu'il me deüst grever, / Ainçoist que g'eüsse geü / Le temps qu'a gesir est deü" (*Le roman du comte d'Anjou*, ll. 4654–66).

37. "Il n'a pas douze jours entiers / Que ma fame d'enfant gesoit / D'un biau filz, si com on disoit, / Et j'estoie hors du païs" (*Le roman du comte d'Anjou*, ll. 5508–11).

38. "Que fame a autre soit piteuse, / Quant la voit povre et soufreteuse, / Mesmement quant si petit a / Que pour enfanter alita" (*Le roman du comte d'Anjou*, ll. 5545–48).

39. "Ha! chastelain, ce dit le conte, / Onques homme n'ot tant de honte, / De mesaises, de bateüres, / De fain, de froit et de laidures, / Con j'ai souffert puis mon partir. / Je ne croi pas qu'il ait martyr / En paradiz si aduré / Qui tant d'angoisse ait enduré / Sanz mort souffrir" (*Le roman du comte d'Anjou*, ll. 6483–91). The countess declines to speak of her pains and travails and prefers to remember the kindnesses of the mayor's wife, who took her in, asked when she had given birth to her child, and took care of her: "Si me mena en sa meson / Et me demanda la saison / Et le temps qu'avoie geü / De cel enfant qu'avoie eü. / Je li diz, si en fu piteuse; / Et sachiéz que molt fu soigneuse / De moi aaisier et baignier, / Car en li n'avoit qu'enseignier. / C'est ce qui me sauva la vie" (*Le roman du comte d'Anjou*, ll. 6561–69). She also recounts the kindness of the mistress of the Hotel Dieu, who knew that she had not completed her lying-in, and who bathed her and cared for her: "Tantost connut que pas n'avoie / Geü tant comme je devoie / Gesir pour mon enfantement; / Le baig fist fere vistement, / Aaisier me fist et baignier / Pour ma sancté regaaignier, / Tant qu'en bon point fui erraument" (*Le roman du comte d'Anjou*, ll. 6609–15).

40. The bishop thinks she is more beautiful than Paris and Helen—a curious comparison (ll. 4651–53).

41. However, the mother's reconciliation with her husband is not unlike the way that churching functioned for unmarried or improperly married women as a moment in which she might publicly repent of her sin and thereby receive permission to be churched (the ritual was forbidden to unmarried women), and through churching take her place as a member of the community. Paula M. Reider, "The Implications of Exclusion: The Regulation of Churching in Medieval Northern France," *Essays in Medieval Studies* 15 (1999): 76.

42. Cited by Clarissa W. Atkinson, *The Oldest Vocation: Christian Motherhood in the Middle Ages* (Ithaca, N.Y.: Cornell University Press, 1991), 60. Christiane Klapish-Zuber emphasizes the tension between concerns about lineage and concerns about the characteristics transmitted by milk in the context of wet-nursing in Italy. *Women, Family and Ritual in Renaissance Italy*, trans. Lydia Cochran (Chicago: University of Chicago Press, 1985), 161–62.

43. Cited by Carolyn A. Nadeau, "Blood Mother/Milk Mother: Breastfeeding, the Family, and the State in Antonio de Guevara's *Relox de Príncipes* (*Dial of Princes*)," *Hispanic Review* 69 (2001): 155–56.

44. Miri Rubin, *Gentile Tales; The Narrative Assault on Late Medieval Jews* (New Haven, Conn.: Yale University Press, 1999), 99. Rubin notes that this report raises the problem of the exact nature of how and whether the host was digested and disposed from the body. *Corpus Christi: The Eucharist in Late Medieval Culture* (Cambridge: Cambridge University Press, 1991), 37–38.

45. Atkinson cites the example of Katarina of Sweden, *The Oldest Vocation*, 60, 180. See also Donald Weinstein and Rudolph M. Bell, *Saints and Society: The Two Worlds of Western Christendom, 1000–1700* (Chicago: University of Chicago Press, 1982), 24–25.

46. "Bien cuide qu'il soit deceü / Et qu'il ait prise unne meschine / De bas lieu et de basse orine / Dont li enfant soient vilain" (*Le roman du comte d'Anjou*, ll. 3048–51).

47. "Unne autre lectre a fet escrire / Par un sien frere chappelain / Sous le non au bon chastelain, / Par quoi au conte senefie / Qu'il devoit bien haïr sa vie, / Qui est de lingnage royal / Et prise a la plus desloial / Fame qui puist morir ne vivre; / Et que n'a pas esté delivre / De droite humaine criature" (*Le roman du comte d'Anjou*, ll. 3398–3407).

48. Though as Laura D. Barefield has shown, while Trevet situates Constance in a "birth narrative that is seldom told in chronicle, explaining the feminine part in producing an heir and in creating and connecting lineage," Chaucer consistently minimalizes her genealogical context and the influence or even power she might derive from it. "Reproducing the Past: Gender and History in Later Middle English Romance and Chronicle," dissertation, University of Wisconsin, 1998, 140. See also Barefield's "Women's Power in the 'Tale of Constance," *Medieval Perspectives* 15 (2000): 27–43.

The Chaucer, Trevet, and Gower versions of the story are different from those cited above in that they do not begin with incest narratives. On this difference, see discussion in Phillip Wynn, "The Conversion Story in Nicholas Trevet's 'Tale of Constance,'" *Viator* 13 (1984): 259–62, esp. 259, n. 3. Carolyn Dinshaw notes that Chaucer's story legitimizes unwanted sexual desire by transferring it from the father to the sultan and that the narrative context is thus "made fully patriarchal: proper marriage is arranged; dynasties are consolidated; heathens are converted" (*Chaucer's Sexual Politics*, 101).

49. Trevet, 172. My translation.

50. For another example of copulation with a demonic being and monstrous offspring, see Jeffrey Jerome Cohen's discussion of *The Anonymous Riming Chronicle* in *Of Giants: Sex, Monsters, and the Middle Ages* (Minneapolis: University of Minnesota Press, 1999), 47–50.

51. Gower, too, makes the wife a fairy ("Thi wife, which is of faierie," [*Confessio Amantis*, 1: 156, ll. 964]).

52. Wynn situates the first conversion episode historically, linking it to a conversion story recounted in an early medieval chronicle entitled *Annales Eutychii* ("The Conversion Story," 265–74). I am suggesting that while the conversion story may be based on a historical story of conversion from Islam to Christianity, the focus on lineage and bloodlines may reflect an anxiety more closely associated with Christian ideas about the impurity threatened by intimate contact with Jews.

53. David Nirenberg, *Communities of Violence: Persecution of Minorities in the Middle Ages* (Princeton, N.J.: Princeton University Press, 1996), 127–65. Nirenberg notes that for Maimonides, miscegenation violated the prohibition against intercourse during menstruation, since "the Sages have decreed that all heathens, whether male or female, are to be regarded as in a permanent state of flux insofar as cleanness and uncleanness are concerned, whether they actually have a flux or not" (134–35).

54. James A. Brundage, "Intermarriage Between Christians and Jews in Medieval Canon Law," *Jewish History* 3, 1 (1988): 31. For a history of the Jewish prohibition of intermarriage, see Shaye J. D. Cohen, *The Beginnings of Jewishness: Boundaries, Varieties, Uncertainties* (Berkeley: University of California Press, 1999), 241–62.

55. In only one version of the story does the father admit that he might have engendered the monstrous child. In *La belle Hélène de Constantinople* the father blames himself: "Pour quoy ne pot mon corps engenrer bien enfant? / Comment font autre gent, chevalier et sergant?" (*La belle Hélène*, ll. 2974–75).

56. "il durement resembla sa mere" (Trevet, 179).

57. *Chaucer's Sexual Politics*, 109.

58. Gower writes that "The king his chiere upon him caste, / And in his face him thoghte als faste / He sih his oghne wif Constance; / For nature as in resemblance / Of face hem liketh so to clothe, / That thei were of a suite bothe" (*Confessio Amantis*, 1: 167, ll. 1373–78).

Chapter 5. The Scene of Parturition

1. "Blood: Cultural Effectiveness of Biological Conditions," in *Sex and Gender Hierarchies*, ed. Barbara Diane Miller (Cambridge: Cambridge University Press, 1993), 84.

2. Pseudo-Albertus, *Women's Secrets: A Translation of Pseudo-Albertus Magnus's* De secretis mulierum *with Commentaries*, trans. Helen Rodnite Lemay (Albany, N.Y.: SUNY Press, 1992), 65.

3. Luke Demaitre and Anthony A. Travill, "Human Embryology and Development in the Works of Albertus Magnus," *Albertus Magnus and the Sciences; Commemorative Essays 1980*, ed. James A. Weisheipl, Studies and Texts 49 (Toronto: Pontifical Institute of Mediaeval Studies, 1980), 416. See also 417–20 on the nature of female and male contributions to conception.

4. Joan Cadden, *Meanings of Sex Difference in the Middle Ages: Medicine, Science and Culture* (Cambridge: Cambridge University Press, 1993), 78–80.

5. "The mooder was an elf, by aventure / Ycomen, by charmes or by sorcerie." *Man of Law's Tale*, in *The Riverside Chaucer*, 3rd ed., gen. ed. Larry Benson (Boston: Houghton Mifflin, 1987), ll. 754–55. Gower, too, makes the wife a fairy : "Thi wife, which is of faierie." *Confessio Amantis* in *The English Works of John Gower*, ed. G. C. Macaulay, 2 vols., EETS e.s. 81, 82 (Oxford: Oxford University Press, 1969 [1900–1901]), 1: 156, l. 964.

6. Jean d'Arras's *Roman de Melusine* was written in prose between 1387 and 1394, and was commissioned by Jean, Duke of Berry, and his sister, Marie, Duchess of Bar. Jean claimed to have found the story in documents provided by the duke and his sister. Jean d'Arras, *Mélusine; Roman du XIVe siècle*, ed. Louis Stouff (Dijon: Publications de l'Université de Dijon, 1932). A second version, closely following the first, but in verse, was composed by the Parisian bookseller Coudrette between 1401 and 1405. *Le roman de Mélusine ou Histoire de Lusignan*

par Coudrette, ed. Eleanor Roach (Paris: Klincksieck, 1982). Coudrette's romance was translated into English and German in the fifteenth century: Thüring von Ringoltingen, *Melusine*, ed. Karin Schneider (Berlin: E. Schmidt, 1958); *The Romans of Partenay, or of Lusignen: Otherwise know as the Tale of Melusine*, ed. Walter W. Skeat, EETS o.s. 22 (London: Kegan Paul, 1899; rpt. New York: Greenwood Press, 1969).

7. Léo Desaivre, *Le mythe de la mère Lusine: Etude critique et bibliographique* (Saint Maixent: Renversé, 1883), 107.

8. The mother's monstrous legacy does not, however, form a monstrous race, as in the example of maternity and monstrosity discussed by Jeffrey Jerome Cohen, *Of Giants: Sex, Monsters, and the Middle Ages* (Minneapolis: University of Minnesota Press, 1999), 48–49.

9. On Gervaise of Tilbury and various other versions of the woman-serpent story, see Jacques LeGoff and Emmanuel Le Roy Ladurie, "Mélusine maternelle et défricheuse," *Annales: Economies, Sociétés, Civilisations* 26 (1971): 587–90.

10. Marie de Frances, *Lais*, ed. Jean Rychner (Paris: Champion, 1966), 76–77, ll. 143–50.

11. ". . . je vous entend a traictier comment la noble et puissant forteresse de Lisignen en Poictou fu fondee par une faee, et la maniere comment, selon la juste cronique et la vraye histoire, sans y appliquer chose qui ne soit veritable et just de la propre matiere" (Jean d'Arras, *Le roman de Mélusine*, 4–5).

12. Coudrette does not begin his narrative with the story of Presine and Helinas, he recounts this episode only late in the story when Mélusine's son, Geoffrey, discovers the tomb of his grandfather, Helinas.

13. *Le roman de Mélusine*, 255. This is the only point in the text where Mélusine's supernatural nature is characterized as malefic, as Sara Sturm-Maddox notes in "Crossed Destinies: Narrative Programs in the *Roman de Mélusine*," in *Melusine of Lusignan: Founding Fiction in Late Medieval France*, ed. Donald Maddox and Sara Sturm-Maddox (Athens: University of Georgia Press, 1996), 24.

14. Douglas Kelly characterizes the monstrous characteristics of Mélusine's sons as mother-marks, marks left on the child by strong emotions during pregnancy or, as in the case of Mélusine, as sign of the child's marvelous parent. "The Domestication of the Marvelous in the Melusine Romances," in *Melusine of Lusignan*, 39–40. He also argues that the characteristics of the sons suggest a progress in Mélusine's transformation into a human. Her youngest sons are not marked like their siblings and they are not emotionally or morally unstable (34–35).

15. Jane H. M. Taylor stresses the extent to which the narrative contains and neutralizes the supernatural origins of Mélusine's children ("Melusine's Progeny: Patterns and Perplexities," in *Melusine of Lusignan*, 180–81).

16. "Maternity and Monstrosity: Reproductive Biology in the *Roman de Melusine*," in *Melusine de Lusignan*, 108.

17. *The Generation of Animals*, in *The Complete Works of Aristotle: The Revised Oxford Translation*, ed. Jonathan Barnes, vol. 1, Bollingen Series 71.2 (Princeton, N.J.: Princeton University Press, 1984), 584b, 28. Cited by Spiegel, "Maternity and Monstrosity," 103–4. Spiegel sees the monstrosity of multiple births as the reason for Presine's interdiction to see her in the childbirth bed.

18. "Maternity and Monstrosity," 104. See also Jean Céard, *La nature et les prodiges. L'insolite au XVIe siècle, en France* (Geneva: Droz, 1977), 5.

19. The forged letter poses as a letter from the husband to his own father: "Serenissimo mio padre prudente / Per quello Idio che governa ogn'imperio, / Mi truovo più ch'i'fussi mai dolente / Considerando come d'adulterio / Ha fatto duo figliuo' la fradulente. / Fagil morir, come è mio desiderio, / Et la lor madre; voglia cmpiacermi; / Quanto che no, pensa non mai vedermi." "Rappresentazione de Stella," in *Sacre rappresentazione dei siecoli XIV, XV, e XVI*, ed. Alessandro d'Ancona, 3 vols. (Florence: Le Monnier, 1872), 3: 346.

20. Marie de France, *Lais*, 44–60; *Le roman du chevalier au cygne et Godefroid de Bouillon*, ed. M. le Baron de Reiffenberg and M. A. Borgnet, 3 vols. (Brussels: Hayez, 1846–54), 1: ll. 214–22, 338–70. See also *The Romance of the Chevelere Assigne*, ed. Henry H. Gibbs, EETS e.s. 6 (London: Oxford University Press, 1868; reprint Millwood, N.Y.: Kraus Reprints, 1975), ll. 60–65.

21. Jean-Jacques Vincensini has studied the interdictions in *Le roman de Mélusine* in the context of folklore and of other kind of interdictions. He locates the importance of the Melusinian interdictions in the way that they construct and disrupt communication, and make visible linguistic and perceptual discontinuities. *Pensée mythique et narrations médiévales* (Paris: Champion, 1996), 182–88.

22. *Le folklore obscène des enfants* (Paris: Maisonneuve et Larose, 1980), cited by Michèle Perret, trans., *Le roman de Mélusine ou l'Histoire de Lusignan* (Paris: Editions Stock, 1979), 326. The association of women, water, menstruation and purification is also made with reference to Mélusine by Danielle Jacquart and Claude Thomasset. *Sexuality and Medicine in the Middle Ages*, trans. Matthew Adamson (Princeton, N.J.: Princeton University Press, 1988), 74.

23. Heldris de Cornäuille, *Le roman de Silence*, ed. Lewis Thorpe (Cambridge: Heffer, 1972), ll. 2000–2008.

24. Gail McMurray Gibson, "Scene and Obscene: Seeing and Performing Late Medieval Childbirth," *Journal of Medieval and Early Modern Studies* 29, 1 (1999): 9. Gibson's study of the cultural performance of childbirth demonstrates the way that public transgressions of the secluded space of pregnancy and childbirth disrupt gender categories. My own focus is a little different: I want to interrogate the different ways that fictions imagine the interdiction of the childbirth scene. See also Gibson's "Blessings from Sun and Moon: Churching as Women's Theater," *Bodies and Disciplines: Intersections of Literature and History in Fifteenth-Century England*, ed. Barbara A. Hanawalt and David Wallace (Minneapolis: University of Minnesota Press, 1996), 149.

25. Chrétien de Troyes, *Guillaume d'Angleterre*, ed. Maurice Wilmotte (Paris: Champion, 1927), ll. 473–78.

26. I am very grateful to Leslie Zarker Morgan for bringing the Beves narratives and their birth scenes to my attention.

27. *Der Anglonormannische Boeve de Haumtone*, ed. Albert Stimming, Bibliotheca Normannica 7 (Halle: Niemeyer, 1899), ll. 2690–2710.

28. "Syr Buys dyd hyr seruyce bede, / Fo to helpe hyr at hyr nede; / 'Gramarcy, syr,' she sayde, 'nay,' / For goddys loue go hens away, / Go and sport you

wyth Terry / And late me worke and our lady: / Shal neuer womans pryuete / To man be shewed for me!'" *The Romance of Sir Beues of Hamtoun*, ed. Eugen Kölbing, EETS e.s. 46, 48, 65 (London: N. Trübner, 1885–94; reprint in one vol., Millwood, N.Y.: Kraus Reprints, 1978), 2: 171, version x, ll. 3367–74.

29. "Seur," che dist Bueves, "je n'os a vous aler / Ne vos dolors vëir ne esgarder / Ne de mes mains toucier ne adeser." *Der Festländische Bueve de Hantone, Fassung 1*, ed. Albert Stimming, Gesellschaft für Romanische Literatur 25 (Dresden: Gedruckt für die Gesellschaft für romanische Literatur, 1911), ll. 7044–49.

30. *Der Festländische Bueve de Hantone, Fassung 1*, ll. 7050–95. A similar version of the childbirth scene is recounted in the version known as Continental 3, ed. Albert Stimming in *Der Festländische Bueve de Hantone, fassung 3*, Gesellschaft für Romanische Literatur 34 (Dresden: Gedruckt für die Gesellschaft für romanische Literatur, 1914), ll. 8736 ff.

31. "Sí come piacque a Dio, a pena avevano compiout di fare gli alloggiamenti, che Drusiana [as Josiane is called in the Italian version] due partorí figliuoli maschi, e Buovo l'aiutava il meglio che poteva e sapeva." Andrea da Barberino, *I reali de Francia*, ed. Giuseppe Vandelli and Giovanni Gambarin (Bari: Giuseppe Laterza and Sons, 1947), book 4: xxxvi, 351). On the seven Italian versions of the story, particularly in relation to Charlemagne narratives, see Leslie Zarker Morgan, "*Bovo d'Antona* in the *Geste Francor* (V 13): Unity of Composition and Clan Destiny," *Italian Culture* 16,2 (1998): 15–38. For the Old French version that does not recount any interdiction to see the childbirth, see *Der Festländische Bueve de Hantone, Fassung 2*, ed. Albert Stimming, Gesellschaft für romanische Literatur 30 (Dresden: Gedruckt für die Gesellschaft für romanische Literatur, 1912), ll. 11527–45.

32. Myriam Greilsammer, *L'envers du tableau; Mariage et maternité en Flandre médiévale* (Paris: Armand Colin, 1990), 223–53. See also Renate Blumenfeld-Kosinski's discussion in *Not of Woman Born: Representations of Caesarean Birth in Medieval and Renaissance Culture* (Ithaca, N.Y.: Cornell University Press, 1990), 15–21, 61–74, 102–3.

33. "Mais de çou est moult esmarie / Que de feme n'a point d'aïe, / Don't ele grant mestier eüst, / Qui mix d'ome aidier li seüst. / Mais tant estoient de gent loing / Que nule feme a cest besoing / N'i peüst mie a tans venir; / S'en estuet le roi convenir" (*Guillaume d'Angleterre*, ll. 465–72).

34. Jacques Gélis asks whether we should "connect repugnance with regard to childbirth to the 'bad blood' which issued forth at such times and which, as everyone knew, was 'impure and corrosive,' like menstrual blood?" *History of Childbirth: Fertility, Pregnancy and Birth in Early Modern Europe*, trans. Rosemary Morris (Boston: Northeastern University Press, 1991), 107.

35. For other societies that hold the fetus to be composed wholly or in part from menstrual blood, see Thomas Buckley and Alma Gottlieb, "A Critical Appraisal of Theories of Menstrual Symbolism," in *Blood Magic: The Anthropology of Menstruation*, ed. Buckley and Gottlieb (Berkeley: University of California Press, 1988), 259, n. 8.

36. *The Body in Pain: The Making and Unmaking of the World* (New York: Oxford University Press, 1985), 188.

Chapter 6. The Grail and Its Hosts

1. Miri Rubin, *Corpus Christi: The Eucharist in Late Medieval Culture* (Cambridge: Cambridge University Press 1991).

2. For studies of the representation of the eucharist in grail romances, see Etienne Gilson, "La mystique de la grace dans *La queste del saint graal*," *Romania* 51 (1925): 321–47; Eugène Anitchkof, "Le saint graal et les rites eucharistiques," *Romania* 55 (1929): 174–94; William Roach, "Eucharistic Tradition in the *Perlesvaus*," *Zeitscrift für Romanische Philologie* 59 (1939): 10–56; W.E.M.C. Hamilton, "L'interprétation mystique de *La queste del saint graal*," *Neophilologus* 27 (1942): 94–110; Myrrha Lot-Borodine, "Le symbolisme du graal dans l'*Estoire del saint graal*," *Neophilologus* 34 (1950): 65–79, and "Les apparitions du Christ aux messes de l'*Estoire* et de la *Queste del saint graal*," *Romania* 72 (1951): 202–23.

3. Chrétien de Troyes, *Le roman de Perceval, ou, Le conte du graal*, ed. Keith Busby (Tübingen: Niemeyer, 1992), l. 3513. Only in the *Perlesvaus* is the grail king's infirmity not explicitly linked to a wound: in this text the king suffers from a mysterious illness, a "*langor.*" *Le haut livre du Graal, Perlesvaus*, ed. William A. Nitze and T. Atkinson Jenkins, 2 vols. (Chicago: University of Chicago Press, 1932), 1: 116. My translations.

4. As, for example, in the *Estoire del saint graal* and Wolfram von Eschenbach's *Parzival*, both of which I discuss below.

5. On the gendering of the figure of Christ in the eucharist in the *Queste*, see E. Jane Burns, "Devilish Ways: Sexing the Subject in the *Queste del saint graal*," *Arthuriana* 8, 2 (1998): 16–18.

6. Miri Rubin, *Corpus Christi*, 136. Roach traces the development of this representation in "Eucharistic Tradition in the *Perlesvaus*."

7. On the form of the grail in the *Estoire del saint graal* and earlier romances, see Carol Chase, "The Vision of the Grail in the *Estoire del saint graal*," *Old and New Philologies. Essays in Honor of Peter Florian Dembowski*, ed. Joan Tasker Grimbert and Carol Chase (forthcoming). I am grateful to Carol Chase for sharing this essay with me before its publication.

8. *L'estoire del saint graal*, ed. Jean Paul Ponceau, 2 vols. (Paris: Champion, 1997). My translations throughout. The *Estoire* has long been thought to postdate the *Queste del saint graal*. See Michelle Szkilnik, *L'archipel du graal: Etude de l'*Estoire del saint graal (Geneva: Droz, 1991), 2–3. However Ponceau dates the romance to the third decade of the thirteenth century, and claims it was composed before or at about the same time as the *Queste* (Ponceau, *L'estoire del saint graal*, xi–xiv).

9. Chase discusses the relationship between *L'estoire* and the verse and prose versions of the twelfth-century *Joseph d'Arimathie* attributed to Robert de Boron ("The Vision of the Grail," typescript, 1–4).

10. Szkilnik describes the trials of the voyage from Orient to Occident as a series of rites of passage, a formulation that captures the ritualistic and symbolic nature of action in this romance as well as the movement and displacement that she analyzes (*L'archipel du graal*, 27).

11. See Colette-Anne Van Coolput, "La poupée d'Evalac ou la conversion

tardive du roi Mondrain," in *Continuations: Essays on Medieval French Literature and Language in Honor of John L. Grigsby*, ed. Norris J. Lacy and Gloria Torrini-Roblin (Birmingham, Al.: Summa, 1989), 163–72. Carol Chase suggests that the Evalach's statue recalls the decorated statues of the Virgin in medieval churches, and she convincingly suggests that Evalac's statue may be a transposition of a Christian image into a pagan context. "Des Sarrasins à Camaalot," *Cahiers de recherches médiévales (XIIIe–XVe s.)* 5 (1998): 50–51.

12. See my "Chaste Subjects: Gender, Heroism, and Desire in the Grail Quest," in *Queering the Middle Ages*, ed. Glenn Burger and Steven F. Kruger (Minneapolis: University of Minnesota Press, 2001), 123–42; and Burns, "Devilish Ways," 11–32.

13. Other men wounded in the thigh in the *Estoire* include Ganor, who dreams he is wounded by a wild boar (436–37); Joseph himself, who is wounded by an enemy (464–501); King Arfasan, wounded in battle (563–64); and King Pellehan, the Roi Mehaigné, also wounded in battle (566).

14. Wolfram von Eschenbach, *Parzival*, trans. A. T. Hatto (London: Penguin, 1980), 244.

15. *Sone von Nausay*, ed. Moritz Goldschmidt (Tübingen: Litterarischer Verein in Stuttgart, 1899), ll. 4769–76, 4855–56.

16. *The Elucidation: A Prologue to the Conte du graal*, ed. Albert Wilder Thompson (New York: Institute of French Studies, 1931).

17. Mary Douglas notes that in Leviticus "the Hebrew word for thigh, referring to the femur of the body, is displaced euphemistically to the genital organs." *Leviticus as Literature* (Oxford: Oxford University Press, 1999), 56. Howard Eilberg-Schwartz notes the use of the thigh as a metaphor for the male organ in the J narrative in Genesis, and gives examples of descriptions of children issuing from the thigh in Genesus, Exodus and Judges. *The Savage in Judaism: An Anthropology of Israelite Religion and Ancient Judaism* (Bloomington: Indiana University Press, 1990), 168.

18. On the representation of Saracens in this romance, see Chase, "Des Sarrasins à Camaalot," 43–53, and on the conversion of women and the continuation of lineages through converted Saracen women, see Chase's "La conversion des païennes dans l'*Estoire del saint graal*," in *Arthurian Romance and Gender*, ed. Fredriech Wolfzettel (Atlanta: Rodopi, 1995): 251–64, esp. 257, 261–62.

19. On the development of this characterization in Latin texts, see Jeremy Cohen, "The Jews as Killers of Christ in the Latin Tradition, from Augustine to the Friars," *Traditio* 39 (1983): 1–27.

20. Irven M. Resnick, "Medieval Roots of the Myth of Jewish Male Menses," *Harvard Theological Review* 93 (2000): 252.

21. Willis Johnson, "The Myth of Jewish Male Menses," *Journal of Medieval History* 24,3 (1998): 275.

22. Peter Biller, "Views of Jews from Paris Around 1300: Christian or 'Scientific'?" *Studies in Church History* 29 (1992): 192.

23. Arnold of Villanova, *Opera Omnia, cum Nicolai Taurelli Medici et philosophi in quosdam libros annotationibus* (Basel, 1585), cited and translated by

Johnson, "The Myth of Jewish Male Menses," 289. Roger de Baron concurs: "just as women menstruate each month, so some men suffer from the hemorrhoidal flux each month, some four times a year, some once a year. This flux ought not to be restrained, because it cleans the body of many superfluities." Roger de Baron, *Pratica maior* (Venice, 1519), cited and translated by Monica H. Green, ed. and trans., *The Trotula: A Medieval Compendium of Women's Medicine* (Philadelphia: University of Pennsylvania Press, 2001), 215, n.82. See also Danielle Jacquart and Claude Thomasset, *Sexuality and Medicine in the Middle Ages*, trans. Matthew Adamson (Princeton, N.J.: Princeton University Press, 1988), 73. For early modern views of the positive medical value of male menstruation, see Gianna Pomata, "Menstruating Men: Similarity and Difference of the Sexes in Early Modern Medicine," in *Generation and Degeneration: Tropes of Reproduction in Literature and History from Antiquity to Early Modern Europe*, ed. Valeria Finucci and Kevin Brownlee (Durham, N.C.: Duke University Press, 2001), 109–52.

24. Green, *Trotula*, 20; Johnson, "The Myth of Male Menses," 289.

25. *History of Jerusalem*, cited by Resnick, "Medieval Roots," 259. For the early modern belief that Jewish men menstruated, see David S. Katz, "Shylock's Gender: Jewish Male Menstruation in Early Modern England," *Review of English Studies* n.s. 50, 200 (1999): 440–62; and James Shapiro, *Shakespeare and the Jews* (New York: Columbia University Press, 1996), 38.

26. Joshua Trachtenberg, *The Devil and the Jews: The Medieval Conception of the Jews and Its Relation to Modern Antisemitism* (New Haven, Conn.: Yale University Press, 1943), 50 and 148.

27. Dyan Elliott, *Fallen Bodies: Pollution, Sexuality, and Demonology in the Middle Ages* (Philadelphia: University of Pennsylvania Press, 1999).

28. "Rewriting Perceval's Sister: Eucharistic Vision and Typological Destiny in the *Queste del San Graal*," *Women's Studies* 21 (1992): 211–14.

29. Chase, "La conversion des païennes," 261–62.

30. Dyan Elliott, "Pollution, Illusion, and Masculine Disarry: Nocturnal Emissions and the Sexuality of the Clergy," in *Constructing Medieval Sexuality*, ed. Karma Lochrie, Peggy McCracken, and James A. Schultz (Minneapolis: University of Minnesota Press, 1997), 16.

31. Johnson emphasizes that medieval accounts of Jewish men's bleeding are accounts of an illness ("The Myth of Jewish Male Menses," 290).

32. "das heisse Sündenblut entquillt, / ewig erneu't aus des Sehnen's Quelle, / das, ach! keine Büssung je mir stillt!" *Parsifal: A Festival-Drama by Richard Wagner*, trans. M. H. Glyn (London: Shott, n.d.), 24. Linda Hutcheon and Michael Hutcheon explain the wound as a syphilitic sore. *Opera: Desire, Disease, Death* (Lincoln: University of Nebraska Press, 1996), 61–93. I am interested here not in the nineteenth-century medical context of the opera, but in its representation of medieval mystical contexts.

33. "Amfortas! / Die Wunde! Die Wunde! / Sie brennt in meinem Herzen . . . Die Wunde sah' ich bluten: / nun blutet sie mir selbst." *Parsifal*, 42.

34. *Parsifal*, dir. Hans Jürgen Syberberg, TMS Film (München), 1982.

35. For the idea that Amfortas's blood is like menstrual flow in Wagner's rendition of the story, see Norma M. Darr, "Reading the Body and Blood of Parsifal: A Performance at Hellerau," *Music Quarterly* 80, 4 (1996): 636.

36. "The Wound Is Healed Only by the Spear That Smote You': The Operatic Subject and Its Vicissitudes," *Opera Through Other Eyes*, ed. David Levin (Stanford, Calif.: Stanford University Press, 1993), 196.

37. Caroline Walker Bynum, *Jesus as Mother: Studies in the Spirituality of the High Middle Ages* (Berkeley: University of California Press, 1982), 161, 129–69; *Holy Feast and Holy Fast: The Religious Significance of Food to Medieval Women* (Berkeley: University of California Press, 1987), esp. 150–86; "The Female Body and Religious Practice in the Later Middle Ages," in *Fragmentation and Redemption: Essays on Gender and the Human Body in Medieval Religion* (New York: Urzone, 1989), 186–88.

38. Karma Lochrie, "Mystical Acts, Queer Tendencies," in *Constructing Medieval Sexuality*, 189, citing Wolfgang Riehle, *The Middle English Mystics*, trans. Bernard Standring (London: Routledge and Kegan Paul, 1981), 46. See also David Aers's discussion of James of Milan's *Stimulus Amoris* in relation to Julian of Norwich's *Revelation of Love* in Aers and Lynn Staley, *The Powers of the Holy: Religion, Politics, and Gender in Late Medieval English Culture* (University Park.: Pennsylvania State University Press, 1996), 91–103.

39. Lochrie, "Mystical Acts," 194.

Conclusion: Bleeding for Love

1. "The Personal Letters Between Abelard and Heloise," ed. J. T. Muckle, *Mediaeval Studies* 15 (1953): 90–91; Betty Radice, *The Letters of Abelard and Heloise*, trans. Betty Radice (New York: Penguin, 1974), 150; Janice Delaney, Mary Jane Lupton, and Emily Toth, *The Curse: A Cultural History of Menstruation* (Urbana: University of Illinois Press, 1988).

2. Nancy G. Sirasi provides a discussion of the medieval practice of phlebotomy in *Medieval and Early Renaissance Medicine: An Introduction to Knowledge and Practice* (Chicago: University of Chicago Press, 1990), 137–41.

3. Peter Brain, *Galen on Bloodletting; A Study of the Origins, Development and Validity of his Opinions, with a Translation of the Three Works* (Cambridge: Cambridge University Press, 1986), 1–15. For an overview of representations of bloodletting in medieval fiction, see Eve Derrien, "Le sang et la saignée dans le roman médieval en vers," *Lettres Romanes* 51, 1–2 (1997): 3–18.

4. Brain points to the anomalous position of blood, which unlike the other three humors is not seen as a pathological substance (*Galen on Bloodletting*, 7–8). See also Sirasi, *Medieval and Early Renaissance Medicine*, 105–6.

5. Brain, *Galen on Bloodletting*, 11.

6. Brain, *Galen on Bloodletting*, 25–26.

7. *Medieval and Early Renaissance Medicine*, 115.

8. Marie de France, *The Lais of Marie de France*, trans. Glyn S. Burgess and Keith Busby (New York: Penguin, 1999), 57.

9. Marie de France, *Lais*, ed. Jean Rychner (Paris: Champion, 1966), 35.

10. Lovesickness is not merely a literary invention; see Mary Wack, *Lovesickness in the Middle Ages: The Viaticum and Its Commentaries* (Philadelphia: University of Pennsylvania Press, 1990).

11. On the bath as a symbolic object that commemorates a negative reciprocity, see Donald Maddox, *Fictions of Identity in Medieval France* (Cambridge: Cambridge University Press, 2000), 45–46. Maddox notes that the lady's plot provides a central transition in the lai; I am interested in the way the plot transforms the false privacy of bleeding (which allows the king to meet his lover) into the actual practice of bleeding (which unites the king with his seneschal). John M. Bowers offers a convincing reading of the influence of medieval notions of trial by ordeal on Marie's use of the scalding bath in "Ordeals, Privacy, and the *Lais* of Marie de France," *Journal of Medieval and Renaissance Studies* 14, 1 (1994): 16–20.

12. On Marie's judgment of courtly love in this lai, see Robert B. Green, "Fin'amors dans deux lais de Marie de France: *Equitan* et *Chaitivel*," *Le Moyen Age* 81 (1975): 265–72.

13. "New Philology and Old French," *Speculum* 65, 1 (1990): 38–58.

14. Because of Marie's emphasis on bleeding as a therapeutic procedure, I cannot agree with Green's claim that the repeated bleedings are a symbol of the king's growing weakness ("Fin'amors dans deux lais de Marie de France," 269).

15. Green, "Fin'amors dans deux lais de Marie de France," 267; Maddox, *Fictions of Identity*, 46

Bibliography

Primary Texts

Abelard. See Heloise.

Ami et Amile, chanson de geste. Ed. Peter F. Dembowski. Paris: Champion, 1969.

Amis and Amiloun. Ed. Eugen Kölbing. Heilbronn: Henninger, 1884.

Amis and Amiloun. Ed. MacEdward Leach. EETS o.s. 203. London: Oxford University Press, 1937.

Andrea da Barberino. *I reali di Francia*. Ed. Giuseppe Vandelli and Giovanni Gambarin. Bari: Giuseppe Laterza and Sons, 1947.

Ansëys de Mes According to Ms. N (Bibliothèque de l'Arsenal 3143). Ed. Herman J. Green. Paris: Les Presses Modernes, 1939.

Der Anglonormannische Boeve de Haumtone. Ed. Albert Stimming. Bibliotheca Normannica 7. Halle: Niemeyer, 1899.

Aristotle. *On the Generation of Animals*. In *The Complete Works of Aristotle: The Revised Oxford Translation*. Ed. Jonathan Barnes. Vol. 1. Bollingen Series 71, 2. Princeton, N.J.: Princeton University Press, 1984.

Aucassin et Nicolette; chantefable du XIIIe siècle. Ed. Mario Roques. Paris: Champion, 1925.

Bar, Francis. *Les épitres latines de Raoul le Tourtier (1065?–1114?): Etude de sources, La légende d'Ami et Amile*. Paris: Droz, 1937.

La belle Hélène de Constantinople; chanson de geste du XIVe siècle. Ed. Claude Roussel. Geneva: Droz, 1995.

Béroul. *The Romance of Tristan*. Ed. and trans. Norris J. Lacy. Garland Library of Medieval Literature Series A, 36. New York: Garland, 1989.

Carr, Caleb. *The Angel of Darkness*. New York: Random House, 1997.

Chaucer, Geoffrey. *The Riverside Chaucer*. 3rd ed. Gen. ed. Larry Benson. Boston: Houghton Mifflin, 1987.

The Chester Mystery Cycle. Ed. R. M. Lumiansky and David Mills. 2 vols. EETS s.s. 3, 6. London: Oxford, 1974–86.

Le Chevalier au cygne et Godefroid de Bouillon. Ed. M. le Baron de Reiffenberg and M. A. Borgnet. 3 vols. Brussels: Hayez, 1846–54.

Chrétien de Troyes. *Le chevalier de la charrete*. Ed. Mario Roques. Paris: Champion, 1958.

————. *The Complete Romances of Chrétien de Troyes*. Trans. David Staines. Bloomington: Indiana University Press, 1990.

————. *Guillaume d'Angleterre*. Ed. Maurice Wilmotte. Paris: Champion, 1927.

————. *Philomena*. Ed. Anne Berthelot. In *Oeuvres complètes*. Gen. ed. Daniel Poirion. Paris: Gallimard, 1994. 917–52.

————. *Le roman de Perceval, ou, Le conte du graal*. Ed. Keith Busby. Tübingen: Niemeyer, 1993.

The Continuations of the Old French Perceval of Chrétien de Troyes. Ed. William Roach. 5 vols. Philadelphia: University of Pennsylvania Press and the American Philosophical Society, 1949–83.

Cooper, Alice. *Welcome to My Nightmare*. Atlantic Recording Corporation, 1975.

Coudrette. *Le roman de Mélusine ou L'Histoire de Lusignan par Coudrette*. Ed. Eleanor Roach. Paris: Klincksieck, 1982.

Eidelberg, Shlomo, ed. and trans. *The Jews and the Crusaders: The Hebrew Chronicles of the First and Second Crusade*. Hoboken, N.J.: KTAV Publishing, 1996.

The Élucidation: A Prologue to the Conte du graal. Ed. Albert Wilder Thompson. New York: Institute of French Studies, 1931.

Eneas, roman du XIIe siècle. Ed. J.-J. Salverda de Grave. 2 vols. Paris: Champion, 1925–29.

L'estoire del saint graal. Ed. Jean-Paul Ponceau. 2 vols. Paris: Champion, 1997.

Der Festländische Bueve de Hantone, Fassung 1. Ed. Albert Stimming. Gesellschaft für Romanische Literatur 25. Dresden: Gedruckt für die Gesellschaft für romanische Literatur, 1911.

Der Festländische Bueve de Hantone, Fassung 2. Ed. Albert Stimming. Gesellschaft für Romanische Literatur 30. Dresden: Gedruckt für die Gesellschaft für romanische Literatur, 1912.

Der Festländische Bueve de Hantone, Fassung 3. Ed. Albert Stimming. Gesellschaft für Romanische Literatur 34. Dresden: Gedruckt für die Gesellschaft für romanische Literatur, 1914.

Florence de Rome: Chanson d'aventure du premier quart du XIIIe siècle. Ed. Axel Wallensköld. 2 vols. Paris: Firmin-Didot, 1909.

"Flourence de Rome: A Critical Edition and Literary Study." Ed. Sarah Crisler. Dissertation. University of Texas, 2000.

G.I. Jane. Dir. Ridley Scott. Hollywood Pictures, 1997.

Gordon, Neil. *Sacrifice of Isaac*. New York: Random House, 1995.

Gower, John. *Confessio Amantis*. In *The English Works of John Gower*. Ed. G. C. Macaulay. 1900–1901. 2 vols. EETS e.s. 81, 82. Oxford: Oxford University Press, 1969.

Hartmann von Aue. *Der arme Heinrich*. Ed. Erich Gierach and John Knight Bostock. 4th ed. Oxford: Blackwell, 1965.

Le Haut Livre du Graal: Perlesvaus. Ed. William A. Nitze and T. Atkinson Jenkins. 2 vols. Chicago: University of Chicago Press, 1932.

Heldris de Cornäuille. *Le roman de Silence*. Ed. Lewis Thorpe. Cambridge: Heffer, 1972.

Heloise. "The Personal Letters Between Abelard and Heloise." Ed. J. T. Muckle. *Mediaeval Studies* 15 (1953): 47–94.

————. "The Letter of Heloise on Religious Life and Abelard's Reply." Ed. J. T. Muckle. *Mediaeval Studies* 17 (1955): 240–81.

————. *The Letters of Abelard and Heloise*. Trans. Betty Radice. Baltimore: Penguin, 1974.

Hildegard of Bingen. *Hildegardis Causae et Curae*. Ed. Paul Kaiser. Lipsiae: B. G. Teubneri, 1903.

Huon de Bordeaux. *Esclarmonde, Clarisse et Florent, Yde et Olive: Drei Fortsetzungen der Chanson von Huon de Bordeaux*. Ed. Max Schweigel. Marburg: Elwert, 1889.

Innocent III. *Lotharii Cardinalis (Innocentii III) De Miseria Humane Conditionis*. Ed. Michele Maccarrone. Lugano: Thesauri Mundi, 1955.

La istoria de la filla de l'emperado Contasti. Ed. Hermann Suchier. *Romania* 30 (1901): 519–38.

Jean D'Arras. *Mélusine: Roman du XIVe siècle*. Ed. Louis Stouff. Dijon: Bernigaud et Privat, 1932.

————. *Le roman de Mélusine ou l'Histoire de Lusignan*. Trans. Michèle Perret. Paris: Editions Stock, 1979.

Jourdain de Blaye. Ed. Peter F. Dembowski. Paris: Champion, 1991.

Maillart, Jean. *Le roman du comte d'Anjou*. Ed. Mario Roques. Paris: Champion, 1931.

Ludus Coventriae or the Plaie called Corpus Christi. Ed. K. S. Block. EETS e.s. 120. London: Oxford University Press, 1922.

Marie de France. *Lais*. Ed. Jean Rychner. Paris: Champion, 1966.

————. *The Lais of Marie de France*. Trans. Glyn S. Burgess and Keith Busby. New York: Penguin, 1999.

Miracles de Nostre Dame par personnages. Ed. Gaston Paris and Ulysse Robert. 7 vols. Paris: Firmin-Didot, 1879.

Le mistére du Viel Testament. Ed. James de Rothschild. 6 vols. Paris: Firmin Didot, 1878.

The Nibelungenlied. Trans. A. T. Hatto. London: Penguin, 1965.

Sefer Nizzahon Yashan. In *The Jewish Christian Debate in the High Middle Ages; A Critical Edition of the* Nizzahon Vetus *with an Introduction, Translation, and Commentary*. Ed. David Berger. Philadelphia: Jewish Publication Society of America, 1979.

"Noinden Ulad." "Uber die irische Sage Noinden Ulad." Ed. Ernst Windisch. In *Berichte über die Verhandlungen der Königlich Sächsichen Gesellschaft der Wissenschaften zu Leipzig: Philologisch-Historische Classe* 36 (1884).

Nouveau recueil de contes, dits, fabliaux et autres pièces inédites des XIIIe, XIVe et XVe siècles. Ed. Achille Jubinal. 2 vols. Paris: Edouard Pannier, 1839.

Nouvelles françoises du XIIIe siècle. Ed. L. Moland and C. D'Héricault. Paris: Jannet, 1856.

Ovid. *Metamorphoses*. Trans. Frank Justus Miller, rev. G. P. Goold. Cambridge, Mass.: Harvard University Press, 1977.

Ovid. *Three Ovidian Tales of Love:* Piramus et Tisbé, Narcissus et Danaé, *and* Philomena et Procné. Trans. Raymond Cormier. New York: Garland, 1986.

Ovide moralisé : Poème du commencement du quatorzième siècle. Ed. Charles de Boer. Amsterdam: J. Müller, 1915–38.

Ovide Moralisé en prose. Ed. Charles de Boer. Amsterdam: North Holland Publishing Company, 1954.

Parsifal. Dir. Hans-Jürgen Syberberg. TMS Films, 1982.

Philippe de Rémy. *Oeuvres poétiques de Philippe de Remi, Sire de Beaumanoir.* Ed. Hermann Suchier. 2 vols. Paris: Firmin Didot, 1884–85.

The Poetic Edda. Trans. Lee M. Hollander. Austin: University of Texas Press, 1962.

Procès de condamnation et de réhabilitation de Jeanne d'Arc dite la Pucelle. Ed. Jules Quicherat. 5 vols. Paris: Renouard, 1841–49.

Procès en nullité de la condamnation de Jeanne d'Arc. Ed. Pierre Duparc. 5 vols. Paris: Klincksieck, 1977–88.

Pseudo-Albertus. *Women's Secrets; A Translation of Pseudo-Albertus Magnus's De secretis mulierum with Commentaries.* Trans. Helen Rodnite Lemay. Albany, N.Y.: SUNY Press, 1992.

La queste del saint graal. Ed. Albert Pauphilet. Paris: Champion, 1923.

Rodulfus Tortarius. *Rodulfi Tortarii Carmina.* Ed. Marbury B. Oble and Dorothy M. Schullian. Papers and Monographs of the American Academy in Rome 8. Rome: American Academy in Rome, 1933.

Le roman d'Apollonius de Tyr. Ed. Michel Zink. Paris: Union Générale d'Editions, 1982.

The Romance of Sir Beues of Hamtoun. Ed. Eugen Kölbing. EETS e.s. 46, 48, 65. London: N. Trübner, 1885–94; reprint in one vol. Millwood, N.Y.: Kraus Reprints, 1978.

The Romance of the Chevelere Assigne. Ed. Henry H. Gibbs. EETS e.s. 6. London: Oxford University Press, 1868; reprint Millwood, N.Y: Kraus Reprints, 1975.

The Romans of Partenay, or of Lusignen: Otherwise known as the Tale of Melusine. Ed. Walter W. Skeat. EETS o.s. 22. London: Kegan Paul, 1899; reprint New York: Greenwood Press, 1969.

Sacre rappresentazioni dei secoli XIV, XV, e XVI. Ed. Alessandro d'Ancona. 3 vols. Florence: Le Monnier, 1872.

Saga Heiðreks Konungs Ins Vitra/The Saga of King Heidrek the Wise. Ed. and trans. Christopher Tolkien. London: Thomas Nelson, 1960.

Saxo Grammaticus: The History of the Danes. Ed. and trans. Peter Fisher and Hilda Ellis Davidson. Cambridge: D.S. Brewer, 1979.

Saxonis Gesta Danorum. Ed. C. Knabe and Paul Herrmann, rev. Jørgen Olrik and H. Raeder. Copenhagen: Levin and Munksgaard, 1931.

Shakespeare, William. *The Norton Shakespeare.* Gen. ed. Stephen Greenblatt. New York: Norton, 1997.

Snorri Sturluson. *Edda.* Trans. Anthony Faulkes. London: Dent, 1987.

Sone von Nausay. Ed. Moritz Goldschmidt. Tübingen: Litterarischer Verein in Stuttgart, 1899.

Táin Bó Cúalnge from the Book of Leinster. Ed. and trans. Cecile O'Rahilly. Irish Texts Society 44. Dublin: Dublin Institute for Advanced Studies, 1967.

The Táin Translated from the Irish epic Táin Bó Cuailnge. Trans. Thomas Kinsella. Oxford: Oxford University Press, 1969.

Théâtre français au moyen-age. Ed. L. J. N. Monmerqué and Francisque Michel. Paris: H. Delloye and Firmin Didot, 1839.

Thomas Aquinas. *Summa Theologica.* Trans. Fathers of the English Dominican Province. 19 vols. London: Burns Oates and Washbourne; New York: Benziger, 1911–22.

Thüring von Ringoltingen. *Melusine.* Ed. Karin Schneider. Berlin: E. Schmidt, 1958.

The Towneley Plays. Ed. George England. EETS e.s. 71. London: Oxford University Press, 1897.

"Trivet's Life of Constance." Ed. Margaret Schlauch. In *The Sources and Analogues of Chaucer's Canterbury Tales.* Ed. W. F. Bryan. Chicago: University of Chicago Press, 1941. 165–181.

The Trotula: A Medieval Compendium of Women's Medicine. Ed. and trans. Monica H. Green. Philadelphia: University of Pennsylvania Press, 2001.

Wagner, Richard. *Parsifal : a sacred festival-drama / Parsifal : ein Bühnenweihfestspiel,* Trans. M. H. Glyn. London and New York : Schott & Co., n.d.

Wolfram von Eschenbach. *Parzival.* Trans. A. T. Hatto. London: Penguin, 1980.

York Mystery Plays. Ed. Lucy Toulmin Smith. 1885. New York: Russell and Russell, 1963.

Ystoria regis franchorum et filie in qua adulterium comitere voluit. Ed. Hermann Suchier. *Romania* 39 (1910): 61–76.

SECONDARY TEXTS

Aers, David and Lynn Staley. *The Powers of the Holy: Religion, Politics, and Gender in Late Medieval English Culture.* University Park.: Pennsylvania State University Press, 1996.

Anitchkof, Eugène. "Le saint graal et les rites eucharistiques." *Romania* 55 (1929): 174–94.

Aronstein, Susan. "Rewriting Perceval's Sister: Eucharistic Vision and Typological Destiny in the *Queste del San Graal.*" *Women's Studies* 21 (1992): 211–30.

Atkinson, Clarissa W. *The Oldest Vocation: Christian Motherhood in the Middle Ages.* Ithaca, N.Y.: Cornell University Press, 1991.

Barefield, Laura D. "Reproducing the Past: Gender and History in Later Middle English Romance and Chronicle." Ph.D. dissertation, University of Wisconsin, Madison, 1998.

———. "Women's Power in the 'Tale of Constance.'" *Medieval Perspectives* 15 (2000): 27–34.

Beckerling, Philippa. "Perceval's Sister: Aspects of the Virgin in *The Quest of the Holy Grail* and Malory's *Sankgreal.*" In *Constructing Gender: Feminism and Literary Studies,* ed. Hilary Fraser and R. S. White. Nedlands: University of Western Australia Press, 1994. 39–54.

Benkov, Edith Joyce. "Hyginus' Contribution to Chrétien's *Philomena.*" *Romance Philology* 36, 3 (1983): 403–6.

Berthelot, Anne. "Sang et lèpre, sang et feu." In *Le sang au moyen âge*, ed. Marcel Faure. Cahiers du CRISMA 4. Montpellier: CRISMA, 1999. 25–37.

Bettelheim, Bruno. *Symbolic Wounds: Puberty Rites and the Envious Male*. London: Thames and Hudson, 1955.

Biale, David. "Blut und Glauben: Uber Jüdisch-christliche Symbiose." In *Wissensbilder: Strategien der Uberlieferung*, ed. Ulrich Raulff and Gary Smith. Berlin: Akamedie Verlag, 1999. 145–68.

Biale, Rachel. *Women and Jewish Law*. New York: Schocken Books, 1984.

Biller, Peter. "Views of Jews from Paris Around 1300: Christian or 'Scientific'?" *Studies in Church History* 29 (1992): 187–207.

Bloch, R. Howard. "New Philology and Old French." *Speculum* 65, 1 (1990): 38–58.

Bluestine, Carolyn. "The Power of Blood in the *Siete Infantes de Lara*." *Hispanic Review* 50 (1982): 201–17.

Blumenfeld-Kosinski, Renate. *Not of Woman Born: Representations of Caesarean Birth in Medieval and Renaissance Culture*. Ithaca, N.Y.: Cornell University Press, 1990.

Blumreich, Kathleen M. "Lesbian Desire in the Old French *Roman de Silence*." *Arthuriana* 7, 1 (1997): 47–62.

Boswell, John. *The Kindness of Strangers: The Abandonment of Children in Western Europe from Late Antiquity to the Renaissance*. New York: Vintage, 1988.

Bourke, Joanna. *An Intimate History of Killing: Face to Face Killing in Twentieth-Century Warfare*. New York: Basic Books, 1999.

Bowen, Charles. "Great-Bladdered Medb: Mythology and invention in the Táin Bó Cuailnge." *Eire-Ireland* 10, 4 (1975): 14–34.

Bowers, John M. "Ordeals, Privacy, and the *Lais* of Marie de France." *Journal of Medieval and Renaissance Studies* 14, 1 (1994): 1–24.

Brain, Peter. *Galen on Bloodletting; A Study of the Origins, Development and Validity of His Opinions, with a Translation of the Three Works*. Cambridge: Cambridge University Press, 1986.

Brissaud, Y.-B. "L'infanticide à la fin du moyen âge: Ses motivations psychologiques et sa répression." *Revue historique de droit français et étranger* 50 (1972): 229–56.

Brown, Peter. *The Body and Society: Men, Women, and Sexual Renunciation in Early Christianity*. New York: Columbia University Press, 1988.

Brundage, James A. *Law, Sex, and Christian Society in Medieval Europe*. Chicago: University of Chicago Press, 1987.

———. "Intermarriage Between Christians and Jews in Medieval Canon Law." *Jewish History* 3, 1 (1988): 25–40.

Buckley, Thomas and Alma Gottlieb. "A Critical Appraisal of Theories of Menstrual Symbolism." In *Blood Magic: The Anthropology of Menstruation*, ed. Buckley and Gottlieb. Berkeley: University of California Press, 1988. 3–50.

Bullough, Vern L. and Bonnie Bullough. *Cross Dressing, Sex, and Gender*. Philadelphia: University of Pennsylvania Press, 1993.

Burns, E. Jane. *Bodytalk: When Women Speak in Old French Literature*. Philadelphia: University of Pennsylvania Press, 1993.

————. "Devilish Ways: Sexing the Subject in the *Queste del saint graal.*" *Arthuriana* 8, 2 (1998): 11–32.

Burt, John R. "The Bloody Cucumber and Related Matters in the *Siete Infantes de Lara.*" *Hispanic Review* 50 (1982): 345–52.

Busby, Keith. *Gauvain in Old French Literature.* Amsterdam: Rodopi, 1980.

Bynum, Caroline Walker. *Fragmentation and Redemption: Essays on Gender and the Human Body in Medieval Religion.* New York: Zone Books, 1991.

————. *Holy Feast and Holy Fast: The Religious Significance of Food to Medieval Women.* Berkeley: University of California Press, 1987.

————. *Jesus as Mother: Studies in the Spirituality of the High Middle Ages.* Berkeley: University of California Press, 1982.

Cadden, Joan. *Meanings of Sex Difference in the Middle Ages: Medicine, Science, and Culture.* Cambridge: Cambridge University Press, 1993.

Calin, William. *The Epic Quest: Studies in Four Old French* Chansons de Geste. Baltimore: Johns Hopkins University Press, 1966.

Carney, James. *Studies in Irish Literature and History.* Dublin: Dublin Institute for Advanced Studies, 1955.

Céard, Jean. *La nature et les prodiges: L'insolite au XVIe siècle, en France.* Geneva: Droz, 1977.

Chase, Carol. *"La conversion des païennes dans l'Estoire del saint graal."* In *Arthurian Romance and Gender*, ed. Fredreich Wolfzettel. Atlanta: Rodopi, 1995. 251–64.

————. "Des Sarrasins à Camaalot." *Cahiers de recherches médiévales (XIIIe–XVe s.)* 5 (1998): 44–53.

————. "The Vision of the Grail in the *Estoire del Saint Graal.*" In *Old and New Philologies: Essays in Honor of Peter Florian Dembowski*, ed. Joan Tasker Grimbert and Carol Chase. Forthcoming.

Clover, Carol. "Maiden Warriors and Other Sons." *Journal of English and Germanic Philology* 85 (1986): 35–49.

————. "The Politics of Scarcity: Notes on the Sex Ratio in Early Scandinavia." *Scandinavian Studies* 60 (1988): 147–88.

————. "Regardless of Sex: Men, Women, and Power in Early Northern Europe." *Speculum* 68, 2 (1993): 363–87.

Cohen, Jeffrey Jerome. *Of Giants: Sex, Monsters, and the Middle Ages.* Minneapolis: University of Minnesota Press, 1999.

Cohen, Jeremy. "The Jews as the Killers of Christ in the Latin Tradition, from Augustine to the Friars." *Traditio* 39 (1983): 1–27.

————. "Philosophical Exegesis in Historical Perspective: The Case of the Binding of Isaac." In *Divine Omniscience and Omnipotence in Medieval Philosophy: Islamic, Jewish, and Christian Perspectives*, ed. Tamar Rudavsky. Dordrecht: D. Reidel, 1985. 135–42.

Cohen, Shaye J. D. "Menstruants and the Sacred in Judaism and Christianity." In *Women's History and Ancient History*, ed. Sarah B. Pomeroy. Chapel Hill: University of North Carolina Press, 1991. 273–99.

————. *The Beginnings of Jewishness: Boundaries, Varieties, Uncertainties.* Berkeley: University of California Press, 1999.

Combarieu du Grès, Micheline de. "Une extrême amitié." In *Ami et Amile. Une chanson de geste de l'amitié*, ed. Jean Dufournet. Paris: Champion-Slatkine, 1987. 15–38.

Crane, Susan. "Clothing and Gender Definition: Joan of Arc." *Journal of Medieval and Early Modern Studies*. 26, 2 (1996): 297–320.

Crawford, Patricia. "Attitudes to Menstruation in Seventeenth-Century England." *Past and Present* 91 (1981): 47–73.

Cressy, David. "Purification, Thanksgiving and the Churching of Women in Post-Reformation England." *Past and Present* 141 (1993): 106–46.

Dannenbaum [Crane], Susan. "Insular Tradition in the Story of Amis and Amiloun." *Neophilologus* 67 (1983): 611–22.

Darr, Norma M. "Reading the Body and Blood of Parsifal: A Performance at Hellerau." *Music Quarterly* 80, 4 (1996): 629–47.

D'Avray, D.L. and M. Tausche. "Marriage Sermons in *Ad Status* Collections of the Central Middle Ages." *Archives d'histoire doctrinale et littéraire du moyen âge* 47 (1980): 71–119.

Delaney, Carol. "The Meaning of Paternity and the Virgin Birth Debate." *Man* n.s. 21 (1986): 494–513.

———. *Abraham on Trial: The Social Legacy of Biblical Myth*. Princeton, N.J.: Princeton University Press, 1998.

Delaney, Janice, Mary Jane Lupton, and Emily Toth. *The Curse: A Cultural History of Menstruation*. Urbana: University of Illinois Press, 1988.

Delbouille, Maurice. "Apollonius de Tyr et les débuts du roman français." In *Mélanges offerts à Rita Lejeune*. Gembloux: J. Duculot, 1969. 1171–1204.

Demaitre, Luke and Anthony A. Travill. "Human Embryology and Development in the Works of Albertus Magnus." In *Albertus Magnus and the Sciences; Commemorative Essays 1980*, ed. James A. Weisheipl. Studies and Texts 49. Toronto: Pontifical Institute of Mediaeval Studies, 1980. 405–50.

De Pauw, Linda Grant. *Battle Cries and Lullabies: Women in War from Prehistory to the Present*. Norman: University of Oklahoma Press, 1998.

Derrien, Eve. "Le sang et la saignée dans le roman médiéval en vers." *Lettres Romanes* 51, 1–2 (1997): 3–18.

Desaivre, Léo. *Le Mythe de la mère Lusine: Etude critique et bibliographique*. Saint Maixent: Renversé, 1883.

Devilbiss, M. C. "Women in Combat: A Quick Summary of the Arguments on Both Sides." *MINERVA: Quarterly Report on Women and the Military* 8, 1 (1990): 29–33.

DeVries, Kelly. "A Woman as Leader of Men: Joan of Arc's Military Career." In *Fresh Verdicts on Joan of Arc*, ed. Bonnie Wheeler and Charles T. Wood. New York: Garland, 1996. 3–18.

———. *Joan of Arc: A Military Leader*. Stroud: Sutton Publishing, 1999.

Dictionary of the Irish Language Based Mainly on Old and Middle Irish Materials. 4 vols. Dublin: Royal Irish Academy, 1913–76.

Dillon, Myles. *Early Irish Literature*. Chicago: University of Chicago Press, 1948.

Dinshaw, Carolyn. *Chaucer's Sexual Poetics*. Madison: University of Wisconsin Press, 1989.

Dembowski, Peter F. "Autour de Jourdain de Blayes, aspects structuraux et problèmes connexes." *Neophilologus* 51 (1967): 238–45.

Doueihi, Milad. *A Perverse History of the Human Heart*. Cambridge, Mass.: Harvard University Press, 1997.

Douglas, Mary. *Implicit Meanings*. London: Routledge and Kegan Paul, 1975.

————. *Leviticus as Literature*. Oxford: Oxford University Press, 1999.

————. *Purity and Danger: An Analysis of the Concepts of Pollution and Taboo*. London: Routledge and Kegan Paul, 1966.

Eilberg-Schwartz, Howard. *The Savage in Judaism: An Anthropology of Israelite Religion and Ancient Judaism*. Bloomington and Indianapolis: Indiana University Press, 1990.

Elliott, Dyan. *Fallen Bodies: Pollution, Sexuality, and Demonology in the Middle Ages*. Philadelphia: University of Pennsylvania Press, 1999.

————. "The Physiology of Rapture and Female Spirituality." In *Medieval Theology and the Natural Body*, ed. Peter Billar and A. J. Minnis. York: York Medieval Press, 1997. 141–73.

————. "Pollution, Illusion, and Masculine Disarray: Nocturnal Emissions and the Sexuality of the Clergy." In *Constructing Medieval Sexuality*, ed. Karma Lochrie, Peggy McCracken, and James A. Schultz. Minneapolis: University of Minnesota Press, 1997. 1–23.

Enders, Jody. *Rhetoric and the Origins of Medieval Drama*. Ithaca, N.Y.: Cornell University Press, 1992.

Feimer, Joel N. "The Figure of Medea in Medieval Literature: A Thematic Metamorphosis." Ph.D. dissertation, City University of New York, 1983.

————. "Jason and Medea in Benoit de Sainte-Maure's *Le roman de Troie*: Classical Theme and Medieval Context." In *Voices in Translation: The Authority of "Olde Bookes" in Medieval Literature*, ed. Deborah M. Sinnreich-Levi et al. New York: AMS, 1992. 35–51.

————. "Medea in Ovid's *Metamorphoses* and the *Ovide moralisé*: Translation as Transmission." *Florilegium* 8 (1986): 40–55.

Finke, Laurie and Martin B. Shichtman. "No Pain, No Gain: Violence as Symbolic Capital in Malory's *Morte d'Arthur*." *Arthuriana* 8, 2 (1998): 115–34.

Foehr-Janssens, Yasmina. "La mort en fleurs. Violence et poésie dans *Ami et Amile*." *Cahiers de civilisation médiévale* 39 (1996): 263–74.

Fonrobert, Charlotte Elisheva. *Menstrual Purity: Rabbinic and Christian Reconstructions of Biblical Gender*. Stanford, Calif.: Stanford University Press, 2000.

Fraioli, Deborah A. *Joan of Arc: The Early Debate*. Woodbridge: Boydell, 2000.

Francke, Linda Bird. *Ground Zero: The Gender Wars in the Military*. New York: Simon and Schuster, 1997.

Friedman, John Block. *The Monstrous Races in Medieval Art and Thought*. Cambridge, Mass.: Harvard University Press, 1981.

Garber, Marjorie B. *Vested Interests: Cross-Dressing and Cultural Anxiety*. New York: Routledge, 1992.

Gélis, Jacques. *History of Childbirth: Fertility, Pregnancy and Birth in Early Modern Europe*. Trans. Rosemary Morris. Boston: Northeastern University Press, 1991.

Gibson, Gail McMurray. "Blessings from Sun and Moon: Churching as Women's Theater." In *Bodies and Disciplines: Intersections of Literature and History in Fifteenth-Century England*, ed. Barbara A. Hanawalt and David Wallace. Minneapolis: University of Minnesota Press, 1996. 139–54.

————. "Scene and Obscene: Seeing and Performing Late Medieval Childbirth." *Journal of Medieval and Early Modern Studies* 29, 1 (1999): 7–24.

Gilson, Etienne. "La mystique de la grâce dans *La queste del saint graal*." *Romania* 51(1925): 321–47.

Gingras, Francis. "Le sang de l'amour dans le récit médiéval (XIIe–XIIIe siècle)." In *Le sang au moyen âge*, ed. Marcel Faure. Cahiers du CRISMA 4. Montpellier: CRISMA, 1999. 207–16.

Gitton, Bernard. "De l'emploi des chansons de geste pour entraîner les guerriers au combat." In *La chanson de geste et le mythe carolingien: Mélanges René Louis.*, ed. Emmanuèle Baumgartner. 2 vols. Saint-Père-sous-Vezeley: Musée Archéologique Régional, 1982. 1: 3–19.

Golightly, Niel L. "No Right to Fight." *U.S. Naval Institute Proceedings* (December 1987): 46–49.

Gottlieb, Alma. "Rethinking Female Pollution: The Beng Case (Côte d'Ivoire)." In *Beyond the Second Sex: New Directions in the Anthropology of Gender*, ed. Peggy Reeves Sanday and Ruth Gallagher Goodenough. Philadelphia: University of Pennsylvania Press, 1990. 113–38.

Goy-Blanquet, Dominique. *Le roi mis à nu: L'histoire d'Henri VI, de Hall à Shakespeare*. Paris: Didier, 1986.

Gravdal, Kathryn. "Confessing Incests: Legal Erasures and Literary Celebrations in Medieval France." *Comparative Literature Studies* 32 (1995): 280–95.

Green, Robert B. "Fin'amors dans deux lais de Marie de France: *Equitan* et *Chaitivel*." *Le Moyen Age* 81 (1975): 265–72.

Greilsammer, Myriam. *L'envers du tableau: Mariage et maternité en Flandre médiévale*. Paris: Armand Colin, 1990.

Grinnell, Natalie. "Medea's Humanity and John Gower's Romance." *Medieval Perspectives* 14 (1999): 70–83.

Hacker, Barton C. "Women and Military Institutions in Early Modern Europe: A Reconnaissance." *Signs: Journal of Women in Culture and Society* 6, 4 (1981): 643–71.

Hamilton, W.E.M.C. "L'interprétation mystique de *La queste del saint graal*." *Neophilologus* 27 (1942): 94–110.

Hauser-Schäublin, Brigitta. "Blood: Cultural Effectiveness of Biological Conditions." In *Sex and Gender Hierarchies*, ed. Barbara Diane Miller. Cambridge: Cambridge University Press, 1993. 83–107.

Hoffman, Lawrence A. *Covenant of Blood: Circumcision and Gender in Rabbinic Judaism*. Chicago: University of Chicago Press, 1996.

Hogbin, Ian. *The Island of Menstruating Men: Religion in Wogeo, New Guinea*. Scranton, Pa.: Chandler, 1970.

Hotchkiss, Valerie R. *Clothes Make the Man: Female Cross Dressing in Medieval Europe*. New York: Garland, 1996.

Howard, Jean E. and Phyllis Rackin. *Engendering a Nation: A Feminist Account of Shakespeare's English Histories*. New York: Routledge, 1997.

Hubert, Henri and Marcel Maus. *Sacrifice: Its Nature and Function*. 1898. Trans. W.D. Halls. Chicago: University of Chicago Press, 1964.

Huchet, Jean-Charles. *Tristan et le sang de l'écriture*. Paris: Presses Universitaires de France, 1990.

Hume, Kathryn. "*Amis and Amiloun* and the Aesthetics of Middle English Romance." *Studies in Philology* 70 (1973): 19–41.

Jackson, Gabriele Bernhard. "Topical Ideology: Witches, Amazons, and Shakespeare's Joan of Arc." *English Literary Renaissance* 18 (1988): 40–65.

Jacquart, Danielle, and Claude Thomasset. *Sexuality and Medicine in the Middle Ages*. Trans. Matthew Adamson. Princeton, N.J.: Princeton University Press, 1988.

Jaeger, C. Stephen. *Ennobling Love: In Search of a Lost Sensibility*. Philadelphia: University of Pennsylvania Press, 1999.

Jay, Nancy. *Throughout Your Generations Forever: Sacrifice, Religion, and Paternity*. Chicago: University of Chicago Press, 1992.

Jeay, Madeline. "Consuming Passions: Variations on the Eaten Heart Theme. In *Violence Against Women in Medieval Texts*, ed. Anna Roberts. Gainesville: University Press of Florida, 1998. 75–96.

Jesch, Judith. *Women in the Viking Age*. Woodbridge: Boydell, 1991.

Jochens, Jenny. *Old Norse Images of Women*. Philadelphia: University of Pennsylvania Press, 1996.

Johnson, Willis. "The Myth of Jewish Male Menses." *Journal of Medieval History* 24, 3 (1998): 273–95.

Jones, Catherine M. "'Se je fusse hons': les guerrières dans *Ansëys de Mes*." In *Charlemagne in the North: Proceedings of the Twelfth International Conference of the Société Rencesvals*, ed. Philip E. Bennett, Anne Elizabeth Cobby, and Graham A. Runnals. London: Grant and Cutler, 1993. 291–97.

Katz, David S. "Shylock's Gender: Jewish Male Menstruation in Early Modern England." *Review of English Studies* 50, 200 (1999): 440–62.

Kay, Sarah. "Seduction and Suppression in *Ami et Amile*." *French Studies* 44 (1990): 129–42.

———. *The* Chansons de geste *in the Age of Romance: Political Fictions*. Oxford: Clarendon Press, 1995.

Kelly, Douglas. "The Domestication of the Marvelous in the Melusine Romances." In *Melusine of Lusignan: Founding Fiction in Late Medieval France*, ed. Donald Maddox and Sara Sturm-Maddox. Athens: University of Georgia Press, 1996. 32–47.

Kelly, Patricia. "The Táin as Literature." In *Aspects of the Táin*, ed. J. P. Mallory. Belfast: December Publications, 1992. 69–102.

Klapish-Zuber, Christiane. *Women, Family and Ritual in Renaissance Italy*. Trans. Lydia Cochran. Chicago: University of Chicago Press, 1985.

Krappe, Alexandre Haggerty. "La belle Hélène de Constantinople." *Romania* 63 (1937): 324–53.

Kratins, Ojars. "The Middle English *Amis and Amiloun*: Chivalric Romance or Secular Hagiography?" *PMLA* 81 (1966): 347–54.

Krueger, Roberta L. *Women Readers and the Ideology of Gender in Old French Verse Romance*. Cambridge: Cambridge University Press, 1993.

Lancashire, Anne. "Chaucer and the Sacrifice of Isaac." *The Chaucer Review* 9,4 (1975): 320–26.

Le Goff, Jacques and Emmanuel Le Roy Ladurie. "Mélusine maternelle et défricheuse." *Annales: Economies, Sociétés, Civilisations* 26 (1971): 587–622

Legros, Huguette. "Le vocabulaire de l'amitié, son évolution sémantique au cours du XIIe siècle." *Cahiers de civilisation médiévale* 23 (1980): 131–39.

Lemay, Helen Rodnite. "William of Saliceto on Human Sexuality." *Viator* 12 (1981): 165–81.

Levenson, Jon D. *The Death and Resurrection of the Beloved Son: The Transformation of Child Sacrifice in Judaism and Christianity*. New Haven, Conn.: Yale University Press, 1993.

L'Hermite-Leclercq, Paulette. "Le sang et le lait de la vierge." In *Le sang au moyen âge*, ed. Marcel Faure. Cahiers du CRISMA 4. Montpellier: CRISMA, 1999. 145–62.

Lincoln, Bruce. *Death, War, and Sacrifice: Studies in Ideology and Practice*. Chicago: University of Chicago Press, 1991.

Lochrie, Karma. *Margery Kempe and Translations of the Flesh*. Philadelphia: University of Pennsylvania Press, 1991.

——. "Mystical Acts, Queer Tendencies." In *Constructing Medieval Sexuality*, ed. Karma Lochrie, Peggy McCracken, and James A. Schultz. Minneapolis: University of Minnesota Press, 1997. 180–200.

Loraux, Nicole. *Tragic Ways of Killing a Woman*. Trans. Anthony Forster. Cambridge, Mass.: Harvard University Press, 1987.

Lot-Borodine, Myrrha. "Les apparitions du Christ aux messes de l'*Estoire* et de la *Queste del saint graal*." *Romania* 72 (1951): 202–23.

——. "Le symbolisme du graal dans l'*Estoire del saint graal*." *Neophilologus* 34 (1950): 65–79.

Loth, J. "Notes étymologiques et lexicographiques." *Revue celtique* 45 (1928): 173–201.

Lowes, John Livingstone. "Chaucer and the *Ovide moralisé*." *PMLA* 33 (1918): 205–32.

Lupton, Mary Jane. *Menstruation and Psychoanalysis*. Urbana: University of Illinois Press, 1993.

Lynch, Andrew. *Malory's Book of Arms: The Narrative of Combat in* Le Morte Darthur. Arthurian Studies 39. Cambridge: D.S. Brewer, 1997.

Maddox, Donald. *Fictions of Identity in Medieval France*. Cambridge: Cambridge University Press, 2000.

Maddox, Donald and Sara Sturm-Maddox. *Melusine of Lusignan: Founding Fiction in Late Medieval France*. Athens: University of Georgia Press, 1996.

Marchello-Nizia, Christiane. "Amour courtois, société masculine, et figures du pouvoir." *Annales: Economies, sociétés, civilisations* 36, 6 (1981): 969–82.

Marcus, Leah. *Puzzling Shakespeare: Local Reading and Its Discontents*. Berkeley: University of California Press, 1988.

Martin, Emily. *The Woman in the Body: A Cultural Analysis of Reproduction*. Boston: Beacon Press, 1992.

McCracken, Peggy. "'The Boy Who Was a Girl': Reading Gender in the *Roman de Silence*." *Romanic Review* 85 (1994): 517–36.

———. "Chaste Subjects: Gender, Heroism, and Desire in the Grail Quest." In *Queering the Middle Ages*, ed. Glenn Burger and Steven F. Kruger. Minneapolis: University of Minnesota Press, 2001. 123–42.

———. "The Curse of Eve: Female Bodies and Christian Bodies in Heloise's Third Letter." In *Listening to Heloise: The Voice of a Twelfth-Century Woman*, ed. Bonnie Wheeler. New York: St. Martin's Press, 2000. 217–31.

———. "The Poetics of Sacrifice: Allegory and Myth in the Grail Quest." *Yale French Studies* 95 (1999): 152–68.

———. *The Romance of Adultery: Queenship and Adultery in Old French Literature*. Philadelphia: University of Pennsylvania Press, 1998.

McLaughlin, Megan. "The Woman Warrior: Gender, Warfare, and Society in Medieval Europe." *Women's Studies* 17 (1990): 193–209.

Meale, Carole M. "Legends of Good Women in the European Middle Ages." *Archiv für das Studium der Neueren Sprachen und Literaturen* 229, 1 (1992): 55–70.

Meltzer, Françoise. *For Fear of the Fire: Joan of Arc and the Limits of Subjectivity*. Chicago: University of Chicago Press, 2001.

Michaud-Fréjaville, Françoise. "L'effusion de sang dans les procès et les traités concernant Jeanne d'Arc (1430–1456)." In *Le sang au moyen âge*, ed. Marcel Faure. Cahiers du CRISMA 4. Montpellier: CRISMA, 1999. 331–40.

Mickel, Emanuel. "The Question of Guilt in *Ami et Amile*." *Romania* 106 (1985): 19–35.

Miramon, Charles de. "Déconstruction et reconstruction du tabou de la femme menstruée (XII–XIIIe siècle)." In *Kontinuitäten und Zäsuren in der Europäischen Rechtsgeschichte: Europäisches Forum Junger Rechtshistorikerinnen und Rechtshistoriker, München 22–24 Juli 1998*. New York: Peter Lang, 1999. 79–107.

———. "La fin d'un tabou? L'interdiction de communier pour la femme menstruée au moyen âge. Le cas du XIIe siècle." In *Le sang au moyen âge*, ed. Marcel Faure. Cahiers du CRISMA 4. Montpellier: CRISMA, 1999. 163–81.

Mitchell, Brian. *Women in the Military: Flirting with Disaster*. Washington, D.C.: Regnery, 1998.

Morgan, Leslie Zarker. "*Bovo d'Antona* in the *Geste Francor* (V 13): Unity of Composition and Clan Destiny." *Italian Culture* 16, 2 (1999): 15–38.

Morse, Ruth. *The Medieval Medea*. Cambridge: D.S. Brewer, 1996.

Niccoli, Ottavia. "'Menstruum Quasi Monstruum': Monstrous Births and Menstrual Taboo in the Sixteenth Century." Trans. Mary M. Gallucci. In *Sex and Gender in Historical Perspective: Selections from* Quaderni Storici, ed. Edward Muir and Guido Ruggiero. Baltimore: Johns Hopkins University Press, 1990. 1–25.

Newman, Barbara. "'Crueel Corage': Child Sacrifice and the Maternal Martyr in Hagiography and Romance." In *From Virile Woman to WomanChrist: Studies in Medieval Religion and Literature.* Philadelphia: University of Pennsylvania Press, 1995. 76–107.

Nirenberg, David. *Communities of Violence: Persecution of Minorities in the Middle Ages.* Princeton, N.J.: Princeton University Press, 1996.

Nolan, Robert J. "The Origin of the Romance of Melusine: A New Interpretation." *Fabula* 15, 3 (1975): 192–201.

Paster, Gail Kern. *The Body Embarrassed: Drama and the Disciplines of Shame in Early Modern England.* Ithaca, N.Y.: Cornell University Press, 1993.

Pernoud, Régine and Marie-Véronique Clin. *Joan of Arc: Her Story.* 1986. Trans. and rev. Jeremy duQuesnay Adams. New York: St. Martin's Press, 1999.

Perret, Michele. "Travesties et transexuelles: Yde, Silence, Grisandole, Blanchandine." *Romance Notes* 25 (1985): 328–40.

Perrot, Jean-Pierre. "Du sang au lait: l'imaginaire du sang et ses logiques dans les passions de martyrs." In *Le sang au moyen âge,* ed. Marcel Faure. Cahiers du CRISMA 4. Montpellier: CRISMA, 1999. 459–70.

Petit, Aimé. "Le traitement courtois du thème des Amazones d'après trois romans antiques: *Enéas, Troie* et *Alexandre.*" *Le Moyen Age* 89 (1983): 63–84.

Pichon, Geneviève. "La lèpre dans *Ami et Amile.*" In *Ami et Amile: Une chanson de geste de l'amitié,* ed. Jean Dufournet. Paris: Champion-Slatkine, 1987. 51–66.

Planche, Alice. "Ami et Amile ou le même et l'autre." In *Beiträge zum romanischen Mittelalter,* ed. Kurt Baldinger. Tübingen: Niemeyer, 1977. 237–69.

Pomata, Gianna. "Menstruating Men : Similarity and Difference of the Sexes in Early Modern Medicine." In *Generation and Degeneration: Tropes of Representation in Literature and History from Antiquity to Early Modern Europe,* ed. Valeria Finucci and Kevin Brownlee. Durham, N.C.: Duke University Press. 109–52.

Ponchelle, Marie-Christine. "L'hybride." *Nouvelle revue de psychanalyse* 7 (1973): 50–61.

Possamaï-Pérez, Marylène. "Chrétien de Troyes au début du XIVe siècle: *Philomena* 'moralisé.'" In *L'oeuvre de Chrétien de Troyes dans la littérature française; Réminiscences, résurgences et réécritures.* Lyon: Université Jean Moulin, 1997. 169–85.

Rackin, Phyllis. *Stages of History: Shakespeare's English Chronicles.* Ithaca, N.Y.: Cornell University Press, 1990.

Remy, Paul. "La lèpre, thème littéraire au moyen âge." *Le Moyen Age* 52 (1946): 195–242.

Resnick, Irven. "Medieval Roots of the Myth of Jewish Male Menses." *Harvard Theological Review* 93, 3 (2000): 241–63.

Rieder, Paula M. "The Implications of Exclusion: The Regulation of Churching in Medieval Northern France." *Essays in Medieval Studies* 15 (1999): 71–80.

Riehle, Wolfgang. *The Middle English Mystics.* Trans. Bernard Standring. London: Routledge and Kegan Paul, 1981.

Roach, William. "Eucharistic Tradition in the *Perlesvaus.*" *Zeitscrift für Romanische Philologie* 59 (1939): 10–56.

Rosenberg, Samuel N. "Lire *Ami et Amile,* le regard sur les personnages féminins." In *Ami et Amile. Une chanson de geste de l'amitié*, ed. Jean Dufournet. Paris and Geneva: Champion-Slatkine, 1987. 67–78.

Ross, D. J. A. "Blood in the Sea: An Episode in 'Jourdain de Blaivies.'" *Modern Language Review* 66 (1971): 532–41.

Roush, Paul E. "Combat Exclusion: Military Necessity or Another Name for Bigotry?" *MINERVA: Quarterly Report on Women and the Military* 8, 3 (1990): 1–15.

Rousselle, Aline. *Porneia: On Desire and the Body in Antiquity*. Trans. Felicia Pheasant. Cambridge, Mass.: Basil Blackwell, 1988.

Rubin, Miri. *Corpus Christi: The Eucharist in Late Medieval Culture*. Cambridge: Cambridge University Press, 1991.

———. *Gentile Tales: The Narrative Assault on Late Medieval Jews*. New Haven, Conn.: Yale University Press, 1999.

Rushton, Peter. "Purification or Social Control? Ideologies of Reproduction and the Churching of Women After Childbirth." In *The Public and the Private*, ed. Eva Gamarnikow et al. London: Heinemann, 1983. 118–131.

Sautman, Francesca Canadé. *La religion du quotidien: Rites et croyances populaires de la fin du moyen âge*. Florence: Olschki, 1995.

Scarry, Elaine. *The Body in Pain: The Making and Unmaking of the World*. New York: Oxford University Press, 1985.

Schlauch, Margaret. "The Allegory of Church and Synagogue." *Speculum* 14 (1939): 448–64.

———. *Chaucer's Constance and Accused Queens*. New York: New York University Press, 1927.

Schibanoff, Susan. "True Lies: Transvestism and Idolatry in the Trial of Joan of Arc." In *Fresh Verdicts on Joan of Arc*, ed. Bonnie Wheeler and Charles T. Wood. New York: Garland, 1996. 31–60.

Schultz, James A. *The Knowledge of Childhood in the German Middle Ages, 1100–1350*. Philadelphia: University of Pennsylvania Press, 1995.

Schulze-Busacker, Elisabeth. "*Philomena*: Une révision de l'attribution de l'oeuvre." *Romania* 107 (1986): 459–85.

Schwarz, Kathryn. *Tough Love: Amazon Encounters in Renaissance England*. Durham, N.C.: Duke University Press, 2000.

Segal, Mady Wechsler. "The Argument for Female Combatants." In *Female Soldiers: Combatants or Noncombatants?* ed. Nancy Loring Goldman. Westport, Conn.: Greenwood Press, 1982. 267–90.

Shapiro, James. *Shakespeare and the Jews*. New York: Columbia University Press, 1996.

Shapiro, Marianne. "*Ami et Amile* and Myths of Divine Twinship." *Romanische Forschungen* 102 (1990): 131–48.

Shichtman, Martin B. "Perceval's Sister: Genealogy, Virginity, and Blood." *Arthuriana* 9, 2 (1999): 11–20.

Sirasi, Nancy G. *Medieval and Early Renaissance Medicine: An Introduction to Knowledge and Practice*. Chicago: University of Chicago Press, 1990.

Sjoestedt, Marie-Louise. *Gods and Heroes of the Celts*. Trans. Myles Dillon. London: Methuen, 1994.

Solterer, Helen. "Dismembering, Remembering the Châtelain de Couci." *Romance Philology* 46 (1992): 103–124.

Spiegel, Gabrielle M. "Maternity and Monstrosity: Reproductive Biology in the *Roman de Melusine*." In *Melusine de Lusignan: Founding Fiction in Late Medieval France*, ed. Donald Maddox and Sara Sturm-Maddox. Athens: University of Georgia Press, 1996. 100–124.

Spiegel, Shalom. *The Last Trial: On the Legends and Lore of the Command to Abraham to Offer Isaac as a Sacrifice: The Akedah.* Trans. Judah Goldin. Woodstock, Vt.: Jewish Lights, 1993.

Stephens, William N. "A Cross-Cultural Study of Menstrual Taboos." *Genetic Psychology Monographs* 64 (1961): 385–416.

Strohm, Paul. *Theory and the Premodern Text.* Minneapolis: University of Minnesota Press, 2000.

Sturm-Maddox, Sara. "Crossed Destinies: Narrative Programs in the *Roman de Mélusine*." In *Melusine of Lusignan: Founding Fiction in Late Medieval France*, ed. Donald Maddox and Sara Sturm-Maddox. Athens: University of Georgia Press, 1996. 12–31.

Suard, François. "Le merveilleux et le religieux dans *Ami et Amile*." *De l'étranger à l'étrange ou la conjointure de la merveille (en hommage à M. Rossi et P. Bancourt).* Senefiance 25. Aix-en-Provence: CUERMA, 1988. 449–62.

Sullivan, Karen. *The Interrogation of Joan of Arc.* Minneapolis: University of Minnesota Press, 1999.

Szkilnik, Michelle. *L'archipel du graal: Etude de l'*Estoire del Saint Graal. Geneva: Droz, 1991.

Taviani, Huguette. "Pouvoir et solidarités dans la principauté de Salerne à la fin du Xe siècle." In *Structures féodales et féodalisme dans l'occident méditerranéen (Xe–XIIIe siècles): Bilan et perspectives de recherches.* Colloques Internationaux du Centre National de la Recherche Scientifique 588. Paris: CNRS, 1980. 587–606.

Taylor, Jane H. M. "Melusine's Progeny: Patterns and Perplexities." In *Melusine de Lusignan: Founding Fiction in Late Medieval France*, ed. Donald Maddox and Sara Sturm-Maddox. Athens: University of Georgia Press, 1996. 165–84.

Thompson, John Jay. "Medea in Christine de Pizan's *Mutacion de Fortune*, or How to be a Better Mother." *Forum for Modern Language Studies* 35 (1999): 158–74.

Thurneysen, Rudolf. *Die irische Helden- und Königsage.* Halle: Niemeyer, 1921.

Tuten, Jeff M. "The Argument Against Female Combatants." In *Female Soldiers: Combatants or Noncombatants?* ed. Nancy Loring Goldman. Westport, Conn.: Greenwood Press, 1982. 237–65.

Tuve, Rosamund. *Allegorical Imagery: Some Medieval Books and Their Posterity.* Princeton, N.J.: Princeton University Press, 1966.

Tuzin, Donald. "Discourse, Intercourse, and the Excluded Middle: Anthropology and the Problem of Sexual Experience." In *Sexual Nature, Sexual Culture*, ed. Paul R. Abramson and Steven D. Pinkerton. Chicago: University of Chicago Press, 1995. 257–75.

Van Coolput, Colette-Anne. "La poupée d'Evalac ou la conversion tardive du roi Mondrain." In *Continuations. Essays on Medieval French Literature and Language in Honor of John L. Grigsby*, ed. Norris J. Lacy and Gloria Torrini-Roblin. Birmingham, Al.: Summa, 1989. 163–72.

Vincensini, Jean-Jacques. *Pensée mythique et narrations médiévales*. Paris: Champion, 1996.

Wack, Mary. *Lovesickness in the Middle Ages: The Viaticum and its Commentaries*. Philadelphia: University of Pennsylvania Press, 1990.

Warner, Marina. *Joan of Arc: The Image of Female Heroism*. Berkeley: University of California Press, 1981.

Wasserfall, Rahel. "Introduction: Menstrual Blood into Jewish Blood." In *Women and Water: Menstruation in Jewish Life and Law*. Hanover, N.H.: Brandeis University Press and University Press of New England, 1999. 1–18.

Webb, James H. "Women Can't Fight." *Washingtonian* (November 1979): 144–48, 273–82.

Weinstein, Donald and Rudolph M. Bell. *Saints and Society: The Two Worlds of Western Christendom, 1000–1700*. Chicago: University of Chicago Press, 1982.

White, Sarah Melhado. "Lancelot's Beds: Styles of Courtly Intimacy." In *The Sower and His Seed: Essays on Chrétien de Troyes*, ed. Rupert T. Pickens. Lexington: French Forum, 1983. 116–26.

Wogan-Browne, Jocelyn. "Chaste Bodies: Frames and Experiences." In *Framing Medieval Bodies*, ed. Sarah Kay and Miri Rubin. Manchester: Manchester University Press, 1994. 24–42.

Woledge, Brian. "*Ami et Amile*: Les versions en prose française." *Romania* 65 (1939): 433–56.

Wood, Charles T. "The Doctors' Dilemma: Sin, Salvation, and the Menstrual Cycle in Medieval Thought." *Speculum* 56 (1981): 710–27.

———. "Joan of Arc's Mission and the Lost Record of her Interrogation at Poitiers." In *Fresh Verdicts on Joan of Arc*, ed. Bonnie Wheeler and Charles T. Wood. New York: Garland, 1996. 19–29.

Wynn, Phillip. "The Conversion Story in Nicholas Trevet's 'Tale of Constance.'" *Viator* 13 (1984): 259–74.

Žižek, Slavoj. "'The Wound Is Healed Only by the Sword That Smote You': The Operatic Subject and Its Vicissitudes." In *Opera Through Other Eyes*, ed. David Levin. Stanford, Calif.: Stanford University Press, 1993. 177–214.

Index

Abelard, 5, 110
Abjection, 2, 7
Abraham, 42, 44–47, 51, 55, 59
Adultery, 10–15, 17–18, 83
Aethelflaed, 33
Ailill, 24–26
Albert the Great, 77–78
Alfonso el Sabio, *Siete Partidas*, 71
Allegory, 19–20
Amazons, 24, 33
Amenorrhea, 4, 22–23, 31–32
Amfortas, 106–8
Amicus and Amelius, 42, 47, 60
Ami et Amile, 47–51, 54, 56, 58
Amis e Amilun, 50
Anfortas, 99–100
Ansëys de Mes, 28–29
Antisemitism, ix, 71, 102
Apollonius of Tyre, 57
Archeology, 27
Aristotle, 4, 56
Aronstein, Susan, 105
Arthur, King, 19, 96

Bademagu, King, 11–12
Beatrice, 15–17
Bede, 67
Belissant, 47–48, 50
Belle Hélène de Constantinople, 66
Bernardino of Siena, 71
Béroul, *Roman de Tristan*, 11
Bettelheim, Bruno, 8
Beves of Hampton, 86–89
Biale, David, 61
Bloch, R. Howard, 115
Blood: in battles, 10, 13, 20, 21–23;
    on bed sheets, 10–17; control of, 4,
    7–8, 57–60, 102, 104; as evidence,

10–17, 77, 89–91; flux, 101–4, 108;
    from anus, 103; from genitals, 100,
    101–2, 109; of Jewish men, xi, 6–7,
    102–4, 108; in Judaism, 6–7,
    61–62; and illness, 101–2, 104, 106,
    108; in medical cures, ix, 3, 5, 9;
    and the sea, 57–58; virgin's, 2–5, 18.
    See also Menstruation; Parturition
Bloodletting, 7–8. *See also* Phlebotomy
Book of Leinster, 24
Bors, 9, 105
Bourke, Joanna, 39
Brown, Peter, 4
Brundage, James, 74
Bynum, Caroline Walker, 4, 107

Camille, 28
Castration, 92, 98, 106
Chastity, 97–98, 99
Chaucer, Geoffrey: *Clerk's Tale*, 51;
    Man of Law's Tale, 59, 64, 73–75,
    78, 82; *Physician's Tale*, 44
Chevalier du cygne, 83
Chrétien de Troyes: *Chevalier de la
    charrete*, 10–15; *Conte du graal*, 92,
    100, 104; *Guillaume d'Angleterre*,
    85–86, 88, 89; *Philomena*, 41, 51–56,
    58, 59–60
Christine de Pizan: *Book of the City of
    Ladies*, 41; *Mutacion de Fortune*, 41
Chronicle of Solomon bar Simson,
    62–63
Circumcision, 6–7
Chester *Abraham*, 44
Churching, 67–69, 70, 88
Conception, ix, x, 63–64, 77–78,
    82–83, 97; of Christ, 3. *See also*
    Monstrous birth

Control. *See* Blood, control of
Constance, 73–75
Conversion, 73–74, 86, 100, 102, 105
Cooper, Alice, 1–2, 18
Cressy, David, 68
Cross-dressing, 29–30, 36
Curse of Eve, ix, 1, 110

Deborah, 33
Delaney, Carol, 45, 47, 55
DeVries, Kelly, 24–25
Dinshaw, Carolyn, 75
Donygild, 73–75, 78
Douglas, Mary, 5

Edda, 41
Eilberg-Schwartz, Howard, xi
Elliott, Dyan, 68, 105, 106
Elucidation, 100
Erembourc, 56–57, 58, 60
Estoire del saint graal, 94–109
Eucharist, ix, x, 3, 92–96, 104

Fairy, 74, 75, 79–85
Fergus, 24–25
Fisher King, 99
Florence, 15–17, 20
Fountain, 18, 80
Freud, Sigmund, 13

G.I. Jane, 22–23, 30
Gaignebet, Claude, 83
Galahad, 9
Galen, 56, 111
Gauvain, 18–20, 93–94
Gervaise of Tilbury
Gésine, 58, 65, 67–72, 80, 101
Gibson, Gail, 68, 85
Gobert Thibaut, 34
Grail, x, 92–100
Gregory the Great, 3, 67–68
Grimhild, 41
Griselda, 51, 59–60
Gudrun, 41
Guenevere, 10–15, 16, 17–18, 20, 113

Gurguran, King, 19

Hagiography. *See Vitae*
Hanser-Schäublin, Brigitta, 77
Hardré, 47–48
Helinas, 80–81, 84
Heloise, 5
Hemorrhoids, 103–4
Heroism, x, 17, 21–23, 23, 30, 110
Heterosexuality, 23
Hildegard of Bingen, 3, 5, 78
Hoffman, Lawrence, 6–8
Howard, Jean, 36
Humors, ix, 111
Huon de Bordeaux, *Yde et Olive*,
    29–30

Impurity. *See* Pollution
Incest, 65, 66
Infanticide, 40, 43, 54–55
Initiation rites, 8
Instinct, maternal, 39–40
Interdiction: of childbirth scene,
    84–89; by fairies, 79–84; of
    intermarriage, 74
Intermarriage, 74–76
Isaac, 44–47
Itys, 41, 53–56

James of Milan, *Stimulus Amoris*, 107
Jay, Nancy, 42
Jean d'Arras, *Roman de Mélusine*,
    79–85, 88
Jean d'Aulon, 31, 37, 39
Jean Maillart, *Roman du comte d'An-
    jou*, 64–67, 73, 75–76, 78
Jephthah, 42, 44
Joan of Arc, 30, 31–39; as mother, 38;
    as witch, 38
Jones, Catherine, 28
Joseph, 96–97
Josephus, 97–99, 100, 104, 106, 108
Jourdain de Blaye, 56–58, 60, 70

Katarina of Sweden, 71–72

Kay, 11, 18, 113
Kriemhild, 41
Kundry, 106

Lactation, 4, 63, 71–72
Lancelot, 10–15, 18, 113
Leprosy, 2–3, 8, 48–51, 63–64
Lesbian, 23
Lincoln, Bruce, 43
Lineage, ix, 43–44, 64–66, 70, 71–76,
    88–91, 96–97
Lochrie, Karma, 107
Lubias, 47–48, 50
Lying in. See *Gésine*
Lynch, Andrew, 10

Macaire, 15–17, 20
Macha, 26
Malleus Maleficarum, 64
Margaret of Anjou, 85
Marie de France: *Equitan*, 112–17;
    Fresne, 83; *Lanval*, 80
Marin le Jaloux, 18–20
Martyr, x, 2, 4–5, 9
Mataquas, 84–85
McLaughlin, Megan, 33–33, 35–36
Medb, 24–26, 30
Medea, 41, 59–60
Méléagant, 11–15, 17–18
Mélusine, 78, 80–83, 85, 89
Menses, 65, 77–78, 83, 90
Menstruation, ix, 2, 3–4, 5–8, 13, 16,
    22–23, 24–26, 30, 31–32, 36–37,
    40, 44, 61–63, 67, 71, 83, 90,
    101–2, 103, 107, 111; and health,
    5, 103; of Jewish men, 104; male,
    7–8
Miramon, Charles de, xi–xii
Mistére du Viel Testament, 45–47, 55
Moore, Demi, 22
Monstrous birth, x, 63–76, 78, 82–83
Morse, Ruth, 59

Newman, Barbara, 42, 51, 60
Nibelungenlied, 41

Nirenberg, David, 74
Nocturnal emissions, 3
Nosebleed, 11–13
Northampton *Abraham*, 45, 55

Old Law, female embodiment of,
    19–20
O'Neil, Lt. Jordan, 22–23, 30
Oriabel, 57–58, 70
Ovid, 41, 51, 52–53
Ovide moralisé, 41

Parsifal, 106–8
Parturition, ix, x, 3, 5, 26, 40, 43–44,
    57–58, 61–91, 111
Paternity, x
Penitentials, 63
Perceval, 2, 9, 19, 105
Perceval's sister, 2, 8–10, 14, 18
Perlesvaus, 18–20, 93–94
Peter the Venerable, 111
Phlebotomy, 111–17
Philippe de Rémi, *Roman de la
    Manekine*, 66, 69
Philomena, 41, 51–56
Pluto, 52–53
Pollution, ix, 3, 5, 58, 61–63, 67–68,
    71–73, 111
Presine, 79–81, 83–85
Procne, 41, 51–56
Procreation, 55, 96–97
Pseudo-Albert, *Secrets of Women*,
    63–64, 77

Queste del saint graal, 2–3, 8–10, 105

Rackin, Phyllis, 36
Rahilly, Cecile, 25
Rape, 100
Raymondin, 81–82
Renier, 56–57
Resemblance, 49–50, 55–56, 107
Riehle, Wolfgang, 107
Roman d'Eneas, 28–29
Roman de Florence de Rome, 15–17

Roman de Silence, 29–30, 85, 89
Rubin, Miri, 92, 93

Sacrifice, x, 2, 8, 19–20, 41–60, 62–63, 78
Sagas, 27, 29, 41
Saint Eupraxia, 4
Saints, 2, 4, 35, 71–72
Saracens, 56–57, 86, 102, 105
Sarah, 44–47, 50
Sautman, Francesca Canadé, 4
Saxo Grammaticus, *History of the Danes*, 27–28
Scott, Ridley, 22
Seed, 56, 78, 81, 83, 89, 90, 96–97, 104
Sefer Nizzahon Yashan, 61–63
Semen, 3–4, 56, 77–78; mixing of, 82
Serpent, 81–82
Shakespeare, William, *Henry VI, part 1*, 32–33, 35–38
Siegfried, 41
Sirasi, Nancy, 111
Sone de Nausay, 100
Spiegel, Gabrielle, 82–83
Strohm, Paul, 12
Syberberg, Hans-Jürgen, *Parsifal*, 107

Taboo. *See* Interdiction
Táin Bó Cúalnge, 24–26, 30, 36–37, 64
Talbot, 32, 37–38
Tereus, 41, 52–53
Thiðrejssaga, 41
Transubstantiation, ix, 91, 92–95
Trevet, Nicholas, *Cronicles*, 73–75
Twins, 83, 86–87

Vagina, 107–8
Vengeance, 41, 51–54, 59
Vikings, 17, 33
Virgin, 2–3, 8–10, 14
Virgin Mary, 3, 4, 62–63, 68, 93
Virginia, 44
Virginity, 4, 12, 31, 37, 44
Vitae, 2, 4

Wagner, Richard, *Parsifal*, 106–8
War, x, 21–40, 110
Wogan-Browne, Jocelyn, 4
Wolfram von Eschenbach, *Parzival*, 99–100, 106
Wound, 10–11, 12, 13, 92, 98–101, 104, 106–8

Žižek, Slavoj, 107

Acknowledgments

One of the greatest pleasures of working on this book was talking about it with colleagues and friends. I am very grateful to David Biale, Caroline Jewers, Catherine M. Jones, Ruth Mazo Karras, Nadia Margolis, Leslie Zarker Morgan, Jerome A. Singerman, and Valerie Traub for suggesting texts and references that turned out to be crucial for my project. This study took its shape in part from these suggestions. For helpful readings of various chapters, I thank Rebecca Bach, Catherine Brown, Matthias Meyer, James A. Schultz, and Zrinka Stahuljak. Doug Anderson, Ross Chambers, and Simon Gaunt read the entire manuscript and offered valuable insights, corrections, and suggestions for revision. Megan Moore was an extraordinary research assistant.

I am also very grateful to Debbie Way and Eileen Jeffers for their enthusiastic interest in my project, and to Karma Lochrie, James A. Schultz, and Catherine Brown for sustaining conversations and email exchanges, and for friendship. My parents offered unfailing support, and Doug Anderson's curiosity and imagination have enriched this project—and my life—in more ways than I can name.

Most of the writing of this project was completed at the Newberry Library with generous funding from the Rockefeller Foundation, and valuable assistance for the final stages was provided by a faculty grant from the Institute for Research on Women and Gender at the University of Michigan.

Earlier versions of Chapters 2 and 3 appeared as "The Amenorrhea of War" in *Signs: Journal of Women in Culture and Society* 28, 2 (2003): 625–44 and "Engendering Sacrifice: Blood, Lineage, and Infanticide in Old French Literature," *Speculum* 77 (2002): 55–75. I am grateful for the anonymous readers' reports I received from these two journals, and to the Medieval Academy and the University of Chicago Press for permission to reprint.

Special thanks to Buckley Hugo at Spirit Music for his generous help in getting "Only Women Bleed" into my book.